The ICSA **Director's Guide**

The ICSA
Director's Guide

5TH EDITION

Martha Bruce

Published by ICSA Information & Training Ltd
16 Park Crescent
London
W1B 1AH

First edition 2003
Second edition 2004
Third edition 2008
Fourth edition 2010
Fifth edition 2013

Typeset in Sabon & ITC Franklin Gothic by
Paul Barrett Book Production, Cambridge

Printed and bound in Great Britain by
Hobbs the Printers Ltd, Totton, Hampshire

British Library Cataloguing in Publication Data

A catalogue record for this book is available from the British Library.

ISBN 9781860724824

Contents

Introduction

Given the extent of their duties, directors face the very difficult task of making sure they stay up-to-date with changes in legislation and commercial practice.

This book is intended as a pocket-sized publication for directors to carry with them and use as a quick reference guide. To achieve this it has been written in a concise, easy to read way so directors and those who advise them can quickly find the basic facts about their duties, responsibilities and what they need to do to comply. It covers essential information about the full range of directors' duties and responsibilities, referring the reader elsewhere for more detail if required.

This fifth edition of the guide incorporates changes that have taken place in corporate law, regulation and recommended 'best practice' guidance since the last edition as well as directors' responsibilities set out in employment, health and safety, consumer protection and environmental law and regulations. It also covers the up-to-date position for the appointment of directors, the need for them to undertake their own due diligence before accepting an appointment, their powers and how they should be exercised in managing the company, as well as the directors' core duties and responsibilities in terms of administration, remuneration and disclosure requirements, restricted transactions, financial accounts and shareholders. In particular, information has been included about the factors and director's behaviours that contribute to achieving an effective board, including diversity of membership, induction, performance evaluation, ongoing training, understanding and achieving a distinction in roles and planning for succession. Reputational damage is covered, as this has emerged as a significant business risk given the speed and global reach of communication through electronic media and the fact that regulators now routinely publicly 'name and shame' those committing environmental, competition, health and safety and financial services offences. This is causing a shift in focus and a widening of directors' responsibilities to more actively encompass the stakeholder group which, through publicity, has greater scope to require directors to account for their behaviour and actions. A number of notable and previously well-respected companies have had their reputations challenged in recent months for internal control failings and for pursuing practices and schemes which, whilst legally legitimate, are considered inappropriate by the public at large.

Writing and updating such a concise guide has proved demanding, not least because of the volume of changes introduced to legislation and recommended practice, but I hope the reader finds it a useful addition to his or her briefcase.

Whilst every effort has been made to ensure the accuracy of this work, neither the author nor the publisher can accept responsibility for any loss arising to anyone relying on the information contained therein.

Martha Bruce FCIS
Director, Bruce Wallace Associates

Abbreviations

AIM	The Alternative Investment Market of the Stock Exchange
BIS	The Department for Business, Innovation and Skills
BOFIs	UK Banks and Other Financial Institutions
CA 1985	Companies Act 1985 (as amended)
CA 2006	Companies Act 2006
CDDA 1986	Company Directors Disqualification Act 1986
CJA 1993	Criminal Justice Act 1993
Code	The UK Corporate Governance Code
COMAH	Control of Major Accidents Hazards Regulations 1999 (SI 1999/743)
COSHH 2002	Control of Substances Hazardous to Health Regulations 2002 (SI 2002/2677)
CPA 1987	Consumer Protection Act 1987
DDA 1995	Disability Discrimination Act 1995
DPA 1998	Data Protection Act 1998
EA 1995	Environment Act 1995
ELCIA 1969	Employers Liability (Compulsory Insurance) Act 1969
ENA 2002	Enterprise Act 2002
EPA 1990	Environmental Protection Act 1990
ERA 1996	Employment Rights Act 1996
ERDRA 1998	Employment Rights (Dispute Resolution) Act 1998
FRC	Financial Reporting Council
FSMA 2000	Financial Services and Markets Act 2000
FTA 1973	Fair Trading Act 1973
HSC	Health and Safety Commission
HSE	Health and Safety Executive
HSWA 1974	Health and Safety at Work, etc Act 1974
IA 1986	Insolvency Act 1986
IA 2000	Insolvency Act 2000
EO	Enforcement Order
ICAEW	Institute of Chartered Accountants in England & Wales
ICSA	Institute of Chartered Secretaries and Administrators
NAPF	National Association of Pension Funds
OFR	Operating and Financial Review

ABBREVIATIONS

OFT	Office of Fair Trading
OPRA	Occupational Pensions Regulatory Authority
PDMR	Person discharging managerial responsibility as set out in the Disclosure and Transparency Rules
PIRC	Pensions Investment Research Consultants Ltd
POCA 2002	Proceeds of Crime Act 2002
Registrar	Registrar of Companies (unless context implies otherwise)
RIS	Regulated Information Service
SAS 600	Statement of Auditing Standards 600, Auditors' reports on financial statements
Schedule	Schedule to the Companies Acts
SDA 1975	Sex Discrimination Act 1975
Stock Exchange	The London Stock Exchange
TDA 1968	Trade Descriptions Act 1968

1   Fundamentals about directors

Most of this book is devoted to making sure directors are fully aware of their obligations and what is expected of them. However, before considering these responsibilities directors need to understand a number of fundamental facts about their role and the mechanics of their appointment. These are covered in this chapter and include:

- Why are directors needed?
- What is a director?
- Who can be appointed?
- How they are appointed?
- Different types and terms for directors
- Lack of formal appointment
- Due diligence, induction and training
- Service contracts and letters of appointment
- Remuneration.

Why does a company need directors?

In simple legal terms a private company cannot be incorporated unless it has at least one director, and a public company at least two (CA 2006, s 154). Directors are therefore needed to satisfy the requirements of incorporation.

In practical terms, a company cannot act on its own as it is merely a legal entity formed 'on paper' through the operation of law. However, through the Memorandum and Articles the subscribers who came together to form the company will give the directors responsibility for managing the company's business. Therefore, following incorporation, the directors will be able to take such actions and do such things as they consider necessary to achieve the objectives and purpose of the company. This might, for example, be the immediate of other officers to whom they delegate certain powers to take actions of behalf of the company.

What is a director?

The only guidance given in the CA 2006 is that a director is 'any person occupying the position of director by whatever name called' (s 250). This makes clear that it is not the title or name they are given, but what a person does that determines whether he or she is a director. Indeed, in many companies the directors are often called governors, trustees, or councillors, etc.

Whilst the exact role a director performs will vary according to the size and type of company to which they are appointed, there are common themes in terms of what is expected from 'the position of a director'. The directors have overall responsibility for how a company is managed and run which means they must oversee, supervise, govern and control the company's activities and operations. Directors also have ultimate responsibility for leading their companies by determining direction and strategy, monitoring and reviewing performance against agreed targets and objectives, making revisions where necessary. Involvement in such matters would indicate that a person is 'occupying the position of director', no matter what title is assigned to them.

Who can be appointed a director?

The CA 2006 does not specify any qualifications that directors must have and most persons and legal entities can hold the position. Exceptions are someone who is:

- an undischarged bankrupt without leave of the court to act;
- subject to a disqualification order or has given a voluntary disqualification undertaking;
- prohibited for failing to pay amounts owing under a county court judgment or administration order;
- a director of an insolvent company and the proposed appointment is to a company with a 'prohibited name';
- secretary of the company and the appointment is as sole director; or
- the auditor of the company.

There is no upper limit regarding the age of a director, but a person may not be appointed unless he or she has attained the age of 16 years (CA 2006, s 157).

Whilst one company can be appointed a director of another company, at least one director of the company must be a natural or actual person (CA 2006, s 155).

Furthermore, a person may be prohibited from appointment by provisions specified in the company's Articles, such as not having the requisite shareholding qualification, suffering from mental disorder, or having entered into an arrangement with creditors.

How are directors appointed?

A company's first directors are appointed by the subscribers to the Memorandum when the company is incorporated (CA 2006, s 12). A statement of proposed officers is submitted with the company's incorporation documents, containing the directors' details and consent to act.

The manner in which subsequent appointments are made is usually determined by provisions in the company's Articles, which may permit:

- the directors to appoint additional directors or to fill casual vacancies;
- the members to appoint directors by ordinary resolution;
- appointment by notice from the holding company where the company is a wholly-owned subsidiary; or
- appointment by a holder of a particular class of share where, for example, the company is a joint venture and each party holds a different class of shares and has the right to appoint one director.

In each case the required approval process will be specified in the Articles and, where there is no mention of directors being able to approve subsequent appointments, only the members will have the right to do so.

When a director is appointed, an entry needs to be made in the register of directors (see Chapter 6) and notification, including the director's details and consent, must be sent to Companies House within 14 days using the prescribed form (AP01 for an individual and AP02 for a corporate director).

The appointment of a director will give rise to various administrative matters, including the need to notify the company's bankers, amend the bank mandate instructions and inform the company's insurers.

Any change in a director's details, for example a change of address or a change of name through marriage, needs to be noted in the company's register of directors and advised to Companies House using the prescribed form.

What types of director are there?

As set out below, directors are given many different names. However, the CA 2006 makes no distinction between directors according to their type or title and prescribes that all directors have the same statutory duties and obligations and must participate in the joint deliberations of the board. Notwithstanding the CA 2006 position, many companies make distinction between directors who have 'executive' status and those who act as 'non-executive' directors. Also, the directors are often permitted by the company's Articles to appoint 'alternate', 'associate', 'managing', or 'nominee' directors, the key points of which are summarised below.

i Executive directors

Full-time working directors are often described as 'executive directors'. In most instances they will enter into a service contract with the company at the time of their appointment which, as well as their employment details, will set out additional executive management functions and any responsibilities they have for specific areas such as operations and production, finance, marketing, human resources or health and safety, etc. However, executive directors should note that their duties and responsibilities extend to the whole of the company's activities and operations and are not limited to their specialist area.

Executive directors will often be given titles such as 'finance director', 'chief financial officer' (CFO), 'marketing director' and so forth and typically possess qualifications and experience relevant to their specialist executive function.

Many boards appoint a 'chief executive officer' (CEO) who is the most senior executive director. In addition to sharing responsibility for leading the company with all other directors, the CEO will be responsible for leading the executive team and delivering the company's stategy.

ii Non-executive directors

Directors who are not employees of the company and who only have to devote part of their time to its affairs are often referred to as 'non-executive directors' (NEDs). A NED will not have an executive function or be involved in the company's day-to-day management but, under the CA 2006, still has the same statutory duties and obligations as any other director. The terms of a non-executive directors' engagement will usually be set out in a letter of engagement, which should state the minimum time that he or she is expected to devote to dealing with the affairs of the company.

Due to the objectivity they can bring when considering a company's options, reviewing performance and making decisions, it is widely recognised that non-executive directors have an important role to play in the governance, direction and control of companies. In particular, they help to:

- balance the interests of shareholders with those of management;
- bring independent judgement to decisions on strategy, performance, use of resources and appointments, etc.;
- mediate over issues in which executive directors may have a personal interest such as directors' remuneration, succession planning, takeovers, etc.;
- monitor performance and ensure sufficient safeguards and controls are in place to protect the interests of the company.

The UK Corporate Governance Code (see Appendix 1), which must be observed by companies with a premium listing of equity securities, requires at least half the board, excluding the chairman, to be independent non-executive directors. Smaller listed companies and those outside the FTSE 350 are required to have just two independent non-executive directors. Listed companies are also required to appoint a 'senior independent non-executive director' (SINED) to work closely with the chairman, communicate with shareholders and meet with other non-executive directors to evaluate the chairman's performance and address succession planning.

The possession of independence puts the non-executive directors in a much better position to openly question and challenge a company's executive directors without putting at risk any business or other ties held with the company. The benefits this can bring for example, by improving the quality of decision-making are worth consideration by all companies, listed or otherwise.

Having said this, the role, effectiveness and need for non-executive directors has been under scrutiny for many years given the numerous high-profile and large-scale corporate collapses involving malpractice. More recently, the banking crisis and worldwide credit crunch have caused the effectiveness of non-executive directors to be called into question. A number of reviews have been commissioned over the years including the Higgs Review, the Tyson Report, the Walker Review and the Davies Report (see Chapter 2). Many of the recommendations from these reviews have been included as principles and provisions in the UK Corporate Governance Code, the main ones being the specification of new principles on their role, the need for an appropriate mix of skills, experience and independence and the time commitment expected.

iii Alternate directors

Whilst there is no provision in CA 2006 or in the Model Articles for a private company, it is common practice for a company's Articles to allow executive or non-executive directors to appoint an 'alternate director' to attend and vote at meetings of the directors on their behalf. Provisions in the Articles will need to be carefully checked as the manner and procedure for appointment of an alternate director can vary considerably.

Alternate directors are subject to all statutory obligations and responsibilities of other directors. Their details must be recorded in the register of directors and Companies House must be notified of their appointment. They must also observe the disclosure requirements detailed in Chapter 5.

iv Associate director

The term associate director has no particular standing in law and is used generically as a courtesy title for senior executives who do not hold a position on the company's board as a way of indicating and validating their seniority. 'Divisional director', 'director of finance', 'director of HR' and 'facilities director' are examples of courtesy associate director titles.

However, the use of such titles can be problematic and it is very important that, where a company's Articles permit the appointment of associate directors, the provisions must make clear that the person is not a member of the board and is not entitled to attend board meetings. In addition, it is important the person knows not to hold themselves out as a director, to others or he or she may be considered a 'de facto director' (see below) and unwittingly accept responsibilities and commit the company to a contract or agreement that cannot be repudiated. This was the situation in *SMC Electronics Ltd v Akhter Computers Ltd [2001] 1 BCLC 433* where the company was held to a contract entered into by the 'Director of Power Supply Unit Sales' even though he was not a director and had exceeded his authority.

v Managing director

Whilst it is not a requirement, the Articles of some companies permit the board both to appoint, and determine what powers are conferred on, a managing director. Where such appointment is made, authority will usually be delegated authorising the managing director to manage the company and take day-to-day decisions, enter into certain contracts and agreements and finalise matters approved 'in principle' by the board. Except where the company has an executive chairman or a CEO, the managing director will be the most senior executive.

In practice a company is unlikely to appoint both a CEO and a managing director and you tend to see managing director appointments in smaller companies and CEO appointments in larger listed companies. Where a group structure exists, a CEO is often appointed by the top company and a managing director in each trading subsidiary.

Where a managing director is appointed, he or she would usually have responsibility for implementing and reviewing:

- operational plans, policies, processes and procedures in pursuit of agreed strategy;
- control and risk management systems; and
- progress towards achieving performance targets.

The managing director would also usually be responsible for building an effective management team, monitoring the executive directors' actions and performance, representing the company and maintaining a dialogue with the company's chairman.

Some Articles exclude the managing director from the requirement to retire by rotation.

vi Nominee director

In some instances a class of shareholders, debenture holders or a major creditor may have the right, expressed in the Articles, shareholders' agreement or other document, to appoint and remove a director. Whilst such person is appointed to broadly represent the appointer's interests. It is important the nominee director observes his or her duty to the company and exercises his or her judgement in the interests of the company without regard to, or on the instructions of, the appointor (see below).

vii Chairman of the company

There is no requirement in CA 2006 for a company to appoint a chairman, but the directors are normally authorised by the company's Articles to appoint one of their number as chairman.

Details of the role, requirements and responsibilities of the chairman will usually be set out in the company's Articles and it is common to find that the chairman:

- has responsibility for running and managing the board, setting the agenda of meetings, ensuring timely, accurate and adequate information is provided on matters to be considered at the meeting, that there is sufficient time for adequate discussion and decision-making and that meetings are properly conducted;
- presides as chairman of general meetings and ensures that such meetings are properly convened and conducted from a procedural perspective, for example in relation to notice given, conduct of voting, rights of proxies, demands for a poll, etc;
- communicates with shareholders, major investors and others; and
- ensures executive directors are aware of their wider responsibilities and that appropriate induction and ongoing training are arranged for all directors.

In addition to the responsibilities listed above, the UK Corporate Governance Code and the FRC's Guidance on Board Effectiveness make clear the importance of the chairman in creating and leading an effective board. Whilst this guidance only directly applies to companies with a premium listing of equity securities, it contains principles relevant to most companies.

It is well recognised that the chairman is fundamental to promoting and encouraging good boardroom behaviour and an open and accepted culture of challenge and debate amongst directors – essential requirements for an effective board. Consequently greater emphasis is being placed on the role of the chairman. In particular, the FRC's Guidance lists a wide range of matters for which the chairman would usually be responsible, namely:

- demonstrating ethical leadership;
- setting the board agenda, primarily focused on strategy, performance, value creation and accountability; ensuring that issues relevant to these areas are reserved for decision by the board and are not delegated;
- ensuring a timely flow of high-quality information;
- determination by the board of the nature, and extent, of the significant risks the company is prepared to take in implementing its strategy and effective oversight of this by the board;
- considering succession planning and composition of the board on a regular basis;
- making certain that the board has effective decision-making processes and sufficiently challenges and debates major proposals;
- ensuring the board's committees are properly structured with appropriate terms of reference;
- encouraging all board members to engage in and contribute to board and committee meetings by drawing on their skills, experience, knowledge and, where appropriate, independence;
- promoting and fostering a relationship founded on mutual respect and open communication between the non-executive directors and the executive team;
- developing productive working relationships with all executive directors, the CEO in particular;
- providing support and advice;
- consulting the senior independent director on board matters in accordance with the UK Corporate Governance Code;
- taking the lead on issues of director development, including thorough induction programmes for new directors and regular directors' performance reviews;
- acting on the results of board evaluations; and
- ensuring effective communication with shareholders and other stakeholders and, in particular, that all directors are made aware of the views of those who provide the company's capital.

From the list set out above, it is clear that the chairman has a key and pivotal role in achieving an effective board and the behaviour he or she demonstrates is fundamental and underpins how the board will operate and behave. This, in turn, will usually have a knock-on effect through the company and the chairman's role is therefore of primary importance.

Lack of formal appointment

There are a number of instances where this may happen, whether by intention or by error and include circumstances where a director not formally appointed would be referred to as a:

i De facto director

This describes a person who acts like a director, is held out by the company as a director and who claims to be a director, without having been formally appointed to the board or whose appointment is later found to be improper (*Re Hydrodam (Corby) Ltd [1994] 2 BCLC 180, [1994] BCC 161*).

Such person is a director by virtue of 'occupying the position of director' and consequently is subject to the same responsibilities that apply to properly appointed directors. Furthermore, a de facto director, whose conduct is considered 'unfit' under CDDA 1986, s 6 may be disqualified as a director (*Re Sykes (Butchers) Ltd (in liquidation), Secretary of State for Trade and Industry v Richardson [1998] 1 BCLC 110*).

As mentioned above, particular care should be taken when bestowing a courtesy title such as 'divisional' or 'regional' director on a senior executive. It can cause confusion, often to the detriment of the company, as the person may be considered a de facto director. This is not generally recommended.

ii Shadow director

CA 2006, s 251(1) defines a 'shadow director' as 'a person in accordance with whose directions or instructions the directors of the company are accustomed to act'. This may, for example, include a majority share-holder, secured creditor or banker who, whilst not actually appointed a director, exercises influence over the affairs of the company and decisions made by the board (*Secretary of State for Trade and Industry v Deverell [2000] 2 All ER 365*).

There are instances where, for example, a class of shareholders may have authority either expressed in the company's Articles or in a share-holders' agreement to appoint and remove a 'nominee' director. Whilst in principle there is nothing wrong with appointing someone as director in this way, that person must be left to exercise his or her own judgement in the best interests of the company without any direction or instruction on how to vote by the appointor (*Boulting v ACTT [1963] 2 QB 606, 626, CA*). Where this is not the case, the appointor will be considered a shadow director.

To ensure that people who control companies but avoid appointment as directors do not evade their legal duties and responsibilities, shadow directors are subject to the same rules as properly appointed directors. Where their conduct falls below that reasonably expected of a director, shadow directors may be the subject of disqualification or be caught by wrongful trading provisions. They can also be liable for a breach of their fiduciary duties to the company (*Yukong Line Ltd of Korea v Rendsburg Investment Corp of Liberia and Others [1998] 2 BCLC 485*).

Where it is apparent that a company has a shadow director, the situation should be regularised by formally appointing that person as a director.

Where this is not done, the shadow director will still be treated as a director for the purposes of statutory duties. For example, requirements and restrictions relating to: directors' service contracts (CA 2006, ss 188 and 189), property transactions (CA 2006, ss 190 to 196), loans CA 2006, ss 197 to 214 and payments for loss of office (CA 2006, ss 215 to 222 still specifically apply to shadow directors).

Due diligence, induction and training

Before accepting an appointment as a director it is important from a practical perspective, that an individual undertakes a thorough examination of the company and how it conducts its affairs to ensure that the new appointee is entirely comfortable with how the company and its board operates and has determined that his skills, experience and own standards will fit well. Indeed, one of the recommendations of the Higgs Review 2003 was that a prospective NED should undertake a thorough examination of the company to satisfy himself that he will be well suited to the organisation and it is one in which he would have faith.

The ICSA has produced a Guidance Note entitled *Joining the Right Board: Advice for Prospective Directors* which comprises a list of questions that a director might pose when conducting his due diligence examination (see Appendix 2). These questions are largely based on points from the Higgs Review 2003 and the Model Code.

Some of the information required by the new appointee might be available from public records, but it is likely that much will not and the company secretary would be closely involved in the due diligence process.

Similarly, it is very important for the company as well as the new director that an induction process is carried out. This will ensure that the new director is able to make a valuable contribution to the board at an early stage in full knowledge of what is required of him and the extent of his liabilities. Indeed, the need for induction of directors is an important recommendation from the Walker Review, now embodied in the UK Corporate Governance Code. To assist the board, the ICSA has produced a Guidance Note entitled *Induction of Directors*, an extract of which appears in Appendix 3. Whilst it is important to provide a new director with information about the company, its operations and how it is controlled and run, it is equally important not to overwhelm him and care should be taken to feed information through gradually. It is a good idea to 'drip feed' information to the new director in a structured fashion over an agreed period, allowing time for questions and feedback.

It is also important that consideration is given on an ongoing basis to the board's training needs and the needs of individual directors who might, for example, have specific training requirements in relation to audit, risk and membership of other committees. Directors will be aware that legislation and best practice requirements never stand still and that they need constantly to be kept up to date. This is often achieved by providing the board with a programme of planned, regular technical notes, bulletins, information updates and presentations on general and key topics, backed up with more targeted or individual training where needed.

Indeed, the need for ongoing training is an important recommendation from the Walker Review, now embodied in the UK Corporate Governance Code and directors of companies with a premium listing of equity securities are required to regularly update their skills, knowledge and familiarity with the company's operations and market. The Code requires the chairmen of such companies to regularly review and agree each director's training and development needs and to make sure appropriate resources are available to ensure they can be fulfilled. Clearly, directors also have their own responsibility to identify and bring forward any areas where they feel the need for more information and training.

In addition, as detailed in Chapter 2, the UK Corporate Governance Code requires listed companies to undertake a formal and rigorous evaluation of the performance of the board and of individual directors each year. Where performance issues are identified it might be appropriate for these to be addressed through the provision of specific information and training on particular topics or areas, either to individual directors or the board as a whole.

Service contracts and appointment letters

A director who has been appointed to an executive position would usually be provided with a service contract setting out not only individual rights relating to employment such as remuneration, holidays, entitlement to notice and other benefits, etc., but also the director's duties to the company arising from appointment to the board. These duties may be expressed in general terms, such as the responsibility to:

- promote the interests of the company;
- carry out specific tasks as assigned by the board;
- devote time and attention to the company during agreed hours; and
- observe all competition and confidentiality restrictions.

The contract may also contain specific and more detailed duties agreed between the director and the company relating to executive responsibilities of office, such as 'human resources'. In this example the service contract may specify that the human resources director has responsibility for achieving specific staff turnover targets and responsibility for all personnel matters; ensuring that the company's employment practices and procedures are fully compliant with legislation and current recommendations for 'best practice'; data protection compliance; staff training, etc.

It is also important that provisions are included setting out the terms on termination. There has been considerable concern about large-scale severance payments made to directors of failing companies and it is important to ensure that any compensation awarded reflects performance.

In any event, careful contract negotiation and drafting is essential and the ICSA has produced a concise guidance note *Directors' Service Contracts* (reference 081021) which is recommended reading. An extract of the key provisions the guidance recommends are considered for inclusion in the service contract are set out in Appendix 4.

Whilst NEDs are not employed and it is therefore not appropriate for them to enter into a service contract, it is still important to formally record the terms of their appointment. This usually takes the form of a letter of appointment or engagement. The ICSA has produced a *Sample Non-Executive Director Appointment Letter* (Guidance Note 111214), an extract of which is set out in Appendix 5. Whilst the example letter in Appendix 5 may be much longer and more detailed than companies and directors have been used to in the past, such detail is considered necessary to ensure clarity of understanding about the nature of the relationship and what is expected from the director and the company.

Requirements for approval of service contracts and disclosure requirements are dealt with in Chapter 7.

Remuneration

Given the amount of concern expressed about levels of executive pay, although it is just one element of what is agreed between the company and the director, it merits separate discussion as determining what is appropriate and how the remuneration should be structured is a very complex matter. Essentially the level of remuneration should be sufficient to attract, retain and motivate directors of the quality required to direct, lead and run the company successfully. At the same time it is important not to pay more than is needed which is difficult to determine and there are many widely publicised statistics that suggest remuneration for executive directors has increased at an alarming rate, often out of step with the company's performance and valuation.

The UK Corporate Governance Code sets out recommendations for directors' remuneration for listed companies as follows:

- performance-related elements should form a significant proportion of a director's remuneration, be stretching and designed to promote sustained, long-term success;
- it should reflect the time commitment and responsibilities of the role;
- non-executive directors' remuneration should not include share options but, if it does, shareholder approval should be sought in advance;
- compensation commitments in the event of early termination need to be carefully considered so as not to be too onerous on the company, nor reward poor performance and they should seek to mitigate any loss suffered;

- notice or contract periods are set at one year or less (see Chapter 7);
- shareholders should be invited to approve significant changes to long-term incentive schemes and any new schemes;
- consideration should be given to pay and employment conditions elsewhere in the company, especially when deciding annual salary increases; and
- benchmarking should be considered, being cautious of any tendency for this to act as an upwards ratchet on remuneration.

Including a substantial performance-related element in an executive director's remuneration is an important way of aligning directors' interests with those of the company's shareholders. The company should seek to determine a well-thought-through long-term plan, possibly with short-term staged targets and rewards along the way and directors should only be rewarded where the agreed targets have been achieved.

As much information, whether in the form of survey results or engagement of remuneration consultants, etc. should be obtained as considered necessary in order to make an informed decision and achieve the most successful outcome for the company. Many companies use remuneration consultants and executive search agencies to help identify levels of pay within comparable companies, against which they then set their own remuneration 'benchmark' in terms of whether they want to be at the high, middle or more conservative end of what is being paid to others. This methodology has come under some criticism and needs to be carefully exercised as there might be a tendency to chase the median, resulting in spiralling levels of pay.

It should be noted that the ABI has also issued *Guidelines on Executive Pay* (published 29 September 2011, available at: www.abi.gov.uk) which, whilst aimed at fully listed companies, set out a number of remuneration principles which are worth consideration even by non-listed companies. In particular, the guidelines state that remuneration structures should not be overly complex; focus on long-term delivery of strategy and value creation; have an appropriate split between short-term and long-term targets and fixed and performance-related variable elements of pay; and avoid payments for failure to perform.

Responsibility for setting the non-executive directors' remuneration generally resides with the executive directors, unless the company's Articles require otherwise, and the level of remuneration should reflect the time commitment and responsibilities of the role, including membership of any committees. Remuneration for executive directors may be determined by the board (with the interested parties abstaining) or, in larger and listed companies, more likely by the remuneration committee.

2   Directors' powers, governance and company management

This chapter addresses how directors exercise their powers to manage the affairs of the company to which they are appointed efficiently and effectively by covering:

- Origin of directors' powers
- Conduct of board meetings
- Corporate governance reviews and guidance
- Components of corporate governance
- Board effectiveness
- Risk management and internal controls; and
- Delegation of authority.

Corporate governance recommendations are addressed in this chapter as the board usually has the discretion and authority to determine what structures and systems of governance are needed to ensure the company is well managed and controlled

Origin of directors' powers

A company's Articles will usually give the directors authority to run the company and its business and provide that 'the business of the company shall be managed by the directors who may exercise all the powers of the company'. Indeed Reg 3 of the Model Articles states that, 'subject to the articles, the directors are responsible for management of the company's business, for which purpose they may exercise all the powers of the company'.

However, many companies' Articles, and indeed those in Table A and the Model Articles, often restrict the extent of this authority by requiring that any limitations specified in the Companies Acts, Memorandum and Articles or special resolutions approved by the members are also observed. Article 4 of the Model Articles, for example, permits shareholders to direct the directors by special resolution to take, or refrain from taking, specific action. Another example might be that, whilst the directors usually have authority to enter into contracts on behalf of the company, the Articles may specify an upper limit to the value of such contracts and require that members' approval be sought where a contract exceeds this value.

A director can also only be delegated the powers of the company and they have a duty to check the Memorandum and Articles to see whether there is any limit on the company's capacity or that does not allow for or permit certain transactions. Say, for example, to borrow money or mortgage property. Such limitations would historically appear in a company's Memorandum, but may now be in the Articles and both should be checked before entering into a transaction.

Whilst a company's Articles generally authorise the directors to manage its business as described above, it is important to note that the directors do not have the power to act individually unless powers and responsibilities have been specifically delegated to them by the board. Consequently, directors must make decisions collectively as a board and act in accordance with the decisions made (*Re Haycraft Gold Reduction and Mining Co [1900] 2 Ch 230*).

Where the CA 2006 and other statutes state that the 'directors' have authority, or are required, to do something, in most instances this refers to all the directors acting together, not to individual directors. So, for example, where the directors have authority under CA 2006, ss 550 or 551 to allot shares, an allotment can only take place when decided by the board and not on the instruction of an individual director.

This requirement for directors to act collectively does mean that the board needs to meet periodically to review and discuss the company's progress against agreed targets and to consider options and make decisions about strategy going forward.

Conduct of board meetings

Apart from requiring minutes of all meetings of the board to be kept (CA 2006, s 248), statutory provisions are silent about how board meetings are convened and carried out.

Similarly, although a company's Articles might contain limited provisions governing board meetings, it is not uncommon for them to give the directors a large degree of freedom to call and conduct board meetings as they consider appropriate. For example, Table A, Reg 88 and Reg 16 of the Model Articles for private companies limited by shares and private companies limited by guarantee and Reg 19 of the Model Articles for public companies, provide that the directors 'may regulate their meetings as they see fit'.

ICSA's best practice guide *Good Boardroom Practice* offers further guidance in this area, as does their guidance note *Specimen Board Meeting Etiquette*. The latter was produced in response to concern raised in the Walker Review (see Appendix 6) about inappropriate boardroom behaviour and the negative effect this might have on corporate governance and sets out appropriate types of behaviour expected before, during and after board and committee meetings.

In practice, private and public companies with larger boards tend to hold regular, scheduled and formal board meetings, as they are necessary to address the many facets of their operations and ensure the directors have the necessary information on which to base decisions. In contrast, directors of smaller companies tend to be more closely involved with day-to-day operations and less frequent and informal board meetings often suffice. Furthermore, smaller companies with, say, only two or three directors, generally find it easier to call impromptu board meetings to consider matters as they arise or to arrange for matters to be approved by resolution in writing.

A director has a general duty to attend board meetings when possible, but this does not mean every meeting (*Re City Equitable Fire Insurance Co Ltd [1925] Ch 407, CA*). However, someone who accepts an appointment as a director must be willing and prepared to attend most, if not all, board meetings. The Articles will frequently provide that a director who fails to attend board meetings for a number of consecutive months, without permission from the board for the absence, shall be removed (Table A, Reg 81). The reasoning behind such provision is quite clear: a person who is never present at board meetings cannot be involved in and contribute to discharging the directors' responsibility to collectively manage the company. Indeed, supporting principle B.6.1 of the UK Corporate Governance Code (see Appendix 1) recommends that evaluation of the board's performance takes account of the commitment of time to board and committee meetings and other duties of the director.

It is always necessary to consult and observe provisions in the Articles concerning the conduct of board meetings when calling and holding a meeting. The following general principles may provide additional guidance, especially where the Articles are silent on any particular matter:

i Notice

- All directors must be given notice of a board meeting unless excluded by the Articles, for example when absent from the UK (Table A, Reg 88). However, the Model Articles do not exclude directors absent from the UK from entitlement to receive notice as electronic communication is now such that notice can easily be given to someone overseas (Reg 9). However, a director may waive the right to receive notice, in which case it does not need to be sent.
- Where board meetings are held at a fixed venue at regular pre-determined intervals, it may not be necessary to give notice of each separate meeting as the directors know in advance where and when each meeting will be held.
- Where the Articles do not specify the length of notice required then 'reasonable' notice must be given, based largely on what is normal practice for the company. This might usually be a few days or a weeks' notice, reducing to a matter of hours when a board meeting is needed to address more urgent matters.
- Unless required by the Articles, notice does not need to set out details of the business to be considered but, from a practical point, the benefits of including this information are clear and notice would often take the form of an agenda accompanied by all the supporting documents and papers necessary to consider the items listed on the agenda.
- Article 9(2) of the Model Articles for private companies limited by shares and private companies limited by guarantee state that the notice of board meeting (usually comprising an agenda and supporting documents and papers) must indicate the proposed time and date of the meeting, location and what arrangements have been made for those in other locations to participate.

ii Attendance

- All directors are entitled to attend and, in principle, vote at a board meeting and no director can be lawfully excluded from a board meeting (*Pulbrook v Richmond Consolidated Mining Co (1878) 9 ChD 610*). On some occasions it might not be possible for all directors to attend a meeting, especially where called at short notice. Such meetings are often referred to as 'interim' or 'ad hoc' meetings and as long as the quorum requirement is met (see below) and all directors have been given notice of the meeting, depending on what is to be considered and discussed it does not necessarily matter that they cannot all attend.

iii Quorum

- Where the required quorum is not present, the board meeting cannot proceed.
- Where the articles do not specify what constitutes a quorum it will be a majority, unless the board's usual practice is a different number (*York Tramways Co v Willows (1882) 8 QBD 685, CA*).
- The articles may allow the board to determine the quorum (Table A, Reg 89 or Model Articles Reg 11 private companies limited by shares and private companies limited by guarantee, Reg 10 public companies). This is subject to the Model Articles specifying that it must never be less than two (save where there is only one director).
- Where a private company has only one director, then attendance of the sole director constitutes a quorum although it is usually recommended that decisions of the sole director are recorded by resolution in writing as an alternative to holding a meeting of one person.
- The Articles may require a director to be excluded from being counted in the quorum at a particular point in a meeting where, for example, a director has an interest in a contract under discussion (Table A, Regs 94 and 95 or Model Articles Reg 14 private companies limited by shares and private companies limited by guarantee, Reg 16 public companies), and a check must be made that the meeting remains quorate at that point.

iv Conduct and voting

- The chair (appointed in accordance with provisions in the Articles) has a responsibility to ensure the board meeting is conducted properly and to preserve order and guide the directors through the business of the meeting, making sure that all matters are adequately discussed before decisions are reached.

- Decisions of the board are usually decided by simple majority and each director is entitled to one vote, unless the Articles specify something different.
- The chair only has a casting vote where provided by the Articles.
- A director must ensure that they have no conflict in the matters under discussion and, if there is a conflict, that they disclose the fact. Where a conflict exists, the company's Articles might require the director to abstain from voting and, even where the Articles are silent on this, it might be prudent for the director to do so (see Chapter 4).

v Minutes

- Minutes must be kept of all board meetings (CA 2006, s 248).
- All decisions taken at the meeting must be recorded in the minutes, with a short explanatory narrative to establish how such decisions were reached and the key factors considered.

On some occasions it may not be possible to arrange for all directors to be present at one location to hold a board meeting, due to constraints of time or availability. Many companies' Articles allow:

- directors to hold meetings by telephone or similar electronic media, such as video conferencing (Model Articles Reg 10 private companies limited by shares and private companies limited by guarantee, Reg 9 public companies);
- decisions of the board to be recorded by resolutions in writing signed by all directors (Table A, Reg 93 or Model Articles Reg 8(2) private companies limited by shares and private companies limited by guarantee, Reg 7(b) public companies).

Where directors' meetings are held by telephone, unless the Articles specifically provide for it, a series of telephone calls on a one-to-one basis stretches the common law meeting too far and is unlikely to be permitted. Consequently, it must be possible for directors to speak and be heard by the other directors at the same time so that discussion can be facilitated.

Board meetings provide the ideal opportunity for directors to discuss the company's strategy and direction away from the day-to-day distractions of running the company. In most instances an agenda setting out the matters to be discussed will be prepared and circulated to the directors, accompanied by necessary supporting documents and papers such as monthly management accounts, sales figures, budget reports, draft agreements for consideration, etc. This formal approach enables the directors to come to the meeting prepared and in full knowledge of the facts necessary to reach decisions, often having contacted executives to ask questions and clarify points in the papers presented to improve their understanding of the matters involved. In most instances this can improve the effectiveness and efficiency of board meetings. The alternative is to use the meeting as an opportunity to bring the directors up to speed with developments and then to expect them to make decisions at the end of the meeting, which may not allow adequate time for consideration. Many boards are moving away from the latter approach as it is not a very efficient use of their often limited meeting time.

Corporate governance reviews and guidance

Corporate governance is, quite rightly, a key board priority and directors are increasingly required to demonstrate and report to those with an interest in the company about the procedures, systems and controls they have put in place to achieve results, improve accountability and prevent malpractice or fraud.

Clearly, however, robust and comprehensive corporate governance is difficult to achieve as, despite numerous reviews and refinements to the 'best practice' requirements they each identify (see below), incidents of corporate malpractice and fraud continue to arise. Indeed, the Walker Review was commissioned in 2009 to independently review governance of the UK's banks and other financial institutions following the near collapse of the banking industry, widely attributed to governance failings and excessive risk-taking. More recently, widespread phone hacking at News Corporation and manipulation of the inter-bank lending rate by, amongst others, Barclays and RBS have also been attributed to governance failings and have been subject to investigation.

Nevertheless, over the years numerous 'best practice' recommendations have been made aimed at improving the systems by which listed companies are directed and controlled including, most notably, those contained in the Cadbury Report, Greenbury Report, Hampel Report, Turnbull Report, Higgs Review (now replaced by the FRC's Guidance on Board Effectiveness), FRC Guidance on Audit Committees (formerly known as the Smith Report), Tyson Report, Walker Review and Davies Report.

Whilst directors must decide how best to manage, control and guide their own companies the recommendations in these reviews may be applicable and should be considered by directors of all types of company, whether listed or not. The key recommendations put forward are summarised in the table below.

REPORT	KEY RECOMMENDATIONS
Cadbury Report	– Appointment of 'non-executive' directors. – Appointment of an audit committee to achieve greater control of financial reporting.
Greenbury Report	– Appointment of a remuneration committee to determine directors' remuneration and other pay issues. – Appointment of a nomination committee responsible for appointments to the board.
Hampel Report	– Largely consolidated recommendations of earlier reports into one 'Combined Code' (now the UK Corporate Governance Code, see below). – Improving communication with shareholders. – Redressing the balance between implementing controls and achieving business success by allowing companies discretion to apply corporate governance principles in the manner most suited to their organisation, and to explain deviations from 'best practice' to shareholders through their annual accounts.
Turnbull Report	– Giving directors, rather than operational managers, the responsibility for risk management and maintaining and reviewing a sound system of internal controls. – Basing internal control on a 'risk-based' approach. – Embedding such controls in the company's operations, with procedures for identifying and reporting control weaknesses so that appropriate remedial action can be taken.
Higgs Review 2003 (now replaced by the FRC's Guidance on Board Effectiveness)	– At least half the board, excluding the chairman, to be non-executive directors. – Non-executive directors to serve two three-year terms with annual re-election after nine years.

REPORT	KEY RECOMMENDATIONS
	– Time commitment required for non-executive directors.
	– Non-executive directors to meet once a year without executive directors present.
FRC Guidance on Audit Committees (formerly known as the Smith Report)	– Requirement for an audit committee comprising at least three independent non-executive directors, one with recent relevant financial experience.
	– Audit committee to have clearly defined terms of reference compliant with the Combined Code (now the UK Corporate Governance Code).
Tyson Report	– Greater diversity amongst non-executive directors and by adoption of more rigorous and transparent recruiting procedures and drawing candidates from a wider pool.
Walker Review	– Improve directors' induction and training and provide support for non-executive directors.
	– Increase the time commitment for non-executive directors and the chairman.
	– Board to be re-elected annually.
	– External board performance evaluation once every three years.
	– Creation of a risk committee and chief risk officer, both reporting to the board.
Davies Report	– Chairmen of FTSE 350 companies should set out the percentage of women they aim to have on their board by 2013 and 2015, aiming for a minimum of 25% by 2015, and report this in the corporate governance statement section of the annual report.
	– Disclose the proportion of women on the board, in senior executive positions and in the company as a whole.
	– Establish a boardroom diversity policy with measurable objectives against which performance is measured and performance reported.
	– Include a report in the annual report on how diversity is achieved in the appointment process.

Whilst recommendations in these reports are essentially 'voluntary', meaning directors may exercise discretion over the manner and extent to which they adopt them, many of the best practice recommendations have been adopted by the UK Listing Authority and appended to the Listing

Rules (LR) by way of the UK Corporate Governance Code (formerly Combined Code). This effectively means that directors of companies with a premium listing of equity securities must adopt them and, if they do not, must explain why in a 'corporate governance statement' in their annual accounts (LR 9.8.6(6)), Schedule B to the UK Corporate Governance Code and Chapter 9).

The Higgs Review was commissioned to review the role and effectiveness of non-executive directors and the adequacy of corporate governance arrangements to determine whether measures in the UK were sufficiently robust to prevent corporate failure and malpractice on the scale seen in the USA. At the same time, a review of the make up and responsibility of audit committees was conducted by the FRC the results of which form the FRC Guidance on Audit Committees (formerly the Smith Report, see Appendix 12).

The recommendations of the Higgs Review 2003 (now replaced by the FRC's Guidance on Board Effectiveness) and the FRC Guidance on Audit Committees were largely included in the UK Corporate Governance Code issued by the FRC at the time they were made and have since been preserved in future revisions.

The Turnbull Report is important for determining the actual framework of a 'risk-based approach' to internal control and the UK Corporate Governance Code consolidates these, and other, recommendations made in early reports on corporate governance.

The UK Corporate Governance Code and the Turnbull Report have been reproduced in Appendices 1 and 7 and extracts from the Walker Review appear in Appendix 6. The main recommendations are summarised below.

i Turnbull Report

The Turnbull Report introduced the need for risk management within corporate governance and redefined internal control as the ongoing assessment and management of risks beyond those purely related to financial objectives and auditing.

As can be seen in Appendix 7, the report identifies the broad framework for internal control and risk management as well as requirements for the process by which controls are reviewed. It does not, however, prescribe any 'best' system, recognising that, in reality, this varies depending on the company's culture, objectives, size, business environment, etc. and no one system would fit all companies. Such an approach encourages active consideration of internal controls and risk management by companies, rather than a box ticking exercise to satisfy regulatory requirements.

To the vast majority of companies, the need to manage and control risks will not be new as it has always been carried out (possibly in a more informal manner at an operational level) for companies to survive, overcome changes and keep ahead of competitors. What is possibly new is the need for the board to address, monitor and report on risk management and internal control. Directors, especially those of listed companies, need to:

- determine formally the company's goals and objectives;
- identify the strategic, financial, compliance, contractual, physical, distribution, regulatory and other risks which would prevent the company achieving its goals;
- determine how to identify and measure these risks and the effects they are having on the company;
- establish a risk management structure through which to monitor performance; and
- set up an internal system to manage and control risks to which the company may be or is exposed and review this internal system at least annually.

The Turnbull Report further recommends that the system of control is embedded in the company's operations and that it forms part of its culture. This certainly makes sense operationally as controls need to be integrated and understood throughout the company to ensure risks are identified, managed and mitigated at the earliest opportunity, minimising possible damage to the company and its performance.

In addition, the Walker Review (see Appendix 6 and paragraph (iii) below) recommends that a separate board risk committee is established and a chief risk officer is appointed reporting directly to the board. Whilst this is only of direct relevance to banks and financial institutions, other companies may find their risk management is improved by following these guidelines.

ii UK Corporate Governance Code

As can be seen in Appendix 1, the UK Corporate Governance Code (the Code) contains main and supporting principles as well as provisions. Companies with a premium listing of securities are required to make a disclosure statement in their annual report and accounts stating:

- how the company has applied the main and supporting principles; and
- that it has complied with the provisions of the Code and, where it has not, has provided an explanation of the deviation. The preamble to the UK Corporate Governance Code makes it clear that whilst listed companies are expected to comply the majority of the time where it is appropriate and beneficial, there will be exceptions and occasions where they do not, especially for smaller listed companies. Full explanation should be given by the board of any areas of non-compliance, steering away from 'boiler plate' statements. Those evaluating compliance should take account of the company's size, complexity, challenges and risks and should not adopt a box-ticking approach to their review.

Whilst directors of listed companies will need to consult the text of the UK Corporate Governance Code in full (available at www.frc.org.uk) some of the key principles and provisions contained in the Code include recommendations that:

- at least half the board of a larger listed company be made up of independent non-executive directors;
- except in exceptional circumstances, the chief executive should not become the chairman and that the chairman be independent at the time of appointment;
- no individual be appointed as chairman of a second FTSE 100 company;
- a full-time executive director shall not take on more than one non-executive directorship in a FTSE 100 company, nor the chairmanship of such a company;
- all directors should receive induction on joining the board and regular training to refresh director's skills;
- all directors should be submitted for re-election each year, subject to their performance remaining satisfactory;

- once a non-executive director has served six years, his or her continued appointment should be subject to rigorous review;
- a senior independent non-executive director be appointed and available to communicate with shareholders if required and as a sounding board for the chairman and other directors as required from time to time;
- the chairman should chair regular meetings of the non-executive directors but there should be at least one such meeting each year chaired by the senior non-executive director without the chairman present in order to assess his or her performance;
- the board should state in the annual report how the performance evaluation of the board, its committees and individual directors has been carried out, including determination of diversity;
- board evaluation is conducted externally every three years and the external facilitator of the evaluation is named in the annual report and accounts (FTSE 350 only);
- there are regular director development reviews;
- the board should establish an audit committee of at least three (or two for a smaller company) independent non-executive directors, at least one of whom has recent relevant financial experience (see Appendix 12);
- the audit committee should monitor and review independence of the external auditors and provide information on how they assess the effectiveness of the external audit process;
- greater focus be placed on board behaviours;
- there is an appropriate mix of experience, skills and independence on boards and a report is given on the board's diversity drive in the annual report including measurable objectives and how progress is being made against those objectives;
- directors' remuneration is more closely aligned with long-term interests of the company and risk; and
- a Stewardship Code is introduced for governing shareholder matters (Appendix 8).

The most recent version of the UK Corporate Governance Code, issued in September 2012, applies to accounting periods beginning on or after 1 October 2012. Following review by the FRC, the 'comply or explain' approach is still considered appropriate and will continue for the time being.

iii The Walker Review

The Walker Review was commissioned by the government in February 2009 to independently assess governance in the UK's banks and other financial institutions (together referred to as 'BOFIs') in light of the near collapse of the banking industry and concerns about their governance failings and excessive risk taking. The aim was to determine how to minimise risk-taking behaviour and improve communication and inter-action between companies and their shareholders. Whilst the review focused on the financial sector, many of the best practice recommenda-tions set out in Appendix 6 have much wider application for companies.

Notable recommendations from the review include:

- the need for appropriate induction, training and development of directors and externally facilitated performance evaluation of the board every three years;
- implementation of tougher selection criteria for non-executive directors and a relaxation of the nine-year 'independence' rule;
- non-executive directors to commit between 30 to 36 days to the role per year;
- chairman to commit two-thirds of his or her time to the role and be subject to annual re-election;
- disclosure of employee's remuneration if over £1m in the remuner-ation report;
- chairman of the remuneration committee should be proposed for re-election the following year if the remuneration report secures less than 75% support from shareholders;
- non-executive directors to be subject to tougher selection criteria;
- institutional investors should sign up to a stewardship code;
- separation of risk and audit committees;
- the appointment of a chief risk officer to report to the board; and
- an increase in the long-term element of variable remuneration, with 'claw back' in the event of irregularities.

For more detailed consideration readers should refer to the full text of the Walker Review available at www.hm-treasury.gov.uk. Whilst the review was specific to BOFIs, the FRC has adopted many of the recommendations in the UK Corporate Governance Code, in particular specification of new principles in relation to the non-executive directors' role, the need for an appropriate mix of skill, experience and independence and an increase in the time commitment required of non-executive directors.

Components of corporate governance

Corporate governance is defined as 'the system by which companies are directed and controlled' and the reviews and guidance set out above on corporate governance and what is considered 'best practice' are all useful points of reference for directors in determining what is appropriate and necessary for their companies.

Looking at governance simply, the directors need to carefully consider:

- what the company is trying to achieve and what needs to be done to get there – hence the need for strategic planning and objective setting, filtering down to more detailed plans and targets for particular parts of the business.
- what risks might prevent a company achieving its strategic objectives and how can they be monitored, controlled, avoided or mitigated – achieved by thorough and wide-ranging assessments of possible risk and implementation of risk management systems.
- what review and internal control processes are necessary to ensure everything stays on track and, if not, identify when and what corrective action or measures are needed before damage is suffered to such an extent that it might prevent the company achieving its strategic objectives.

On this simplistic level, corporate governance does not appear complicated and essentially involves planning; anticipating opportunities and problems; and determining whether performance is on track or whether mitigating or corrective action is needed. However, the task becomes complex given the vast number of factors that impact on a company's performance and determining how these can be captured by the corporate governance process.

In determining the appropriate corporate governance framework for their organisation, the directors must pay attention to how direction and control measures flow down through their companies and how reports are generated, reviewed and flow up through the reporting framework. There has been considerable criticism of standards of corporate governance demonstrated by many large companies recently and one thing that is increasingly evident is that the merest 'chink' somewhere in a company's corporate governance framework (where one small, but potentially significant, aspect is not adequately monitored or checked) can have a disastrous effect. Take the Deepwater Horizon oil spill incident in the Gulf of Mexico and the damage to BP, not only in terms of cost, but also to the company's reputation. Many of the required protocols and assessment processes were in place at BP but, for a variety of reasons, they were not observed and the warning signs did not show up and were ignored until it was too late to avert the disaster. This represents a failure and breakdown in BP's systems of corporate governance.

When determining the corporate governance framework and what measures are required and appropriate, the directors need to consider legislative requirements and regulations, approved codes of practice and recommended industry 'best practice', and be able to respond to current experience and developments in their sector and the economy as a whole to ensure the company's measures and controls remain appropriate over time.

Whilst, as a consequence, each company's corporate governance measures will vary there are some components relevant to all companies which are set out below.

i The effective board

There has been considerable focus in recent years on how to achieve an effective board that makes consistent, good-quality decisions. The FRC's Guidance on Board Effectiveness is a useful point of reference for more information on this matter (available at www.frc.org.uk). Clearly there is no 'one size fits all' solution and whether or not a board is effective is derived from a combination of many inter-related factors including:

- *Composition of the board* – Few would dispute that, in most instances, there needs to be a balance of skills, experience, knowledge and independence amongst the members of the board. In many ways, this is no different to what is required in any group, save that the expectations of the board are higher and the consequences of failure greater. A diverse mix of individuals will help the board to generate different ideas, look at things and analyse proposals from many perspectives and challenge what is being presented, drawing on past experiences and skills. This might be diversity in terms of psychological type, personal attributes and character, gender, background, nationality, or experience. Social psychologists studying groups and how they operate identified that members of a group often seek to conform and to gain a sense of unanimity, cohesiveness and belonging ('Groupthink', Irving Janus 1972). It is believed 'groupthink' is behind many bad judgements and decisions and that it is more likely to occur where there is similarity in type of group member, little change in membership, an overbearing leader, inadequate information and pressure for quick decisions.

The need for greater diversity on boards has received particular attention in recent years, which is not surprising given that many boards are comprised of like-minded men of a similar age, from similar educational and social backgrounds. Some years ago the Higgs review recommended more women on boards and the Tyson Report called for directors to be appointed from more diverse backgrounds to decrease the tendency towards appointment of individuals with similar perspectives, backgrounds and experiences. More recently the Davies Report (see table above) concluded that gender-diverse boards were more effective and desirable and FTSE 350 companies should increase female representation on their boards. The main recommendations from the Davies Report have been included in the UK Corporate Governance Code and, whilst this applies to listed companies, it is clear that diversity (including gender) is important when making decisions about composition of the board. In addition, feedback from board evaluation will be important when considering composition of the board and, in turn, this will be important in succession planning.

- *Structure and roles on the board* – Clarity and distinction between roles and responsibilities of those appointed to the board is recommended to ensure that each director knows what is expected and no one director has too much power. The latter is considered by many to have been the fundamental problem in a number of high-profile scandals, the most recent being News Corp where the chairman and CEO were one and the same and the company had no truly independent non-executive directors. Section A of the UK Corporate Governance Code (Appendix 1) sets out detailed recommendations concerning board structure and the need for division of responsibilities and the FRC's Guidance on Board Effectiveness contains more detail about specific roles, both of which are recommended for reference as they address issues such as the need to separate the role of chairman and CEO, the role and need for non-executives and chairman, etc.

- *Meetings* – These need to be held as often as necessary for the board to discharge its responsibilities for setting strategy as well as directing, managing and controlling the company. It is recommended that there is a formal schedule of regular meetings, to consider and discuss matters such as strategy, planning, resource allocation, risk management and internal controls, etc. and that these are supplemented by such interim meetings as necessary depending on the needs of the business. Each meeting should have an agenda, with such supporting documents and papers as necessary to consider the agenda items, and sufficient time be allowed for consideration and debate. It is also suggested that a list of matters requiring decision by the board is drawn up which would usually be worked into the planned meeting timetable (see Delegation of authority, paragraph iii below).

  The board's conduct at meetings is also extremely important and the chairman has a fundamental part in promoting good boardroom behaviour as set out in Chapter 1. In particular, there needs to be adequate time and openness amongst directors to allow matters on the agenda to be fully debated without rushing to make ill-informed decisions.

  In addition, in most companies how the board behaves has a knock-on effect throughout the company and so, if high standards of corporate governance are expected at all levels within the company, such standards must be demonstrated by the board.

- *Information and reporting* – The board needs to consider what information is required and the frequency and content of reporting in order that it can discharge its duty to oversee and control the company's business and performance. It is very important for the board and its committees to receive suitable and sufficient information in a timely manner in order that informed decisions can be made about the company and how to best deploy its assets for maximum long-term benefit. Usually the chairman will be instrumental in ensuring the board receives the required information and that it is accurate, timely, clear and sufficiently comprehensive.

Particular attention should also be given to when the information is provided to ensure the directors have sufficient time in advance of a meeting to review and consider it in detail and, if necessary, ask initial questions of the preparer, so each can attend the board or committee meeting with a comprehensive understanding of the issues faced, ready to discuss and debate the matters on the agenda.

The company secretary has an important role in supporting the board and ensuring there are good information flows amongst the board and committees and between executives and the non-executive directors. Again, this free flow of information makes perfect sense in terms of improving understanding, ensuring transparency and encouraging openness and debate by the board at their meetings.

- *Development* – As set out in Chapter 1, it is recommended that all new directors receive a formal, tailored induction on joining the board; that the existing directors' training and developments needs are periodically assessed; and that appropriate training is provided so they remain valuable members of the board. By keeping directors up-to-date with changes in legislation and best practice, they will continue to be in a position to make a valuable contribution as individuals and at board and committee level. To further this aim, directors should also have 'appropriate knowledge' of the company and its operations and be kept advised of changes.
- *Performance evaluation* – Given the board's role in leading, directing and controlling the company for which it is responsible and that the extent to which it is successful in doing this can vary tremendously, it is important for the board to consider and evaluate the effectiveness of its own performance and that of individual directors. The need for formal board evaluation is now a main principle of the UK Corporate Governance Code, which requires:
  - the board to undertake a formal and rigorous annual evaluation of its own performance and that of individual directors and committees of the Board;
  - evaluation of board performance for a FTSE 350 company to be carried out externally at least once every three years;
  - individual evaluation of each director, which should identify whether he or she contributes effectively to the board and the extent of his or her commitment. The Code also goes further

and requires the chairman to act on the results of performance
evaluation;
–   that the chairman's performance be evaluated by the
    non-executive directors; and
–   that the annual report should contain a statement from the
    board on how performance evaluation has been conducted.
Even where a company does not have to comply with the Code,
the benefits of conducting an evaluation of board performance
as a means of determining whether individual directors and the
board are doing what is required of them effectively and, insofar
as they are not, to identify areas where improvement is needed,
is self-evident. Indeed most executives who have reached board
level will have pursued careers during which their individual and
group performance have been regularly and actively evaluated and
assessed and, where necessary, performance training and development programmes have been put in place to help them improve
and move to the board. It is therefore extremely important to
continue this evaluation and development process given the importance of decisions made by the board and the disastrous effect a
poorly performing board or series of bad decisions can have on the
success of a company.

There is no prescribed system and the chairman, directors
and board have complete discretion and authority to determine
what needs to be covered in the performance evaluation process.
Certainly from a corporate governance perspective there is now
much greater emphasis on the actual behaviour demonstrated by
directors and their boards and on the distinction between the roles
of the chairman, CEO, executives, non-executives and SINED,
etc and therefore this behaviour will need to be assessed to know
where improvements and help are needed. It might be, for example,
that some board members do not fully understand their roles and
further training for individual directors in these areas is needed.

The FRC's Guidance on Board Effectiveness, whilst not
intending to be exhaustive or prescriptive, lists some areas that a
board evaluation might cover and are worth consulting.

However, one thing that is clear is that unless a formal
assessment is carried out it is very easy for problems to go
unrecognised or unacknowledged for a considerable time, which

is of no benefit to the directors, the board, or the company. At best, it might mean under-performance and at worst, a corporate disaster. For example, the board evaluation might identify that the quality of papers presented to the board is poor, they lack detail and are received only a few hours before meetings. By identifying and then rectifying this problem, the board is less likely to reach an ill-informed or hasty decision that it might later regret.

In addition, an externally facilitated board evaluation can give opportunity for a fresh, objective and independent evaluation by a third party which might be of benefit, not only in terms of external validation, but also by encouraging openness and an unaffected outsider reviewing performance from a different perspective.

- *'Refreshment' of the board* – It is recognised that membership of a board usually needs to be periodically 'refreshed' to prevent a tendency towards 'group think' where directors become too cosy and unwilling to constructively challenge colleagues (see Composition of the board above), This should be considered at the time of a director's appointment (see Chapter 1) and be addressed when considering succession planning (see Chapter 3). The UK Corporate Governance Code requires all directors of FTSE 350 companies to offer themselves for election at each AGM, whilst directors of other companies would, subject to the Articles, usually be re-elected at the first AGM following their reappointment and thereafter at intervals of no more than three years. The Code also recommends that where a non-executive director is to be reappointed for a term beyond six years, this should be subject to rigorous review as it might affect determination of independence.

ii Risk management and internal controls

All directors will recognise the importance of identifying, monitoring and, as far as possible, either avoiding or mitigating risks that might impact the company's performance or prospects. Failure to do so would effectively leave the success of a company to chance which is a luxury none can afford and no shareholders are likely to support.

However, even in recent months, there have been numerous reports of corporate governance and risk management failings in very sizeable companies. Two such examples widely reported in the press include the manipulation of the inter-bank lending rate by Barclays and lax controls at HSBC over bearer share company accounts making it possible for them to be used to launder Mexican drug money around the world. Incidents such as these have raised public awareness and considerable concern has been expressed about how it is possible for such problems and issues to go undetected, often for prolonged periods of time.

The need for risk management and implementation of effective internal controls is common to all companies. Depending on the nature of a company's operations, the risk identification and management process may be much more straightforward in a small organisation where the directors are closer to operations and have a working knowledge of the risks and control issues. In contrast, the risk assessment and risk management process in large companies and those with complex operations will usually involve delegation of much of the process, for which the board remains responsible.

The duty of the board to present a balanced and understandable assessment of the company's position and prospects is a main principle in the UK Corporate Governance Code. The Code also requires the board to determine the nature and extent of significant risks faced by the company as a consequence of the board's approved strategy and to identify the level of risk they are willing to accept to achieve the strategy. Directors are required to include a statement in the annual report and accounts, immediately preceding the audit report, explaining their responsibility for preparing accounts and commenting on the company's internal system of risk management and control (see Chapter 9). Coupled with this is the requirement, at least once a year to review and report to shareholders on the effectiveness of the company's risk management, corporate reporting and internal control systems. This review must cover all aspects of corporate reporting, internal control and risk management including operational and compliance issues and not just purely financial matters.

For the vast majority of companies the need to manage and control risks has always been known and addressed, possibly informally, at a more operational level. However, the Turnbull Guidance introduced the requirement for the board to be responsible for determining risk management and internal control and reviewing and reporting on its effectiveness once a year (see paragraph i above).

It is particularly important for the board to promote and encourage the right culture and attitude within the company to ensure that the need to observe systems, procedures and control measures is recognised, understood and observed at all times and at all levels within the company without any temporary lapses. With this in mind it is important for directors to remember that whilst they might not be directly involved or responsible for the action resulting in loss or damage to the company, they will be held accountable if they failed to identify a potential risk, did not implement sufficient controls or failed to put in place appropriate reporting requirements from which it would have been apparent.

Adequate consideration must be given to the content and frequency of monitoring and reporting to ensure risks are identified, managed and mitigated as soon as they arise, thereby minimising any damage or adverse consequences for the company. Risk management and control systems must also be responsive to the need to change and adapt in light of the emergence of new risks and the experience of others. For example, recently there has been a shift in focus towards:

- companies identifying and managing 'show-stopping' strategic risks, which alone or together could totally undermine the company's ability to achieve it's strategic objectives or cause it to fail;
- recognition of the need to combine risks and risk events, as well as determining the 'net' effect of each individually, so total potential exposure can be gauged; and
- active consideration of potential reputational risks and the need for crisis management policies, given that in today's electronic world bad news is transmitted virtually instantaneously.

iii Delegation of authority

Except where the company is very small and the directors are also effectively the operational managers of the business, it is unlikely they would be able to attend personally to all matters that concern the board. Where this is the case, the directors can delegate responsibility for carrying out certain tasks. However, they must ensure that persons to whom they delegate have the necessary knowledge, experience, skills and understanding to carry out the tasks properly as the board will remain ultimately responsible for their actions. ICSA has published

Guidance Note 071011 *Matters Reserved for the Board* to help directors to determine what it is appropriate to delegate. For example, the board would usually decide matters such as strategy, business plans and budgets; dividend payments; approval of the report and accounts; formal shareholder communications; extension or change of business activities; remuneration policy; and determination of committees and their terms of reference, etc. In practice, the board will often delegate authority to the following:

Committees

The company's Articles usually empower the directors to delegate their powers to committees consisting of one or more directors and to impose regulations by which such committees operate (Table A, Reg 72 or Model Articles Regs 5 and 6). However, where the Articles are silent on this matter, the directors have no such power of delegation.

The board resolution establishing a committee must be carefully drafted to ensure the committee's status and functions are clearly defined. For example, it must be clear whether the committee has been authorised to reach decisions and put them into effect itself, or merely to consider a range of options and make recommendations to the board. To achieve this, 'terms of reference' setting out the committee's structure, membership, constitution, role and requirements for meetings and other matters would usually be determined and approved by the board. Terms of reference would typically include:

- details of and requirements for membership;
- details of how meetings are to be conducted in relation to the quorum, frequency, notice required and recording of minutes;
- duties of the committee; and
- the authority of the committee and details of any limitations on the powers delegated by the board.

Committees frequently found in companies' management structures include audit, risk, remuneration and nomination as well as share allotment and standing committees and those set up on an ad hoc basis to consider specific issues such as health and safety, environmental matters, acquisitions or disposals, etc.

ICSA has issued guidance notes containing model terms of reference for audit, risk, remuneration and nomination committees, copies of which are available at www.icsa.org.uk, and directors of listed companies should also refer to recommendations set out in the UK Corporate Governance Code and FRC Guidance (see Appendices 1 and 12).

The board can revoke any delegation of powers at any time by recording the decision in the board meeting minutes.

Managing or other director

As set out in Chapter 1, paragraph v, it is usual for provisions in a company's Articles to permit the board to appoint a 'managing director' and for the board to confer any or all of its powers of management to the appointee by simple resolution (Table A, Regs 84 and 72). This is often necessary for practical reasons where the board meets formally only, say, once or twice a month and day-to-day matters need to be approved in the meantime. Where this is an issue, the board may delegate authority to the managing director, for example to enter into contracts or agreements on behalf of the company, either generally or limited to certain transactions. Similar provisions relating to the appointment of a 'managing director' are not contained in the Model Articles, although companies may insert such provisions.

A company's Articles may also allow the directors to delegate such of their powers as they consider fit and desirable to any director holding another executive office (Table A, Reg 72). Regulation 5 of the Model Articles goes further than this by stating that powers can be delegated to any person or committee, using any means (including power of attorney), to any extent in relation to such matters or territories, and on such terms and conditions as the board of directors thinks fit. Regulation 5 also states that the directors may authorise further delegation of powers by any person to whom they are delegated. For example, the operations directors may be delegated authority for signing commercial contracts on behalf of the company up to a specified monetary limit without need for formal board approval each time.

Agents

Table A, Reg 71 permits the directors to appoint any person, by power of attorney or otherwise, to be the agent of the company for such purposes and on such conditions as they determine. For example where presence in person is required overseas, delegation of power to an agent may be used, with the solicitor or attorney who represents the company acting as appointed agent. Similar provisions are contained in Reg 5 of the Model Articles.

Company secretary

Whereas a public company must have a secretary (CA 2006, s 271) a private company is not required to have a secretary (CA 2006, s 270(1)) although the functions performed by the secretary will still need to be carried out. In practice, the directors delegate many tasks of a legal, compliance and administrative nature to the secretary as well as relying on the secretary for technical, legal, compliance, management or adminis-trative advice.

Whilst company secretaries' roles vary tremendously, in many cases they assist the directors by:

- ensuring, as far as they are able, that all corporate compliance and administrative work is carried out;
- advising them of the requirement to promote the success of the company and to be able to demonstrate that they have done so;
- keeping them aware of their responsibilities towards shareholders, employees, creditors and other stakeholders and the implications of decisions on these other parties;
- ensuring compliance with legal, regulatory and contractual requirements;
- properly recording decisions of the board and ensuring actions are pursued and the outcome recorded;
- ensuring high standards of governance are maintained;
- informing directors of their obligations and assisting with infor-mation disclosed; and
- assisting with induction of new directors into the business to enable them to determine the extent of their new role and responsibilities, as well as providing information to new directors carrying out their own due diligence on the company.

However, whilst responsibilities may be delegated to the company secretary to the extent indicated above, the directors remain ultimately responsible for ensuring that all legal requirements are being met. It is therefore important that directors periodically check the company secretary is carrying out delegated tasks satisfactorily.

The importance of the company secretary in a company's management was endorsed by inclusion in the UK Corporate Governance Code of the requirement that:

- all directors should have access to the advice and services of the company secretary, who is responsible to the board for ensuring that board procedures are followed and that applicable rules and regulations are complied with;
- under direction of the chairman, the company secretary is responsible for ensuring good information flows within the board and its committees and between senior management and non-executive directors;
- the company secretary facilitates the induction of new directors and assists with the professional development of existing directors; and
- the company secretary is responsible for advising the board, through the chairman, on corporate governance matters (see Appendix 1, B.5.2).

In addition, the FRC's Guidance on Board Effectiveness goes a little further and states that the company secretary should ensure high-quality information is presented to the board and its committees, be involved in giving or arranging directors' induction and training and for advising and periodically reviewing board governance matters.

3   Length of service

There is nothing in CA 2006 that limits the time a director may remain in office.

A director may continue in office successfully for many years.

However, there may be circumstances where:

- the director decides to resign, for example because of time pressures, a parting of the ways with fellow directors who take no account of his or her views or opinions, or simply because another more attractive opportunity has emerged;
- the shareholders do not wish the director to continue in office, for example where they are concerned about the director's performance or motivation or the direction in which he or she is taking the company, and either seek to remove the director from office, or not to reappoint him or her at the next AGM;
- there are specific restrictions in the company's Articles that prevent the director from continuing in office after, say, a given time or where the director ceases to be eligible and is required to vacate office;
- a non-executive director was appointed for a specified term, that period is up and a board review determines that re-election is not appropriate.

This chapter looks at the mechanics of changing directors and the need for periodic refreshment of the board by covering:

- Succession planning
- Resignation
- Removal
- Retirement by rotation
- Vacating office.

Succession planning

It is very important that board composition and succession planning are regularly reviewed on a formal basis, taking account of the needs of the company going forward, each director's length of tenure and the need to refresh membership of the board, as well as feedback from the board evaluation process on where improvements could be made. Clearly it is important to have an appropriate level of stability and continuity in a company and an organised approach to succession planning can help avoid situations where the company's chairman, CEO and finance director announce with little advance warning that they intend to leave at or around the same time. Substantial change is likely to cause concern amongst a company's employees and shareholders and the resulting uncertainty, unrest and publicity could be very damaging. By conducting formal succession planning at least once a year it is more likely these situations can be pre-empted, enabling implementation of more orderly solutions and for directors' changes to be carefully planned around each other to ensure, as far as possible, they do not coincide.

Succession planning is important not only for the board, but also for the membership of board committees and senior executives, who will be in the frame for appointment as executive directors. It might be, for example, that a senior executive is suitable for appointment to the board provided certain aspects of the person's skills and abilities are improved. The succession plan provides a formal means of addressing this and providing a timescale within which the improvements need to be achieved. Training and personal development programmes can then be put into place to ensure the senior executive is ready for appointment to the board at the appropriate time.

In a listed company the nomination committee, with the involvement of the chairman, would usually be responsible for recruitment of directors and succession planning. In smaller, unlisted companies such matters would normally be addressed by the board or by an ad hoc committee of the board formed for the purpose.

Composition of the existing board should be considered when reviewing succession planning to ensure it is clear what skills, experience, background, characteristics, etc. are required of the new appointee to complement and further improve the existing balance on the board. Feedback from the board evaluation process will be important as there might be particular areas of concern that could be addressed by well-timed and careful recruitment of a replacement director.

Consideration also needs to be given to the challenges faced by the company in light of decided strategy. It might be, for example, that the board is gearing the company up for an acquisition or listing, in which case appointment of an independent non-executive director with corporate finance experience is considered necessary and desirable. Alternatively, it might be that the new director is also to join the audit committee in which case recent, relevant financial experience might be required.

Non-executive directors are usually engaged for a limited term given the need to preserve their independence and consequently they need to be periodically replaced. Their maximum length of tenure should be worked into the succession planning process.

Once the company's succession plan has been determined, parts will need to be distilled out into action plans for managing succession of particular roles. A detailed and agreed specification of the required role is needed, setting out the skills, knowledge, experience and personal attributes required of the replacement. Decisions will need to be made about who will lead and who will be involved in the succession planning process. For example, it will usually be led by the chairman and the head of HR, company secretary, CEO, and certain executive directors might be involved and responsible for different stages of the process. However, where it is the chairman's succession, the senior independent director will usually lead the process.

The need for and timing of additional nomination committee meetings (or board meetings, depending on how succession is being addressed) will need to be considered, planned and organised. In addition the timetable, allowing time for hand-over and to re-start the process if initial candidates are not suitable, and need for and timing of public announcements must be determined. Given the length of time that recruitment would normally takes, it is important to identify and put dates to key milestones in the process and to determine how to monitor and report progress against them. This is important to ensure an appointee is lined up, ready for succession, at the appropriate time.

The form the recruitment process will take is important as, in the interests of achieving diversity, it is important to go beyond the usual known channels and executive search agencies and head hunters will need to be given a brief detailing what is required of them and the breadth of search they are to undertake. Where it is thought the replacement will come from the company's senior executive, such agency might be required to undertake a benchmarking exercise.

Resignation

Notwithstanding any restrictions in any contract of service, directors have the right to resign simply by tendering their resignation to the company (Table A, Reg 81(d), Model Articles for private companies limited by shares and private companies limited by guarantee, Reg 18(f) and Model Articles for public companies, Reg 22(f)). Such resignation would normally need to be in writing and be addressed to the company's registered office.

The Articles usually require directors to give reasonable notice of their resignation, but, in the absence of any such provision, a director can resign without the need for notice (*OBC Caspian Ltd v Thorp 1998 SLT 653, OH*).

A director's resignation must be noted in the register of directors. Notification must be sent to Companies House, using prescribed Form TM01 (where the director is an individual) or TM02 (where the director is a corporate entity), within 14 days.

Removal

The members of a company may, at any time and notwithstanding anything in the company's Articles or any service contract with the director, remove a director from office by ordinary resolution approved in a general meeting of which special notice has been given (CA 2006, s 168). Such removal is initiated when the company receives 'special notice' from a member detailing the member's intention to propose the resolution to remove a director at a general meeting.

Whilst the Articles cannot exclude this statutory right, they may permit removal by an alternative, and often simpler, means. For example, they may allow removal by majority vote of the other directors or merely by written notice from the holding company or the holder of the class of shares that appointed the director.

As removal of a director is a contentious matter and most often takes place when the relationship between the director and shareholders has irretrievably broken down, the remaining directors must ensure that the procedures set out in CA 2006 or those in the Articles are closely observed in order to avoid any recourse by the director so removed.

Retirement by rotation

Although there is no general requirement in CA 2006 for directors to retire by rotation at each AGM, such provision is usually included in the Articles of a public company (Table A, as it applies to a public company Regs 73 to 80, or the Model Articles for public companies, Reg 21). This provision serves to restore the balance of power between the shareholders and directors by giving the shareholders an opportunity to vote against a resolution to reappoint a particular director.

Prior to the AGM, the directors will need to check the provisions on rotation in the company's Articles, as they vary tremendously. In many instances private and subsidiary companies, and those which have directors appointed by the holders of different classes of shares, will not require retirement by rotation.

Table A as it applies to public companies requires all directors (except a managing director or director holding any other executive office) to retire by rotation and offer themselves for re-election at the company's first AGM. Thereafter any directors appointed during the year must retire by rotation, together with one-third of the existing directors. Under Reg 21 of the Model Articles for public companies all the directors must retire from office at the first AGM. Thereafter any directors who have been appointed by the directors since the last annual general meeting, or who were not appointed or reappointed at one of the preceding two annual general meetings must retire from office and may offer themselves for reappointment by the members. In addition, the UK Corporate Governance Code requires that directors of fully listed companies offer themselves for re-election every year.

Where applicable, the selection of which directors are due to retire by rotation will be based upon who has been longest in office since they were last reappointed. Where the director is willing to continue, wording of the resolution will be along the lines of 'That Mr XYZ, retiring by rotation in accordance with the Articles of Association, offers himself for reappointment as a director of the company'. The resolution will be proposed as an ordinary resolution and be passed (or fail) on a simple majority.

Where the resolution for reappointment is approved, the director will continue in office. Where the resolution is not approved, the director will remain in office only until the end of the AGM, following which he or she will cease to be a director. This fact must be recorded in the register of directors and be notified to Companies House using prescribed Form TM01 or TM02, for individual and corporate directors respectively.

Private companies are no longer required to hold an AGM unless a specific requirement to the contrary is contained in the Articles and the mere mention of rotation of directors in the Articles is not necessarily sufficient to require an AGM to be held for this purpose.

Vacating office

A company's Articles will usually provide that, when a person becomes prohibited from holding office as a director (see Chapter 1), the office of director shall be vacated.

The Articles may also specify other circumstances in which a director is required to vacate office, for example where the director:

- in the opinion of a registered medical practitioner who is treating that person he or she has become physically or mentally incapable of acting as a director and may remain so for more than three months and this opinion is confirmed in writing (Model Articles for private companies limited by shares and private companies limited by guarantee, Reg 18(d), Model Articles for public companies, Reg 22(d));
- fails to attend board meetings for six months without permission for absence (Table A, Reg 81(e));
- ceases to hold a shareholding qualification; and
- has been in office for the maximum period specified in the Articles.

4   Statutory statement of directors' duties

In an attempt to make directors' duties more accessible and easier to understand CA 2006 contains a statutory statement of directors' general duties which draws together and updates various common law rules and principles (CA 2006, ss 170–181). Whilst the statutory statement replaces these common law rules and principles, they remain important for determining how the duties in the statutory statement are interpreted and applied (CA 2006, s 170). It should be noted that requirements in the statutory statement of duties extend to de facto and shadow directors and, in some instances, to former directors of a company.

Directors need to understand the duties placed upon them by the statutory statement and this chapter covers:

- content of the statutory statement
- origins of directors' duties – common law.

It should also be noted that this statutory statement of directors' duties does not cover all the duties that a director may owe to the company. Many duties are expressed elsewhere in legislation, such as the duty to keep accounting records and to protect the health and safety of employees, etc. Information on directors' other duties beyond this statement of 'general' duties is contained in the chapters that follow.

Should a director breach any of these statutory duties, CA 2006, s 178 states that the consequences would be the same as if the common law rule or equitable principle had been breached, namely civil remedy and this is addressed in Chapter 13.

Content of the statutory statement

The statutory statement comprises seven duties. These are based on, but replace, certain common law rules and principles owed by directors to the companies to which they are appointed.

The seven duties

These require directors to:

i Act within their powers

A director must act within his powers under the company's constitution and only exercise his powers for the purpose for which they were conferred (CA 2006, s 171). This is largely a re-statement of a well recognised common law principle and means, for example, that a director should only consider allotting more shares in the company where it is in the company's interests to do so, not as a means of preventing a takeover purely to preserve his or her own remunerated position.

ii Promote the success of the company

A director must 'act in a way he considers, in good faith, would be most likely to promote the success of the company for the benefit of its members as a whole' (CA 2006, s 172). This duty applies to all directors' actions, not just those exercised at board meetings.

In response to concern about how 'success' is interpreted (as it is different from the known common law requirement for acting in the best interests of the company) the government confirmed it will usually mean a 'long-term increase in value' of the company (although depending on the nature and purpose of the company 'value' could be interpreted in many ways).

When making decisions, directors must ensure they have regard to the likely consequences of the decision over the long term, which means they must take account of the:

- interests of employees;
- impact on the community and environment;
- need to foster business relationships with suppliers, customers and others;
- need to act fairly between members; and
- need to maintain a reputation for high standards of business and conduct.

The requirement to observe these factors is set out in CA 2006, s 172(1)(a) to (f), formalising the need for directors to consider and balance the interests of the company's members with those of other 'stakeholders' when deciding what actions should be taken to promote the success of the company.

A great deal of concern was initially expressed about this duty, the need to consider the five factors listed above and its implications. However, given that the interests of employees, customers, the environment, and suppliers, etc. are to an extent already intrinsically linked to achieving success in the commercial environment, it is probable that many directors instinctively consider these matters when making decisions and this process, and the need for it, has simply been formalised.

The directors must decide, using their own business judgement, what weight is given to the five factors listed above from CA 2006, s 172(1) when decisions are being made. It is not intended that these requirements will delay the decision-making process or create the need for a paper trail of factors considered when making decisions, although there might be situations where this is appropriate. Neither is it intended, or appropriate, that minutes of the company's board meeting record whether each factor was considered.

From a practical perspective most decisions taken by the company's directors, certainly in larger companies, follow a review and proposal process and are supported by background papers or briefing notes. It is therefore important that, as well as the directors considering the factors set out in CA 2006, s 172 in whatever manner they determine appropriate, the factors are also properly considered when options are evaluated background papers are prepared and recommendations are made to the board by the management or executive team. The directors therefore have a duty to ensure that such persons are fully aware of the requirements of CA 2006, s 172.

iii Exercise independent judgement

A director must exercise independent judgement (CA 2006, s 173). This duty largely codifies the requirement in common law for directors to exercise their powers independently, without subordinating their powers to the will of others and without fettering their discretion. For example, where a director is appointed in accordance with the company's Articles to represent a particular class of shareholders, the director must still exercise his or her own judgement when considering what action is necessary to promote the success of the company.

A director is still able to seek advice where appropriate and the director's duty to exercise independent judgement is subject to restrictions contained in any agreements entered into by the company or in the company's constitution, including resolutions of the shareholders.

iv Exercise reasonable care, skill and diligence

A director must exercise such reasonable skill, care and diligence as would be exercised by a reasonably diligent person with:
- the general knowledge, skill and experience that could reasonably be expected from a person carrying out the director's functions; and
- the director's actual general knowledge, skill and experience (CA 2006, s 174).

This two-step test is not new as it largely mirrors the common law standard and the tests already laid down in IA 1986, s 214.

v Avoid conflicts of interest

A director has a statutory duty to avoid any situations in which he has, or could have, a direct or indirect interest that conflicts, or could conflict, with the interests of the company (CA 2006, s 175). This applies, in particular, to the exploitation of property, information or opportunity regardless of whether the company could take advantage of it. It applies to a conflict of duty, as well as a conflict of interest and includes the interests of 'connected persons'.

This is increasingly referred to as a 'situational conflict' and includes circumstances where, for example, a director is involved with a competitor, major shareholder, customer or supplier, is an adviser to the company or a competitor, is a trustee of the company's pension scheme, or owns property adjacent to the company's premises. This list is not exhaustive and there may be other circumstances giving rise to a situational conflict.

Each individual director must determine his or her own situational conflicts and seek to avoid them. However, in some instances, avoidance might not be possible or even beneficial to the company, in which case the director must immediately notify the company of the situational conflict and seek prior approval of the circumstances and the existence of the situational conflict. Thereafter, the director must advise the company of any change in the nature of a previously notified conflict.

Provided a public company has the requisite provisions in its Articles of Association, the board may authorise a conflict of interest notified to it by a director.

Where a private company was incorporated before 1 October 2008, authorisation may be given by the directors provided a resolution to this effect has been approved by the shareholders or the company's Articles of Association have been amended to include such authority. For any private company incorporated on or after 1 October 2008, authorisation may be given by the board provided there is no provision stating otherwise in the company's Articles of Association.

Where a public company does not have the required provision in its Articles, or a private company incorporated before 1 October 2008 has not passed the necessary shareholders' resolution or amended its Articles, approval by the shareholders of any director's conflict situations will be needed. For many companies it would be costly, time-consuming, inconvenient and impractical to arrange shareholder meetings to approve such matters and most companies have ensured the directors have been given the necessary authority.

Authorisation of a conflict of interest is only effective if the quorum requirement for the meeting at which it is to be approved is met without including the relevant director, or would have been authorised without including the relevant director's votes. A transaction which has been validly authorised by the directors, as permitted by the company's articles or resolution of the shareholders, does not need further authorisation by a company's shareholders (CA 2006, s 180(1)).

Authorisation by the directors of a company under s 175 cannot be retrospective and only applies to the actual conflict situation, not to a breach of duty. This means that where a conflict situation had been validly authorised this does not absolve the director from his duties to act in a way he considers most likely to promote the success of the company (CA 2006, s 172).

A problem which many directors who have conflicts of interest may encounter is in relation to confidential information. Where there has been a valid authorisation of the conflict, and the director receives confidential information as a result of that conflict, he can be excused from having to disclose that information to the company. The director may also be excused from the whole or part of board meetings at which the matter giving rise to the conflict is discussed.

Companies need to consider directors' conflicts on a case-by-case basis and approval must only be given in accordance with the general directors' duties as set out in CA 2006, in particular where approval is thought necessary to promote the success of the company. There are various options the board can consider:

- excluding the director from receipt of relevant information and discussions on the matter;
- excluding the director from the board in relation to the matter; and
- requiring the director to remove him or herself from the conflict situation or resign.

Companies should maintain a register of authorisations, containing information about the conflict and what the authorisation related to, when it was approved, any limitations or restrictions that apply and when the authorisation will expire. In order to do this, documentation recording the director's situational conflict should include:

- details of the matter which has been authorised;
- the duration of the authority (usually subject to annual review) and a statement to the effect that the authority can be revoked at any time;
- the circumstances under which the director must refer back to the board for the authority to be reviewed;
- provisions, where appropriate, stating that the director may not receive information relating to the conflict or participate in board discussions in relation to the matter; and
- provisions, where appropriate, that where the director obtains information as a result of the conflict he will not be obliged to disclose that information to the company or to use the information in relation to the company's affairs. It may also be useful, if another company is involved in the conflict, to ascertain and ensure that they have also allowed the same provision.

Whilst it is recognised that the duty to avoid and seek prior approval of a situational conflict rests with individual directors, companies often seek to gather this information and encourage disclosure by, for example, carrying out a formal six-monthly or annual review often based on a questionnaire for completion by the directors. It is also usual practice to remind the directors at the beginning of each meeting of the need for them to disclose any interests they might have in the matters on the agenda. Both of these are useful ways of flushing out situational conflicts that need to be notified.

vi Not accept benefits from third parties

A director has a statutory duty not to accept a benefit from a third party which is given because of the position held by the director or because of anything the director has done in his capacity as a director (CA 2006, s 176).

In brief, acceptance of benefits is not subject to any 'de minimis' limit and is only permitted where the matter is approved by the company's members or it can reasonably be regarded that it will not give rise to a conflict of interest with the company.

Given the questions this raises with regard to corporate hospitality and gifts, companies would be well advised to consider their policies on this and to ensure all directors are given guidance and are fully informed about what is acceptable. This will very much depend on the type of business the company is in, industry practice and the accepted norm. Timing of the receipt of corporate hospitality is also important, as it might be appropriate to decline if in the midst of contract or supply negotiations.

Maintenance of a register to record benefits offered, their approval and details of receipt will help to demonstrate compliance with this duty.

vii Declare interests in transactions or arrangements

A director of a company has a statutory duty to disclose any direct or indirect interest he has in a proposed transaction or arrangement with the company (CA 2006, s 177). Furthermore, the director has a duty under CA 2006, s 182 to declare any interest held, direct or indirect, in an existing transaction or arrangement.

In both instances, the director will need to disclose the nature and extent of his interest to the other directors either at a meeting of the directors or in writing (and it is either sent to each director or presented at a meeting or the directors). However, no disclosure is needed where the interest does not give rise to a conflict of interest, the other directors are already aware of the interest, or it concerns the director's service contract. It is advisable for companies to keep a record of directors' interests disclosed and to make sure directors are aware of the need to notify any change in the nature of their interest.

A declaration required under CA 2006, s 177 must be made to the board prior to the company entering into the transaction or arrangement. However, a declaration required by CA 2006, s 182 may be made either at a meeting of the board, by written notice under CA 2006, s 184 or by a general notice under CA 2006, s 185 as soon as possible.

Where an interest has been declared, provisions in the company's Articles must be checked to determine whether the director may still be included in the quorum and vote on the matter in which the interest is held. Having said this, notwithstanding what is permitted by the Articles, there may be situations where it is better for the director not to be involved in discussions and decisions reached on the conflicted matter.

Another important point is that formal disclosure and approval of a director's conflict of interest in a transaction can help secure refusal by the court for a derivative action to proceed (see Chapter 13). For example, in *Kleanthous v Paphitis & Others [2011] EWHC 2287*, heard in October 2011, application by a shareholder for a derivative action was refused as all transactions concerned had been approved by the company's board and the board had also been made fully aware of, and had approved, the particular director's conflict of interest that was being called into question. This matter involved a director of Rymans Group (Rymans) pursuing the acquisition of La Senza once Rymans had decided not to proceed, which a shareholder of Rymans claimed was a conflict of interest from which he received personal benefit.

Origins of directors' duties – common law

It has long been established in common law that a director owes two types of duty to the company: a 'fiduciary duty' and a 'duty of skill and care' and it is important these principles are understood. Where a director breaches these duties, the company has been able, through common law, to take action to recover its property or to obtain payment of damages from the director as compensation for the loss incurred, and to recover any personal profit made by the director.

Interpretation of these common law duties is embodied in a vast number of cases which are not easy for directors to find and understand, hence the introduction of the statutory statement of directors' duties.

i Fiduciary duty

The need for directors to observe their fiduciary duty to the company when contributing to and making decisions as part of the board has in the past meant that directors always needed to:

- act in good faith and in the best interests of the company;
- use the powers conferred on them for the proper purpose;
- not put themselves in a position where they have an actual or potential conflict of interest with the company; and
- not make any secret personal profit from opportunities that arise from their position as a director.

As can be seen from the above, these common law duties largely gave rise to a negative obligation requiring directors not to do anything or make any decisions that conflicted with the interests of the company.

The need for directors to observe their fiduciary duty is best illustrated by some sample cases.

CASE	DETAILS
Bhullar v Bhullar, Re Bhullar Bros Limited [2003] All ER (D) 445 (Mar)	One family which part-owned a limited company through which their grocery business was run became aware that the property adjacent to the company's premises was for sale and bought it. The Court of Appeal held that the directors had breached their duty to communicate the availability of the property to the company and confirmed that it should be transferred to the company at purchase price.
British Midland Tools v Midland International Tooling [2003] All ER (D) 174 (Mar)	It was held that a number of directors had breached their fiduciary duties to the company where they knew a potential competitor was poaching the company's employees and did nothing to prevent it in the period prior to them joining the competitor.
Extrasure Travel Insurances Ltd v Scattergood [2003] 1 BCLC 598	Directors who transferred money from one group company to another merely to satisfy a pressing creditor had breached their fiduciary duties as it was not in the interests of the company to transfer the money. They were held liable accordingly.

CASE	DETAILS
JJ Harison (Properties) Ltd v Harrison [2001] 1 BCLC 158	A director used company resources to obtain planning permission on land which he bought from the company without informing his fellow directors of the planning status and without obtaining a market valuation. The director was held to have breached his duty to act in the best interests of the company and was required to account to the company for profits made.
Hogg v Cramphorn Ltd [1967] Ch 254	Directors who issued shares with enhanced voting rights to forestall a takeover bid, whilst they were acting in good faith, had breached their duty by making improper use of their powers to issue shares.

ii Duty of skill and care

Directors have been required under common law to exercise whatever skill they possessed and reasonable care when acting in the company's interests.

Whilst traditionally (based on judgment in *City Equitable Fire Insurance Co Ltd [1925] Ch 407, CA*) the degree of skill required of a director was only that expected of an 'ordinary man' without the need for him to be an expert, to possess any particular skills or to devote his continuous attention to the company's business, the requirements have been changing to take account of the fact that:

- many directors are full-time executives employed under contracts of service who are expected to bring particular skills and expertise to the company in exchange for sizeable remuneration; and
- when determining whether a director should be personally liable for wrongful trading, IA 1986, s 214 applies a 'reasonable director' standard to determine what is expected of someone carrying out the director's function within the company.

As a consequence, more objective tests of the level of skill required of directors were being applied. This is illustrated in *Bairstow v Queens Moat Houses plc [2000] 1 BCLC 549* where the court held that an executive director is expected to bring to his work a level of competence commensurate with his responsibilities and for which he receives substantial remuneration.

In terms of the time and degree of attention a director was required to devote to the affairs of the company, there was a difference in what is expected from an executive director as opposed to a non-executive director. For non-executive directors, principles in City Equitable that directors were not required to give continuous attention to the affairs of the company and that their duties are intermittent could still be applied.

However, in contrast, executive directors would usually be required to devote their time and attention to the business of the company on a full-time basis, although the size and nature of the company would determine which matters received personal attention.

Where the size of the company made it impossible for directors to attend to all matters personally, delegation was permitted, provided there was adequate supervision (see Chapter 2). In *Re Barings plc; Secretary of State for Trade and Industry v Baker (1998) BCC 5 83*, when making a disqualification order the judge made it clear that, whilst directors may delegate functions, given the responsibilities of their office they must adequately supervise those carrying out the work even where they trust their competence and integrity. Furthermore, where directors seek professional advice, they must not rely solely upon the advice received without exercising their own judgement as they cannot absolve themselves entirely of responsibility by delegation (*Re Bradcrown Ltd [2001] 1 BCLC 547*).

5 Disclosure requirements

There are a number of statutory duties arising under CA 2006 that require directors to disclose certain information to the company, to the shareholders in the accounts and to investigators appointed by the Secretary of State.

This chapter covers:

- Interest in contracts and transactions
- Interest in shares
- Investigations.

Interest in contracts and transactions

Directors must not put themselves in a position where there is a conflict between their personal interests and their statutory duty to the company. Similarly, directors cannot make a secret profit from a contract with the company (see Chapter 4).

To address this, under CA 2006, ss 177 and 182, a director who has any direct or indirect interest in a contract or proposed contract, transaction or arrangement with the company must disclose this to the board. Provided disclosure has been made, the transaction is not voidable and the director will not be required to account for any benefit gained.

Failure to disclose such interest is a finable offence (CA 2006, ss 183(1) and (2)) and the director will in most instances be required to repay any personal profit made to the company (*Regal (Hastings) Ltd v Gulliver [1942] 1 All ER 378*).

It should also be noted that the board of directors has a corresponding duty to ensure that, when a director has disclosed an interest, it is recorded. Failure to do so exposes the company and every officer in default to a fine (CA 2006, s 248(4)).

Disclosure must:

- be made by all directors of private and public companies, including 'shadow directors' (see Chapter 1) (CA 2006, ss 182 and 187);
- be made at the earliest opportunity;

- include the nature of the interest;
- be made at a meeting of the board of directors, not to a committee meeting (*Guinness plc v Saunders [1990] 2 AC 663*) and it is not sufficient to record disclosure by resolution in writing (CA 2006, ss 182(2), 184(5) and 185(4));
- be made and recorded in the minutes of the relevant board meeting even where the company has only a sole director (*Neptune (Vehicle Washing Equipment) Ltd v Fitzgerald [1995] 1 BCLC 352*); and
- be given by the director of such matters that might be relevant to the company's audited accounts (CA 2006, s 412(5)).

A director who is a member of another firm or company can disclose general notice of an interest without need for further disclosure at subsequent meetings.

Whilst the disclosure requirements of CA 2006, ss 177 and 182 cannot be abrogated by a company's Articles, the Articles can impose stricter requirements.

The Articles might also state whether a director who has disclosed an interest can be counted in the quorum and vote on the matter under consideration. However, Rule 11.1.7(4)(a) of the Listing Rules requires that listed companies ensure that where a director or person connected to a director has an interest in a transaction (making it a related party transaction), the director does not vote on the matter.

Save for small and medium-sized companies which are exempt, companies must disclose information about directors interests in contracts and arrangements in their annual accounts.

Interest in shares

The obligations under CA 1985, s 324 for directors and shadow directors to disclose to the company their interest in shares and debentures have been repealed and there is no corresponding provision in CA 2006. This means that, while for the reasons set out below, directors of companies listed on the Official List, AIM and PLUS Market continue to be required to notify their companies of their interests in the companies' shares, directors of other companies have no such duty.

i Listed on the Official List

DTR 3.1 of the Disclosure and Transparency Rules requires persons discharging managerial responsibilities (PDMRs) and their connected persons to notify the company in writing of all transactions conducted on their account in the shares of the company, derivatives or any financial instruments relating to the shares. The notification must be made by the PDMR in writing within four business days of the transaction and include:

- the name of the PDMR;
- the reason for responsibility to notify;
- the name of the company;
- where applicable, a description of the financial instrument;
- the nature of the transaction (acquisition/disposal);
- the date and place of the transaction; and
- the price and volume of the transaction.

In addition, the director's disclosure of an interest must be announced by the company via a Regulatory Information Service, as soon as possible after notification by the PDMR and no later than the end of the next business day following receipt of the notification. The notification must include all the information provided by the PDMR as set out above as well as confirmation of the date the company was notified by the PDMR.

A listed company must also include in its annual financial report, usually in the directors' report, a statement of each person who has been a director of the company during the period's interest and any changes in their interest during the period under review, distinguishing between beneficial and non-beneficial interests. If there has been no change in a director's interest in the period under review, this must be stated. This information must be made up to a date not more than one month prior to the notice of the company's annual general meeting and is usually disclosed in the directors' report.

Furthermore, directors of listed companies must also be mindful that dealings by directors of listed companies in their own companies' securities are regulated by the Listing Rules. Before they deal in the securities of their listed company they, and other PDMRs and persons connected to them, are, unless the transaction is exempt, required by the Model Code to seek clearance to deal (see Appendix 9). Except in certain very limited circumstances, clearance will not be given where the listed company is in a close or prohibited period, or where the transaction is of a short-term nature.

ii AIM companies

AIM Rule 17 requires an AIM company to announce any deals by directors without delay and Schedule 5 of the AIM Rules requires the disclosure to include:

- the director's identity;
- the date the disclosure was made;
- the date of dealing;
- the price, amount and class of securities;
- the nature of the transaction; and
- the nature and extent of the director's interest in the transaction.

Where the transaction has taken place in a 'close period' or concerns a related financial product, additional disclosures would be required.

iii PLUS Market

A company whose shares have been admitted to the PLUS-quoted market is required by paragraph 34 of the PLUS Rules for Issuers to ensure that a deal by a director, member of his family, or a connected person is announced as soon as possible. The announcement must contain details of the following:

- the name of the person who has the obligation;
- the nature of the transaction;
- the resulting number of voting rights held by the notifying person;
- the date of the transaction;
- the date on which the company was notified;
- the number and class of securities concerned;
- where relevant, the name of the family member or connected person;
- the price paid for the shares; and
- any other information required under a DTR notification.

Investigations

The Secretary of State for Business, Innovation and Skills (BIS) has the power to investigate a company's affairs and membership and, where the company is subject to investigation, the company and all officers have a duty to co-operate with the investigation and to disclose such information as is required by the investigators (CA 1985, ss 431 to 434, as amended by CA 2006, s 1035). These self-standing provisions of the CA 1985 remained in force with some minor changes following the enactment of CA 2006.

There are many reasons for such investigations. For example, they may be initiated where it appears:

- the company's affairs have been conducted with intent to defraud creditors and others for a fraudulent, unlawful or prejudicial purpose (CA 1985, s 432);
- that those involved in formation of the company or management of its affairs are guilty of fraud, misconduct or misfeasance towards the company or its members (CA 1985, s 432);
- members have not been given all the information they might ordinarily be expected to receive (CA 1985, s 432);
- there has been a contravention of restrictions on directors' dealing in share options of quoted securities (CA 1985, s 323);
- there is an apparent need to determine the people interested in shares of controlling the company;
- insider dealing has taken place, in contravention of CJA 1993, s 52 and FSMA 2000; or
- the proceeds of crime have been used (POCA 2002) or money laundering is taking place (Regulations 36–41, Money Laundering Regulations 2007).

An investigation may lead to civil or criminal proceedings for a breach of duty or other statutory offences, a petition for the company to be compulsorily wound up, or a petition for relief by minority shareholders.

Once inspectors have been appointed, the company's directors, officers and agents have a duty to provide all assistance they could reasonably be expected to give to help the investigation. This includes disclosing and producing documents and information recorded in any form and attending before the inspectors when required to give evidence (CA 1985, s 434(1) and CA 2006, s 1038). Past and present officers may also be required to explain the content of documents provided (CA 1985, s 447). When an investigation is under way, it is an offence for directors to:

- fail to comply with a requisition to produce information or provide an explanation or statement of circumstances or to obstruct the inspector's right to search the premises, and they may be liable to a fine (CA 1985, s 447(6)). Where they persistently fail to co-operate, directors may be held 'in contempt of court' and punishment will be at the discretion of the court (CA 1985, s 436). For example, in *Re An Inquiry into Mirror Group Newspapers plc [2000] Ch 194 [1999] All ER(D) 255*, a director who refused to co-operate was held 'in contempt of court' and was not entitled to refuse to answer questions;

- attempt to destroy, mutilate or falsify documents or make any false entries in any document or books of account. Where found guilty such a person will be liable to a fine, imprisonment, or both (CA 1985, s 450);
- make a false statement or to provide a false explanation of events (CA 1985, s 451).

6   Administrative duties

The general duties of directors contained in common law are augmented by an extensive range of specific duties imposed by statute. This chapter concentrates largely on administrative and compliance duties imposed by CA 2006, including the directors' responsibility for:

- Appointing and removing officers
- Maintaining statutory records
- Filing requirements
- Retaining documents
- Displaying company name and details
- Paying dividends
- Political donations
- Bank accounts
- Paying tax
- Identifying money laundering
- Arranging insurance
- Takeovers and mergers.

Whilst many of these are duties for which the company as a whole is responsible the directors, by virtue of their position and the authority they hold as policymakers, are ultimately responsible for ensuring compliance. Even if the directors delegate responsibility to the company secretary (see Chapter 2), as is common practice, the directors retain responsibility and in many instances will be liable with the company for contravention of statutory requirements. Furthermore, the directors may face disqualification for failing to fulfil these duties.

Appointing and removing officers

The directors have a duty to shareholders and others who have dealings with the company to ensure that officers required by statute are appointed. These include:

i Directors

Chapters 1 and 3 cover the need and mechanics for appointment, resignation and removal of directors. When such changes are being considered, the directors must ensure that requirements for any minimum or maximum number of directors contained in the Articles are observed or risk the validity of their acts being called into question. Where the number of directors falls below the minimum required by the Articles, the remaining directors do not have a right to continue to act unless this is specifically provided for in the company's Articles (*Re Alma Spinning Co (1880) 16 ChD 681*). Most Articles contain such a right, but in most instances it is limited to allowing the directors either to fill the vacancy themselves or to convene a general meeting for this purpose (Table A, Reg 90).

ii Auditors

Unless the directors of a private company decide otherwise, on the grounds that audited accounts are not required, a company must appoint an auditor for each financial year (CA 2006, ss 485(1) and 489(1)).

The directors of a private company have authority by CA 2006, s 485(3) to appoint the first auditor and to fill any casual vacancies and, when doing so, must ensure the person or firm is properly qualified and eligible for appointment. The same is required for a public company (CA 2006, s 489(3)).

The directors of a public company must ensure that the auditors' reappointment and remuneration are approved each year at the general meeting at which accounts are laid before the members (CA 2006, s 489(2)). However, a private company is no longer required to reappoint auditors each year, unless this is required by provisions in the company's Articles. Consequently the auditor's appointment for a private company will be 'deemed' to continue until such time as determined by the directors or members (CA 2006, s 487(2)). Directors need to be aware that auditors of a private company cannot be deemed to be reappointed where the company has received notice from holders of at least 5% of the company's total voting rights that they should not be reappointed (CA 2006, s 488(1)). Should this happen, the directors would need to arrange for members to vote on the matter by ordinary resolution, bearing in mind that special notice and a general meeting would still be required should dismissal of the auditor be proposed.

Any change of auditor needs to be notified to Companies House by submitting the auditor's resignation letter and any statement from them of relevant circumstances connected with their resignation which, if received, needs also to be circulated to the members (CA 2006, ss 517 and 521). In addition, where a new auditor is appointed during the year, special notice must be given to members of the resolution proposing their re-appointment. Copies of the special notice must also be sent to the outgoing as well as the incoming auditor (CA 2006, s 511).

Directors of listed companies should also be aware that the UK Corporate Governance Code recommends that a company's audit committee should oversee and manage the relationship with the external auditors, and monitor and review their performance and the extent of their independence (see Chapter 2).

iii Company secretary

Every public company must ensure there is a secretary of the company, and that the company secretary is not the same person as a sole director. However, since 6 April 2008, a private company has not been required to have a company secretary (CA 2006, s 270(1)). It is usual for the Articles to give authority to the directors to appoint and remove the company secretary (Table A, Reg 99).

The directors of a public company have a specific duty to ensure the person appointed has the requisite knowledge or qualifications to fulfil the position satisfactorily (CA 2006, s 273). This is also important with private companies that choose to still appoint a secretary, as the person to whom the directors delegate many statutory duties must be capable of such tasks.

Maintaining statutory records

The term 'statutory records' is frequently used to refer to a company's minute books and registers, the size and complexity of which normally depends on whether the company is public or private, the size of its share capital, the number of shareholders and directors, the size of the company, the volume of movement in share ownership and the level of trading activity. Details and extracts from the registers are the source of most information available on the public record and there are various alternatives available to directors when considering how best to maintain the statutory records.

Directors of small, family-owned, private companies often choose to maintain the statutory records in-house themselves in hard copy, book format as this is a simple and often cost-effective solution where matters are straightforward and few changes are anticipated during the year. An increase in the volume of compliance work necessary for a larger private company, group of companies or public company may warrant the company holding the records electronically and setting up a specialist secretariat department or, alternatively, out-sourcing some or all of the work to a specialist firm of chartered secretaries or the company's accountants, solicitors or registrars thereby freeing up internal resource.

CA 2006, s 1148 permits a company's statutory records to be kept in computerised form provided information can be extracted and printed in legible form when required. A wide range of dedicated computer systems are available to directors which vastly speed up and reduce the administrative burden of statutory compliance matters, particularly now that it is possible to generate and file many forms electronically direct from such systems. Use of computers in maintaining statutory records has provided large-scale benefits, taking the time needed and tedium out of many of the updating tasks. At the same time computer systems enable increased use of information stored to produce useful and meaningful management reports and can be used to check that compliance matters have been carried out.

The directors must ensure the company's statutory records are kept up-to-date and are complete. Whilst this responsibility is a routine compliance matter, directors should give it as much attention as other matters. This was highlighted in *Re Bath Glass Limited (1987) 4 BCC 130*, where the decision to disqualify the director was in part for failure to maintain the register of directors. Failure to ensure compliance with these requirements will, in most instances, render the company, the directors and any officer in default liable to a fine.

Statutory records can be kept at the company's registered office or single alternative inspection location and comprise the following.

i Register of secretaries

Whilst details of a company's directors and secretary have historically been recorded in one register, two separate registers are now required (CA 2006, ss 162 and 275). The register of secretaries must contain details of the secretary's name (and any former names used for business purposes in the last 20 years), the secretary's service address (see sub-paragraph ii below), date of appointment and, where relevant, date of resignation. The registered number and place of incorporation must also be recorded for a corporate secretary. The register must be open for inspection as set out in sub-paragraph (iv) below.

ii Register of directors

This register, contains details of current and past directors, their service address, date of birth, nationality and occupation and must be kept and be available for inspection by the company's shareholders or members of the public (CA 2006, s 162).

Directors and company secretaries are now able to use a service address for the purpose of the public record. This change has been welcomed by directors and company secretaries who are able not only to protect their privacy by restricting access to their residential addresses, but also to preserve a greater degree of separation between their work and home lives.

A director or company secretary can use any address as a service address without the need to demonstrate a threat of serious violence or intimidation, as was required under the old confidentiality order regime. The service address can be the director or secretary's residential address or, alternatively, can be changed to his or her usual office address, the company's head office or any other suitable address.

However, an important point to note is that it must be possible to physically serve documents at the chosen address and, where required, for delivery to be acknowledged by, for example, obtaining a signature. This is particularly important as, if it becomes evident to the Registrar that documents cannot be effectively served there, the Registrar has power to restore the director's residential address to the public record. It must also be ensured that there is an effective system or procedure for dealing with any official correspondence received at the service address for the director or secretary to avoid it being lost in the 'ether' or the filing records of a large office.

The director's or secretary's address recorded in a company's registers of directors and secretaries and appearing on the public record at Companies House immediately prior to 1 October 2009 is deemed to be the service address, save where a confidentiality order was already in place and the existing service address for the director automatically became the new service address. For directors and secretaries appointed after 1 October 2009, the service address needs to be recorded in the relevant register of directors and secretaries and notified to Companies House.

iii Directors' residential addresses

It is now necessary to record a director's residential address in a separate register kept for that purpose (CA 2006, s 165). There is no corresponding requirement for company secretaries as only their service address is to be recorded. This register is not open to inspection by the public.

The director's residential address must be notified to Companies House, but will not form part of the public record. In addition, where a director's service address is the same as his residential address, nothing on records available from Companies House will show this is the case.

Unless the service address is a director's home address, the residential address will be 'protected information' and restrictions on use and disclosure will apply. This means that a company must not use or disclose protected information about one of its directors unless it is communicating with the director, sending particulars to the Registrar in compliance with a requirement of the Companies Acts, required to do so under court order where, for example, effective service of documents has not been possible at a director's service address, or consent has been obtained from the director.

Similarly, the Registrar must not use or disclose protected information unless communicating with the director or required to do so under court order. The Registrar will, however, be permitted to disclose protected information to a specified public authority in response to receipt by the Registrar of a statement confirming that the information will only be used for performance of that authority's public function. These public authorities might include the FSA, the HSE, the Charities Commission, or HMRC, amongst others.

Additionally the Registrar may disclose protection information to a credit reference agency – subject to that agency satisfying certain conditions, largely based on data protection principles and provided the director does not already have a service address under the existing confidentiality order regime. The credit reference agency must deliver a statement to the Registrar confirming that the information will only be used by it to assess a director's financial standing; in connection with money laundering requirements and the need to verify a director's identity; to conduct conflict of interest checks required by enactment; or to provide information to a public authority or other credit reference agency which has satisfied the relevant conditions and requirements.

A person who is, or is to become, a director can apply to the Registrar, in prescribed form and on payment of a single fee, to stop protected information being disclosed by the Registrar to a credit reference agency (CA 2006, s 243). To be successful, the director must be able to demonstrate in the application that either he or she, or any person living with the director, will be at serious risk of violence or intimidation as a result of the directorship; or he or she has been or is employed by a relevant organisation (which includes the police, armed forces and so on). Where the application is successful, the Registrar will be required to refrain from disclosing protected information to a credit reference agency. This restriction will remain in place indefinitely, unless revoked.

However, where a director had a confidentiality order in place immediately prior to 1 October 2009, he or she was automatically treated as if a successful s 243 application had been made restricting the Registrar from disclosing protected information to a credit reference agency.

In addition, where desired, an application under s 1088 of the Act can be made to the Registrar for the director's residential address to be made unavailable on the register. A fee is payable, the amount of which will depend on the number of documents on which the address is to be suppressed.

This is only possible where the address was placed on the register on or after 1 January 2003. For the application to be successful, a director must be able to demonstrate either a serious risk of violence or intimidation or employment by a relevant organisation. The s 1088 grounds will also, on application, be deemed satisfied where the director has already successfully made a s 243 application. In addition, where a director has a confidentiality order in place immediately prior to 1 October 2009, he or she will be automatically treated as if a successful s 1088 application has been made, without the need for an application by the director.

The director must disclose the service address that is to replace the residential address and, where successful, the s 1088 restriction will continue indefinitely unless revoked by the Registrar.

Many directors have already taken advantage of being able to register a service address that is different from their home address, Others might be waiting, perhaps, until they move house especially where they would not satisfy the criteria for suppressing availability of their home address as it currently appears on the public record.

As explained above, the service address can be any address at which it is possible to serve official documents and can be the company's registered office address. If a director's residential address is the same as his or her service address (and it does not just state that it is the company's registered office in the register of directors), the register can merely record this fact.

iv Register of members

Every company must maintain a register containing details of members' names and addresses and the number of shares held (CA 2006, s 113).

The directors must ensure that the register is available for inspection at the registered office or such other place as notified to Companies House, for example the offices of a share registration agent (CA 2006, s 114).

The register must be open to inspection by any member of the company without charge or by any member of the public on payment of the prescribed fee (CA 2006, s 116). A person wishing to inspect or copy the register must make the request to the company and provide their name and address and state the purpose for which the information is required. The company must either comply with the request within five working days or apply to the court on the basis that the request for inspection has not been made for a proper purpose (CA 2006, s 117). The right of inspection is subject to a 'proper purpose' test and the ICSA has produced a Guidance note *Access to the Register of Members: The Proper Purpose Test* to assist companies and their directors to determine how to deal with such a request. This can be downloaded from www.icsa.global.com.

Failure to provide a copy of the register without sanction of the court not to do so is a fineable offence (CA 2006, s 118).

v Allotments and transfers

Whilst there is no statutory requirement to maintain such registers, it is both usual and good practice to keep them, to explain changes in the register of members and to assist with completion of the annual return and disclosures to be made in the accounts each year.

vi Directors' interests

Whilst the requirement for companies to maintain a register containing the directors' interests in any shares or debentures of the company embodied in CA 1985 was repealed and not replaced in CA 2006, companies listed on the Official List, AIM or the PLUS Market may still find it useful to keep this register in order to comply with the Disclosure and Transparency, AIM and PLUS Market Rules, as applicable (see pp 62 to 64, interest in shares).

vii Substantial interests

On 20 January 2007, ss 198–211 of CA 1985 were repealed and replaced by the Disclosure and Transparency Rules which, in the UK, only apply to listed, AIM and PLUS companies. This means that other public companies are no longer required to maintain a register and disclose substantial interests in their shares.

DTR 5.1.2 requires a person to notify the listed, AIM, or PLUS company where the percentage of voting rights that person holds as a shareholder reaches, exceeds or falls below 3, 4 or 5% and each percentage point up to 100% as a result of an acquisition or disposal of shares. In addition, save for some exceptions, investment managers, unit trusts and open-ended investment companies must disclose their interests at both 5 and 10% but not at increments in between. The need for notification at 5 and 10% levels also applies to treasury shares.

Where a shareholder has a notification obligation, the notification must be made to the company (and to the FSA electronically) as soon as possible, but within two days of the obligation arising for a UK issuer. The company is then obliged to announce the notification to the market via an RIS as soon as possible but, in any event, by the end of the trading day following receipt of the notification (DTR5.8.12).

To facilitate the calculation of shareholders' percentage voting rights required in the notification, DTR 5.6.1 requires the company to make an announcement via an RIS at the end of each calendar month where there has been any increase or decrease in the company's total voting rights.

Whilst neither CA 2006 nor the DTRs require listed, AIM or PLUS companies to routinely keep a register of substantial interests, the Listing Rules require listed companies to make a statement in their annual report and accounts of all information disclosed about the interests in the company's shares (DTR 9.8.6(2) and CA 2006, Part 22). This being the case, good practice would suggest it is necessary to maintain a register of substantial interests.

However, where it appears that a member of a public company has acquired an interest in shares of the company, the directors of the public company may issue notice to that person to investigate the situation and determine the beneficial owner of those shares (CA 2006, s 793).

The company must then keep a register of information received by it in response to the investigation permitted by s 793 (CA 2006, s 808). This register must be available for inspection.

viii Debenture holders

Whilst there is no statutory obligation to maintain a register containing details of debenture holders, it will help the directors keep accurate and reliable records. If such a register is maintained, it must be kept at the registered office or such other location where the company's records are available for inspection as notified to Companies House (CA 2006, s 743) and be available for inspection by members and the public.

ix Mortgages and charges

If there are fixed or floating charges, a register of mortgages and charges must be kept, together with a copy of every instrument creating the charge (CA 2006, s 876). The register must be available for inspection by members, creditors and the public. If it is not made available, any officer in default will be liable to a fine (CA 2006, s 877).

The directors have a corresponding duty to notify Companies House of the creation of a charge (CA 2006, s 860). Failure to comply with the registration requirement will render the company and its officers liable to a fine.

x Minute books

Every company is required to keep minutes of all general and class meetings, directors' meetings and meetings of managers (CA 2006, ss 248 and 355). The Articles would usually specify that minutes of committee meetings must also be kept.

Minutes of general meetings would usually be kept separately from other minutes as they must be available for inspection by the members or members may request copies (CA 2006, s 358). Board minutes must be available for inspection by the auditors and the directors (CA 1985, s 237 and *McCusker v McRae 1966 SC 253*).

Filing requirements

As well as being responsible for maintaining the statutory books and records of the company, the directors have a corresponding duty to ensure that key changes in the company's location, structure and management are notified to Companies House on prescribed forms within specified periods. Most will be triggered by changes in the content or location of statutory records, for example:

- a change in registered office (CA 2006, s 87);
- a change in directors or the secretary, or their details (CA 2006, ss 167 and 276);
- creation of a charge (CA 2006, s 870);
- allotments of shares (CA 2006, s 554);
- changes to share capital (CA 2006, ss 619, 621 and 689);
- purchase by a company of its own shares (CA 2006, s 307);
- certain ordinary resolutions (such as removal of a director or auditor, or granting of authority to directors to allot shares) and all special resolutions (CA 2006, ss 29 and 30); and
- if a company amends its articles, it must send a copy of the amended articles within 15 days of the amendment taking effect (CA 2006, s 26).

Resolutions must be submitted within 14 days of being passed and the filing period for forms varies, depending on the type of form. Companies using approved software packages are able to submit an increasing number of forms electronically and the Companies House web-filing system can also be used. To facilitate electronic filing, Companies House issue authentication codes and it is very important that these are kept securely and access is restricted to those authorised to submit documents.

Failure to fulfil the filing requirements will render the directors and every officer in default liable to a fine and, for continued contravention, to a daily default fine.

As well as the forms listed above, every company must submit an annual return to Companies House within 28 days of the return date shown on the form. This contains details of the company secretary, directors, shares and shareholder information, registered office, location of the registers of members and debenture holders and the company's principal business activity (CA 2006, s 54). Failure to submit an annual return within the required period is an offence for which the company, its directors and the secretary may be liable for prosecution. Whilst initial warnings will be issued to the company, letters will be sent to the directors warning them that criminal proceedings may be initiated against them for the default.

A copy of the company's annual report and accounts must also be submitted to Companies House, as described in Chapter 9.

Retaining documents

The volume of documents generated by most companies after a number of years trading means that it is not possible to retain old files and records indefinitely due to limited storage space. In some instances off-site storage is either unavailable or unaffordable and directors must balance the need to reduce the volume of documents placed in storage with the need to ensure documents are retained for as long as needed.

In making such assessment the directors should consider:
- 'Minimum retention periods' specified or implied in statute, which include:
  - minutes of all meetings and resolutions of a company's directors and members must be kept for at least 10 years after the meeting, resolution or decision (CA 2006, ss 248 and 355);
  - employment records – three years (Income Tax (Employment) Regulations 1993, Reg 55);

- documents relating to calculation of national insurance contributions – three years (Social Security (Contributions) Regulations 1979, as amended and Sch 1, para 32(5));
- VAT records where the company is registered for VAT – six years (Value Added Tax Act 1994, s 58 and Sch 11, para 6(3)), although these records may be retained on microfilm, computer or other similar storage medium.
- As a general guide, documents relating to accounts, tax, VAT, personnel and employment details, share registration and health and safety matters have minimum retention periods. Directors must examine specific requirements before documents are destroyed. If there is a minimum retention period, directors must ensure documents are retained at least until this period has passed.

● The need for past records and documents to provide evidence in legal proceedings that the company discharged its duties satisfactorily. Directors should take care to ensure that documents are kept in the appropriate form until expiry of the period within which legal proceedings could be brought (Limitation Act 1980, as amended). These include:
- product liability action within 10 years of the date of supply;
- action for breach of contract within six years of the breach, unless the contract is under seal or executed as a deed, in which case it is 12 years;
- claims for personal injury within three years of the cause of the injury or when the plaintiff becomes aware of the injury; and
- claims for negligence (other than those connected with (c) above), within three years of the damage or loss being discovered.

Furthermore, whilst in most instances the courts accept copies of documents, such as microfilm or CD-ROM, as admissible evidence in legal proceedings (Civil Evidence Act 1968, s 6), some civil and criminal proceedings may require original documents.

● Ongoing commercial and operational needs for the documents as a possible means of reference, etc.

● Retention periods implied or specified in the company's Articles. For example Table A, Reg 108 and the Model Articles (Reg 33 for a private company and Reg 75 for a public company) require unpaid dividends to be held to a shareholder's account and repaid if claimed within 12 years of the date of declaration. Documents relating to dividends must be retained for at least this period.

- The possibility that HMRC might raise a tax assessment, which in normal circumstances can be at any time up to six years after the event (Taxes Management Act 1970, s 34) or, where it suspects avoidance by fraud, wilful neglect or negligence has no time limit (Taxes Management Act 1970, ss 36 and 39).

Where information kept includes 'personal data' about an individual, these requirements must be balanced against data protection principles (Chapter 11 and Appendix 10) which require that data is only kept as long as strictly necessary.

Appendix 11 provides an indication of the statutory and recommended retention periods for documents, which may assist directors when considering whether to retain or dispose of records.

Whilst it is reasonable and acceptable for directors to delegate the 'retain versus dispose' assessment to others within the company, they remain responsible and must ensure such persons have a full understanding of all the legal and commercial requirements for retaining documents. Once the initial assessment is complete, policies and procedures would usually be implemented by the company to ensure that reasoned and informed decisions are made on an on-going and continuous basis about which documents to retain and which to destroy or move into storage.

Displaying company name, other details and websites

Once incorporated every company is required by the Companies (Trading Disclosures) Regulations 2008 (SI 2008/495) and the Amendment Regulations to clearly display the company name:

- At the company's registered office, every office and premises in which business is carried on, and at any location where the company keeps any company records available for inspection.
- Companies that have been dormant since incorporation are exempt from this requirement, as are premises that are primarily used as living accommodation such as a director's home; the offices of an insolvency practitioner, administrator or administrative receiver; where the premises concerned are not the registered office nor an

inspection place, there is a risk that displaying the company's name might attract violent activity; and any office where business is carried out if s 243 restrictions are in place for all directors prohibiting protected information about them being disclosed (see (iii) above).

The company's name must be displayed in characters that can easily be read, continuously displayed and in such position that it can be seen by a visitor to the premises (even outside business hours). If a location is shared by six or more companies then it is permissible for display of the company names to rotate, save that each name must be displayed for a minimum continuous period of 15 seconds in every three minutes.

- On all business letters, notices and official publications, order forms, endorsements, bills of exchange, promissory notes, cheques and orders for money or goods signed on behalf of the company, and on all demands for payment, receipts, invoices and credit notes issued by the company and on all other forms of business correspondence and documentation.

  Failure to comply with these requirements will render the company and its officers liable to a fine. Furthermore, the officer who signed such cheque, promissory note, bill of exchange or order for money or goods without correctly displaying the company name may be liable to a fine and be ordered to account to the holder for the amount concerned if the company fails to honour the payment (see *Barber & Nicholls Ltd v R and G Associates (London) Ltd and Rogers [1981] CA Transcript 455, 132 NLJ 1076*, page 156).
- On any applications for licences to carry on trade or activity.
- On the company's website.
- Where the company has a common seal, the company name must be engraved in legible characters.

With increasing use of electronic mail (e-mail) as a means of communication, Reg 1(2)(d) has confirmed that electronic messages will be treated in the same way as paper-based communications. Consequently, directors must ensure that any business letters, order forms or company documents sent electronically comply with the requirements set out above.

Failure to comply with these regulations without reasonable excuse renders the company and every officer in default liable to a fine (Reg 10, as permitted by CA 2006, s 83).

It should also be noted that there are also potential commercial consequences of default to the extent that, if a company is bringing legal proceedings where it is enforcing its rights under a contract which was made at the time when the company was in breach of the regulations, then the court has power to dismiss the proceedings, if it is considered equitable to do so and the defendant can show that: (i) he has a claim against the company arising out of the contract, which he is unable to purse due to the company's breach of the regulations; or (ii) the defendant has suffered financial loss in connection with the contract by reason of the company's breach of the regulations.

The directors must also ensure that, as well as the company name, the following information is given on all business letters, order forms, invoices, receipts, payment demand notices and websites (Regs 7 and 8, Companies (Trading Disclosure) Regulations 2008):

- any trading name under which business is conducted (as well as the registered company name);
- place of registration (ie England and Wales, or Scotland, etc);
- company's registration number;
- address of the registered office at which documents may be served. Where this is the same as the place of business the address need not be repeated but a statement to that effect must be made on the document. Directors should note that where any change is made to the location of the registered office, the new address must be displayed on documents within 14 days of the change;
- where the company is an investment company, this fact must be stated;
- where the company is a charity and no indication is given in the company name by use of the words 'charity' or 'charitable', then this must be stated;
- where a director's name is given on letters and other documents, the names of every director must be shown. It is important that directors are aware of this requirement when considering the use of personalised stationery and the need to re-order stationery every time the directors change. They should also note that the disclosure requirement for all directors' names includes 'shadow' directors;
- where the company chooses to include details of its share capital on documents, it must state it is the issued and fully paid share capital;

- where the company is exempt from use of the word 'limited' in its name, this must be stated; and
- if applicable and the company is not a public company, a statement that the company is a community interest company.

A company is also required to state its VAT number on all VAT invoices and receipts and to post it clearly on the company's website (regardless of whether or not the website is used for e-commerce transactions).

In practice, much of the information listed above would appear as a pre-printed footnote on headed paper, company documents and emails and the directors must ensure that, before such documents are re-ordered and reprinted, they are checked thoroughly to ensure that none of the statutory information has changed, been omitted or printed incorrectly.

With regard to a company's website, this information can be included and displayed in a number of ways, but the important point to note is that it must be posted clearly and be easy to find. The use of 'footnotes' on all or most website pages, supported by more detailed information in contact and legal disclosure pages, is quite common.

Rule 26 of the AIM Rules sets out website requirements for AIM companies which the directors must ensure are observed.

AIM companies should notify the website address at which the information required by this rule is available. This can be part of another notification. The information must be kept up-to-date and the last date on which it was updated should be included.

The website on which this information is made available should be the company's website, although it is acknowledged that such a site may be hosted by a third-party provider. The information should be easily accessible and a statement that the information is being disclosed for the purposes of Rule 26 should be included.

The information and documents that must be made available on the website, free of charge, include:

- a description of its business and, where it is an investing company, its investing strategy;
- the name of its directors and brief biographical details of each, as would normally be included in an admission document;
- a description of the responsibilities of the members of the board of directors and details of any committees of the board of directors and their responsibilities;

- the main country of operation, being the geographical location from which the company derives (or intends to derive) the largest proportion of its revenues or where the largest proportion of its assets are (or will be) located, as is most appropriate depending on the business of the company;
- its country of incorporation and, where the AIM company is not incorporated in the UK, a statement that the rights of shareholders may be different from the rights of shareholders in a UK incorporated company;
- its current constitutional documents (for example, its Articles of Association);
- details of any other exchanges or trading platforms on which the AIM company has applied or agreed to have any of its securities (including its AIM securities) admitted or traded;
- the number of AIM securities in issue (noting any held as treasury shares) and, insofar as it is aware, the percentage of AIM securities that are not in public hands together with the identity and percentage holdings of its significant shareholders. This information should be updated at least every six months;
- details of any restrictions on the transfer of its AIM securities;
- its most recent annual report published and all half-yearly, quarterly or similar reports published since the last annual report;
- all notifications the company has made in the last 12 months; and
- its most recent admission document together with any circulars or similar publications sent to shareholders within the past 12 months, and details of its nominated adviser and other key advisers.

Where relevant, consideration may need to be given to how to make this information and these documents available in such a way that does not infringe any securities laws for overseas jurisdictions that may apply. Such issues can usually be resolved, for example by the use of appropriate disclaimers and user residence confirmation.

A listed company must also ensure that its annual accounts and reports are made available on a website as soon as reasonably practicable and that they remain available until the annual accounts and reports for the next year are available on the website (CA 2006, s 430).

Directors should also note that provisions in the UK Corporate Governance Code require that the terms of reference for a listed company's nomination, remuneration and audit committees are 'made available' (B.2.1, D.2.1 and C.3.3). This requirement is considered met where the information is displayed on a website, maintained by or on behalf of the company.

Furthermore, where a poll is taken at a general meeting of a listed company, the company must ensure that information is placed on the company's website about the date of the meeting, the text of the resolution or a description of its subject matter and the number of votes cast for and against the resolution (CA 2006, s 341). In addition, where an independent assessor has been appointed to report on a poll, the fact of the assessor's appointment, his identity, the text of the resolution or a description of its subject matter and a copy of the assessor's report must be made available on the company's website (CA 2006, s 351).

Paying dividends

Directors generally have responsibility for a company's dividend policy. It is common practice for a company's Articles to authorise directors to declare and pay an 'interim' dividend, and to require that payment of a 'final' dividend recommended by the directors be approved by the members. Before a dividend is paid, provisions of the Articles must be checked, and any requirements for approval must be met.

Other requirements that directors must ensure are observed before a dividend is declared and paid include:

- the company's operational requirements, for example in terms of the need for re-investment of profits to fund expansion plans or the need to upgrade plant and machinery;
- observing preferential rights where shares of a particular class confer on the holders a preferential right to receive a dividend in preference to any other class of share; and
- only paying a dividend where there are sufficient distributable profits (CA 2006, s 830).

The directors must ensure 'relevant accounts' are prepared so they can accurately determine the distributable profit available. These may comprise the last annual accounts, interim accounts or initial accounts where the company has not completed its first accounting period, subject to CA 2006, s 839.

Directors who allow an 'illegal dividend' to be paid may be personally liable to repay the company (CA 2006, s 847). In *Bairstow v Queens*

Moat Houses Plc [2002] BCC 91 the directors allowed a dividend to be paid out of capital; the Court of Appeal held that they were personally liable to repay £79m to the company even where they were not recipients of the money. In addition, directors who make improper dividend payments based on defective accounts or where they believe such payments cannot be afforded by the company may be liable for disqualification (*Re AG (Manchester) Ltd; Official Receiver v Watson [2008] BCC 497*).

A private company may, where permitted to do so by provisions contained in the Articles (or Memorandum for companies incorporated prior to 1 October 2009), declare a dividend to be paid wholly or partly by the distribution of specific assets to the shareholders, such as shares of a subsidiary company (in a 'demerger') or the freehold or leasehold interest in property. Where such authority exists, approval of the members in general meeting will generally be required, based upon recommendations made by the directors (Table A, Reg 105).

Political donations

Under CA 2006 a company must not make a political donation to a political party or other political organisation or incur any political expenditure unless the donation or expenditure has been approved, in advance, by a resolution of the members of the company (and, where applicable, of the holding company) in accordance with CA 2006, ss 362–379. Where directors allow such payments to be made without the required authorisation by members, the directors will be liable to pay back the expenditure, with interest, and compensate the company for any loss or damage sustained as a consequence of the unauthorised payment (CA 2006, s 369).

Directors should further note that the payment cannot be ratified after the event and access to relief through court process in these instances is specifically excluded.

Bank accounts

One of the first tasks the directors will have to undertake is to open a bank account so that the company can make and receive payments when trading commences. The board must approve opening of the account and the terms and conditions by which the account is operated by the bank. No one director alone has the authority to do this, although the board will usually authorise one director to proceed and finalise the formalities of opening the account once it has been approved. All banks require their standard bank mandate form to be completed and signed for a company to open an account and the mandate is frequently in the form of draft minutes, emphasising the requirement for board approval. The bank will usually require sight of the company's original Certificate of Incorporation and Memorandum and Articles, or certified copies thereof, before opening an account.

Consequently directors have a duty to ensure that, before signing and returning the mandate form to the bank, they have approval of the board and an additional signed copy of the mandate has been placed in the company's minute book as evidence of the board's decision to open the account.

Where an overdraft facility needs to be arranged, banks will normally require security or collateral for this facility and the directors have a duty to ensure that they have the necessary authority, normally contained in the Articles, to borrow money and charge the company's assets before entering into such agreement.

As part of their general duty to look after and protect the assets of the company, the directors must also give consideration to:

- suitable signatories and how to exercise adequate control of the account, for example by requiring a set number of signatures for payments above a certain monetary limit;
- the frequency of bank statements;
- how often and by whom reconciliation of the bank account is carried out, for example monthly and by someone other than a signatory to the account, to keep the directors informed of the company's financial position; and
- informing the bank of changes to the company's officers, especially where they are a signatory to the account and the bank mandate instruction needs to be revised.

Directors must also ensure that the bank is kept advised of changes in directors, secretary, registered office, accounting reference date, auditors, etc, and that the bank mandate instruction is revised as soon as a person leaves and ceases to be eligible as a signatory.

Paying tax

Timely and accurate tax compliance is essential for any company, as severe financial penalties may be incurred where a company is late or inaccurate in making returns and interest may be charged on underpayments, which is obviously not the best use of a company's resources. HMRC's tax departments may also pursue criminal action against anyone guilty of tax evasion, or impose civil penalties for such offences (see Chapter 13).

Principal taxes include corporation tax, VAT, PAYE and national insurance. Whilst the task of computing and making required returns is usually delegated, the directors remain ultimately responsible for tax matters. They must therefore ensure that appropriate tax and accounting systems are in place to make sure that no offences or defaults occur and that whoever carries out these day-to-day tasks is appropriately monitored to identify any irregularities or non-compliance at the earliest opportunity.

Identifying money laundering

Directors have a responsibility under POCA 2002 and The Money Laundering Regulations 2007 to implement procedures within the company to verify the identity of new clients and investors, etc. and to ensure adequate systems are in place for employees to identify and report any suspicion they may have that such client is involved in the laundering of illegally acquired funds.

POCA 2002 largely consolidates and updates money laundering offences in earlier legislation. It also extends the scope of offences to include:

- concealing, disguising, converting, transferring or removing criminal property;
- arranging or facilitating the acquisition or retention of criminal property; and
- acquiring, using or possessing criminal property.

As well as the better recognised money laundering offences, POCA 2002 extends to the proceeds of any crime and would include theft, tax evasion and burglary, etc.

Many companies address this responsibility by implementing a formal procedure to verify the identity of all new clients. For example, where transactions exceed a certain pre-determined amount or are always paid in cash, a company would usually require sight of an individual's passport and a utilities bill or, where the client is a company, carry out its own search of records at Companies House, check credit references and verify the identity of the company's principals in the same manner as for individual clients. Employees should be told who in the company is the 'money laundering reporting officer' to whom they should report any suspicions about clients, events or transactions.

The Money Laundering Regulations 2007 require companies to put in place suitable policies and procedures to identify money laundering and ensure records are kept of client verification checks. In addition they state that where an offence has been committed with the consent or connivance of an officer of the company (including the directors, secretary, managers and others) or was due to their neglect, they shall also be held liable for penalties where they should have known that money laundering was taking place (Reg 47(1)).

Arranging insurance

Insurance policies form an important part of a company's risk management process by allowing a company to mitigate against potential financial loss when control measures implemented to avoid risks have failed. In general, directors should consider the following policies.

i Employer's liability insurance

This insurance must be effected by an employer, and failure to do so is a criminal offence. Typically the insurance will provide cover in respect of claims by employees for illness, bodily injury or disease caused during or arising as a result of their employment. The policy must provide for a minimum indemnity of £5m on any single claim and be on display in the workplace. Whilst the requirement for old certificates of insurance to be kept by employers for 40 years has been removed, companies must carefully consider their continuing liabilities and ensure appropriate records are retained in order that future claims can be met.

ii Product liability insurance

Given the requirement that products must be safe for consumers to use, directors of a company that produces, supplies or imports products should obtain insurance to indemnify the company against the cost of a claim for damage caused by a defect in the product and the cost of having to withdraw or recall products from the market.

iii Directors' and officers' indemnity insurance

Directors can effect insurance against personal liability (CA 2006, s 233) which may arise when, for example, they have been negligent, made mistakes, committed a breach of duty, authority or trust, issued misleading statements or carried on wrongful trading. Such insurance may also cover the directors' costs incurred by investigation into their actions and those arising from disqualification proceedings. Directors, particularly of public companies, have much to gain from effecting such insurance to protect them against claims by shareholders, creditors, etc. where, for example, they consider corporate failure was attributed to the directors' actions or inactions or where they consider the directors' conflict of interest influenced the outcome of a merger or takeover. There are also considerable benefits to the company, as effecting such insurance may encourage the directors to have a more balanced attitude to risk, rather than always preferring the conservative, less risky approach. Indeed, the UK Corporate Governance Code recommends that a copy of this policy is provided to non-executive directors at the same time as their letter of appointment.

Directors should consider whether the breadth of cover provided by this insurance needs to be extended in the light of the increased risk of a claim by a member for a director's negligence, default, breach of duty or breach of trust now possible under CA 2006, ss 206–264. Indeed, whilst a standard policy may allow 'insured versus insured' actions, it might not cover claims by directors against directors.

Recognising that choices over the type of insurance, extent of cover and exclusions can be confusing, ICSA have produced a guidance note on Directors' and Officers' Insurance to alert directors to some of the key issues when selecting a policy. This is available at www.icsa.global.com.

iv Employer's practices liability insurance

This insurance can be effected to provide cover against the cost of arbitration or tribunal proceedings, demands for compensation, punitive damages and defence costs should employment-related claims such as wrongful or unfair dismissal, direct or indirect discrimination, harassment and defamation be made against the company. Given the complexities of employment law and the vastly increased upper limit for awards of damages in successful unfair dismissal claims this insurance can be a valuable means of mitigating against potential loss in an employment-related claim. Commonly the policy will require the company to use a lawyer from the insurer's approved list and follow their recommended action otherwise the policy will be invalidated.

v Environmental insurance policy

It may be necessary to obtain a tailor-made environmental policy where the company's public liability policy does not extend to cover all pollution incidents which have been identified as a potential risk relevant to the company. Gradual pollution is often excluded from public liability policies and typically they only cover a 'sudden, identifiable, unintended and unexpected incident which takes place in its entirety at a specific time and place during the period of the insurance' (suggested ABI wording). Directors need to be aware of this issue and, where, for example, a pollution risk has been identified that will not be covered by the public liability policy, consider and if thought appropriate put in place an environmental policy for the company or site.

vi Extent of cover

Insurance policies' terms, conditions and exclusions vary tremendously and it is important the directors ensure the correct level of cover has been obtained. For example, in *Rexodan International Ltd v Commercial Union (Court of Appeal), [1999] Lloyd's Rep IR 495*, the company's product liability insurance only covered the cost of damaged products and not the cost of recall, loss of profits or packaging purchased that could not be used. This had disastrous financial implications for the company and emphasises the importance of fully understanding the cover in place and ensuring that it is periodically formally reviewed to make sure it remains appropriate and meets the needs of the business. A company's geographic coverage, product offering, and method of distribution etc. are likely to change over time and scheduled reviews of insurance will help to ensure there are no gaps or areas that are inadvertently not covered, exposing the company.

Takeovers and mergers

Directors must be aware that when they are considering or recommending an offer for a takeover or merger with another company or are evaluating an offer that has been received, they have an over-riding obligation to observe their general duties to the company as set out in the statutory statement and act honestly and seek to promote the success of the company to which they are appointed (see Chapter 4). The directors should not, for example, allow their personal interests to influence any advice or recommendations they provide or do anything to frustrate an offer received without approval from the shareholders.

The directors also have a duty to ensure that any information or representations provided during the takeover or merger process are correct, up to date and accurate. Where they fail to do so, they risk action for fraudulent misrepresentation. In *Erlson Precision Holdings Ltd v Hampson Industries PLC [2011] EWHC 1137 (Comm)* the parent company, Hampson Industries, and it's CEO, who was also a director of the subsidiary being sold, provided misleading forecasts and failed to advise the buyer that the subsidiary had lost one of its main customers immediately prior to conclusion of the sale. As a consequence they were found guilty of fraudulent misrepresentation and the buyer, Erlson Precision Holdings, was entitled to rescind the share purchase agreement.

There are also a number of specific additional requirements concerning takeovers and mergers which stem not only from statutory provisions, including the FSMA 2000 (as amended) and CA 2006, but also from the Takeover Code and Listing Rules which the directors must ensure are observed. In addition to these, where the OFT considers a merger might decrease competition, the matter might be referred to the Competition Commission.

i FSMA 2000

FSMA 2000, s 397 applies where the proposed takeover or merger concerns a public company. It requires that all information disseminated to the market is accurate and no false, misleading or deceptive statements are made which might create a false impression of the market or value of the company's shares, thereby inducing persons to buy or sell their shares or to refrain from doing so. Breach of the requirements of the FSMA 2000 is a criminal offence.

ii CA 2006

CA 2006, Part 28 gives the Panel on Takeovers and Mergers certain statutory functions as the 'supervisory authority' and, whilst they are chiefly responsible for regulating takeovers and mergers by listed companies, the Panel's remit also extends to certain unlisted public companies and to private companies where their securities were listed in the previous 10 years.

The Panel determines the rules on takeovers, mergers and others matters concerning change of ownership or control of a company, including provisions in the Takeover Code. The Panel also has power to require companies to provide information and the directors must ensure the requested information is produced and assistance is provided to the Takeover Panel as failure to comply will constitute breach of the Takeover Code (see below).

iii Takeover Code

The Takeover Code sets out a number of general principles and rules governing the manner in which takeovers and mergers of listed companies and certain public companies and private companies are conducted. Failure to observe requirements of the Takeover Code can lead to disciplinary or other action by the Takeover Panel or the relevant regulatory body, such as the Financial Services Authority. This other action might, for example, include a private reprimand or public statement of censure, the effects of which can be very damaging to a company's reputation both within and outside the company.

Directors of the offeror and offeree company have a responsibility to ensure that the requirements of the Takeover Code are complied with and that the limitations imposed by the Code are observed. Failure to do so might result in the director being subject to a fine or being ordered to pay compensation (CA 2006, ss 953(6) and 954).

In addition to specific rules set out in the Takeover Code governing how and when an offer is made, the timing and content of announcements required, responsibilities of the offeror and offeree company and the need to obtain and communicate competent independent advice to shareholders, etc., which must be consulted when a takeover is proposed or an offer received, the directors must ensure the Code's six general principles are observed. These require that:

- members holding shares of the same class are treated equally and, in particular, are protected should someone acquire control of the company;
- shareholders are given sufficient accurate information and time in which to reach an informed decision, such information shall include the views of the directors of the company being acquired on the effects the bid will have on employees, employment conditions, and business locations;
- the board of the offeree acts in the interests of the company as a whole and does not deny the holders of securities opportunity to consider the merits of a bid;
- no false market is created in securities of either the offeror, offeree or any company concerned with the bid;
- directors of the company making the offer only announce it when they are confident it can be implemented and the consideration be met in cash or as otherwise intended; and
- the offeree is not hindered in the conduct of its affairs by the bid for longer than is reasonable.

The directors must also ensure they do not deal in securities of either company when they have access to price-sensitive information. Recognising this, the shareholdings of directors and their dealings in the offeree and offeror companies in the 12 months leading up to the offer must be disclosed. In addition, if any payment as compensation for a director's loss of office is proposed in the offer, this is a restricted transaction and shareholder approval is required as explained in Chapter 7 below.

iv Listing Rules

Listed companies involved in a takeover are required to submit the offer document to the UK Listing Authority for approval. The directors must ensure the offer document is in the prescribed format and contains the information specified in the rules for listed companies.

In addition, the Listing Rules require that when a listed company is involved in a takeover, as the acquirer and the consideration for the acquisition includes the issue of securities for which listing will be sought, the company must notify an RIS as soon as possible after the terms of the acquisition are agreed (LR 10.3.1). Similarly, where the listed company is the subject of a takeover bid, an RIS is required as soon as possible.

Where consideration for the takeover or merger consists of securities for which listing will be sought, it may be necessary to circulate listing particulars, or a summary thereof, to shareholders at the same time as the offer document (LR 3.2).

7   Restricted and prohibited transactions

There are a number of statutory duties arising from CA 2006 restricting directors' actions, either by prohibiting certain acts or by requiring them to be approved in advance by the shareholders.

They include the following, which are covered in this chapter:

- Substantial property transactions
- Loans to directors
- Service contracts
- Payment for loss of office.

There is also a prohibition on a director obtaining financial assistance from a company for purchase of the company's shares, which is touched upon in Chapter 8.

Substantial property transactions

As a general rule a director of a company or of its holding company may not enter into an arrangement to acquire from or transfer to a company a substantial 'non-cash asset' unless the arrangement has been approved by the members of the company by ordinary resolution in general meeting or the agreement is conditional upon such approval being obtained (CA 2006, s 190(1)). This requirement extends to shadow directors and persons 'connected' with a director. It is largely concerned with preventing acquisitions at an inflated price and disposals at less than their full value, which could arise due to a director's conflict of interest.

Approval is required for acquisitions and disposals for valuable consideration, gifts and voluntary dispositions where the value of the 'non-cash' asset is greater than £5,000. Where the asset concerned is valued above £5,000 and exceeds £100,000 or 10% of the company's net asset value, the transaction requires approval.

A 'material' transaction approved in accordance with CA 2006, s 190 must be disclosed in the company's audited accounts unless the company is a small or medium-sized company and is exempt from this requirement.

Where the requirements of s 190 are contravened and a transaction does not receive the necessary approval it may be voidable at the insistence of the company, and the director or connected person and any other directors who authorised the transaction or arrangement will be liable to account to the company for any direct or indirect gain made from the transaction or be required to jointly indemnify the company from any loss or damage arising from the transaction (CA 2006, s 195).

However, where a substantial property transaction has been entered into by a company without the required approval it is possible for it to be affirmed by the members within a reasonable period by resolution (CA 2006, s 196). Directors should note that shareholder approval is not required where:

- the arrangement is between a wholly-owned subsidiary and either the holding company or another wholly-owned subsidiary in the group (CA 2006, s 192(b));
- it is part of an arrangement where the company is being wound up (unless it is a members' voluntary winding-up (see Chapter 12));
- the director is acquiring the asset in his or her capacity as a member of the company and not as a director, e.g. a distribution of assets (CA 2006, s 192(a)); or
- the transaction is conducted through a recognised investment exchange by an independent broker as agent for a director or connected person.

However, even where approval by the shareholders is not required, the director would be required to disclose his or her interest in the transaction to the board (see Chapter 5).

Loans to directors

To discourage directors from borrowing money from a company for their own benefit when it could be put to better use for the company, statutory obligations impose restrictions on loans to directors which they must ensure are observed. A company is not permitted to make a loan to a director, or provide a guarantee or security for any such loan, unless the transaction has been approved by a resolution by the members of the company (CA 2006, s 197).

This restriction applies to shadow directors and also requires that where the director is a director of the holding company and the loan is proposed by a subsidiary, it must also be approved by members of the holding company.

Where the company itself is a public company or is associated with a public company the requirements described above also apply to:

- loans or quasi-loans (CA 2006, s 198);
- credit transactions (CA 2006, s 201); and
- provision of a guarantee or security for a loan, quasi-loan or credit transaction (CA 2006, s 203).

For a public company, the requirement for approval also extends to transactions and arrangements with connected persons.

Exemptions to the requirement for approval by the members include:

- Expenditure on company business, provided the aggregate of the transaction in question and any other relevant transactions or arrangements when taken together does not exceed £50,000 (CA 2006, s 204).
- Providing a director with funds to defend criminal or civil proceedings in connection with alleged negligence, default, breach of duty or breach of trust by him in relation to the company or an associated company or in connection with an application for relief (CA 2006, s 205). The loan must be repaid if the director is convicted in the proceedings, judgment is given against him or an application for relief is refused (CA 2006, s 205).
- Providing a director with funds in order to defend himself in an investigation or an action to be taken by a regulatory authority in connection with alleged negligence, default, breach of duty or breach of trust by him in relation to the company or an associated company (CA 2006, s 206).
- Loans, quasi-loans or for guarantees or security in connection therewith where the value of the transaction or taken together with other relevant transactions or arrangements does not exceed £10,000 (CA 2006, s 207(1)).
- Credit transactions or guarantees or security therewith where the value of that transaction alone or when taken with other relevant transactions or arrangements does not exceed £15,000 (CA 2006, s 207(2)).
- Credit transactions or guarantees therewith where the transaction is entered into by the company in the ordinary course of its business and the value and terms are no more favourable than would have

been offered had the person not been a director (CA 2006, s 207(3)).

- Intra-group transactions where a credit transaction is entered into or a loan or quasi-loan is made to an associated body corporate and the provisions of the guarantee or security in connection therewith (CA 2006, s 208).
- Making a loan or quasi-loan or guarantee or security therewith where the transaction is entered into by the company in the ordinary course of the company's money-lending business and the value and terms are no more favourable than would have been offered had the person not been a director (CA 2006, s 209).

Where a loan is made in contravention of CA 2006, ss 197, 198, 200, 201 or 203, it may be voidable at the instance of the company. Any director who was involved in or authorised the transaction is guilty of an offence and is liable to a fine or imprisonment and may be required to account to the company for any direct or indirect gain made from the transaction and to indemnify it against any loss or damage suffered (CA 2006, s 213). This omission can, to some extent, be rectified by the members affirming the transaction or arrangement within a reasonable period after it has been entered into (CA 2006, s 214).

Subject to a few exceptions, disclosure of transactions described in CA 2006, ss 197, 198, 200, 201 and 203, must be made in the notes to the company's audited accounts and, where the company is part of a group, also in the group accounts (CA 2006, s 412(5)).

Service contracts

Whilst generally a company's board has authority to negotiate the terms and conditions of a director's service contract without referring the matter to the company's members for approval, the following should be noted:

- the Articles may specify particular approval requirements which must be observed, as failure to do so may result in the contract being unenforceable to the detriment of the company (*UK Safety Group Ltd v Heane [1998] 2 BCLC 208*);
- CA 2006, s 188 requires that where a service contract is under consideration for a guaranteed term of more than two years, the directors must obtain prior approval of the members in general meeting. This requirement also extends to:

- contracts for services such as consultancy agreements (CA 2006, s 227);
- contracts which permit the director to extend the contract period to more than two years (CA 2006, s 188(3));
- a contract for services of more than two years in a subsidiary company, in which case approval by members of both the subsidiary and the holding company is required (CA 2006, s 188(2)(b)).

In order to approve the service contract, the members must be provided with a memorandum setting out details of the proposed contract (CA 2006, s 188(5)). Where the requirement for members' approval is not met, the contract will be deemed terminable by the company at any time on reasonable notice (CA 2006, s 189).

Directors of listed companies also have to take into account corporate governance requirements relating to service contracts, embodied largely in recommendations of the UK Corporate Governance Code. These require that remuneration packages for executive directors are determined by the remuneration committee made up of non-executives and that notice periods on service contracts be set at one year or less unless approved by the shareholders. There have been numerous reviews in recent years and there is now considerable focus on the need to limit a company's exposure to large-scale severance payments in situations of poor performance.

In addition to the requirements set out above, CA 2006, s 228 requires that a copy of every director's service contract with the company or any subsidiary company is made available for inspection by members at the company's registered office without charge or such other place notified to Companies House. Listed companies are also required to make copies available at the AGM location.

Directors should be aware that any failure to make service contracts available for inspection or to keep copies at the appropriate location will expose the company and every officer in default liable to a fine, plus a daily default fine where the contravention continues (CA 2006, ss 228(6) and (7)).

The requirement for a service contract also applies to shadow directors, covered in Chapter 3.

Payment for loss of office

Where a director is to receive a payment, by way of compensation for loss of office as a consequence of the proposal, details of the payment (whether in cash or by the transfer of property) must be disclosed to, and approved by, the members of the company (CA 2006, ss 217(1), 218(1) and 219(1)). Particulars of such payments must also be disclosed in documents sent to members (CA 2006, ss 217(3), 218(3) and 219(3)) and as well as compensation for loss of office they could, for example, include a payment made to secure a director's resignation or retirement and be made to a connected person. It should be noted that where payment is proposed by a company to a director of the company's holding company, the payment also needs to be approved by members of the holding company, save where the company is a wholly-owned subsidiary (CA 2006, s 218(4)).

Approval by the members is not required where the amount does not exceed £200 or the payment is being made to comply with a legal obligation or to pay damages for breach of an obligation to the director, is in settlement or as compromise for termination of a person's executive office or employment, or is made by way of pension for past services (CA 2006, s 220).

Failure by the directors to comply with these statutory requirements in relation to loss of office may lead to any director who authorised the payment being jointly and severally liable for any loss resulting to the company, and any unauthorised payment received by a director will be deemed to be held 'on trust' for the members and may need to be repaid (CA 2006, s 222).

8 Shareholders

It is fair to assume that the vast majority of shareholders are very reliant on the directors as they have only limited knowledge about what general meetings are required, how changes in share ownership occur, what decisions require shareholder approval and what information they should be sent by the company. Directors therefore have an important role to play in ensuring that restrictions and requirements in all shareholder matters are observed. In addition, given that shareholders own the companies they have entrusted the directors to run, the need for directors to communicate with shareholders is extremely important and the effects of failing to do this well should not be underestimated. To explain these responsibilities, this chapter covers:

- Share ownership
- General meetings
- Minority interests
- Communication
- Shareholder activism
- Stewardship code.

Share ownership

Shareholders rely on directors to ensure that their rights are observed when any allotment, transfer, purchase or redemption of shares is being considered. Directors must make sure, before proceeding, that any requirements, restrictions or procedures governing such transactions as set out in the company's Articles and in statute are observed. A director who knowingly contravenes such requirements will be liable to civil liabilities and criminal penalties.

i Allotment

The procedure for allotting shares is relatively straightforward, involving approval by the board and the issue of forms of application and acceptance. However, the directors must first check whether:

- the company still has a maximum cap on authorised share capital (abolished on 1 October 2009 but retained as a restriction in some companies' Memorandum and Articles) and, where it does, whether the company has sufficient unissued shares from which to make the allotment. Where it does not, the directors will need to arrange for the authorised share capital to be increased by ordinary resolution approved by the members;
- the directors have the authority to allot shares (CA 2006, s 550). Where they do not, they can arrange for it to be provided by ordinary resolution of the members;
- shares must be offered pro rata to existing shareholders before being offered to other parties (CA 2006, s 561 or by provisions in the company's Articles). Where there are such rights of 'pre-emption' and the proposal is for shares to be allotted other than pro rata to existing members, the directors must obtain:
  - individual consent to the allotment from each shareholder; or
  - approval from the members to a special resolution disapplying their statutory pre-emption rights (CA 2006, ss 569–571) or waiving the provisions in the company's Articles, whichever applies;
- any necessary shareholder qualification in the company's Articles is satisfied before a person can be admitted to membership;
- the allotment involves provision of financial assistance, which is generally unlawful for a public company (CA 2006, ss 678 and 679), although there are certain exceptions to this prohibition which may apply and should be checked (CA 2006, s 672). Where the directors permit shares to be acquired in circumstances where financial assistance is prohibited, they may be liable to a fine and imprisonment (CA 2006, s 680);
- the allotment is for a public company and will involve offering shares to the public. If so, requirements of the DTRs, FSMA 2000 and the relevant market's rules may apply (e.g. the Listing Rules for companies with securities quoted on the main Stock Exchange list) in addition to those of the CA 2006. In general these additional requirements relate to issue of offer documents and details required in the prospectus or listing particulars. The directors may be liable for civil and criminal penalties punishable by fine and/or imprisonment for making a false or misleading

statement in the prospectus, and someone who has relied on this information may seek compensation from the directors (FSMA 2000, s 90);

- shares are to be allotted for cash or by way of a bonus or capitalisation issue, in which case provisions in the company's Articles must be observed and further approval of the shareholders is required. Shares may not be allotted at a discount (CA 2006, s 580) but may be allotted partly paid (observing the minimum requirements of CA 2006, s 586 for a public company) and for consideration other than cash (observing CA 2006, s 582).

Once all these initial requirements have been checked and complied with, the directors may proceed with the allotment of shares, bearing in mind their duty to ensure the allotment is in the best interests of the company and not for any other purpose.

ii Transfer

Shares are essentially property and as such may freely be bought and sold by members as provided in the company's Articles and in any shareholders' agreement (CA 2006, s 544). Directors are responsible for maintaining the company's register of members (see Chapter 6) and, as an extension of this duty, are responsible for registering share transfers.

Whilst there may be additional provisions in a company's Articles, registration of a transfer of shares would usually require approval of the board. However, before such approval is given the directors must ensure:

- the stock transfer form submitted to them is appropriate (Table A, Reg 23 or Model Articles Reg 26 for private companies and Reg 63 for public companies), has been properly executed, and has either been signed on the reverse as 'exempt' from stamp duty or bears evidence that stamp duty has been paid;
- the transferor's share certificate is returned confirming ownership of the shares or, where this has been mislaid, a letter of indemnity is obtained from the transferor; and
- any provisions or restrictions in the company's Articles (and any shareholders' agreement) are observed. For example, the Articles may contain pre-emption on transfer provisions requiring that any shares for sale are first offered to existing members in proportion to the number of shares they already own.

Once the requirements prescribed above have been complied with, the directors may proceed to approve and register the transfer of shares.

It is worth noting that shares of public companies quoted on the Official List, AIM or PLUS Market must be freely transferable. In most instances such companies' registers of members will be maintained by share registration agents and the directors will only be aware of and approve the transfers in batches when produced in reports for board meetings.

iii Purchase and redemption

Every private limited company with a share capital may issue redeemable shares (CA 2006, s 684) and can purchase its own shares from the company's distributable profits, the proceeds of a new issue (CA 2006, s 690) or out of capital (CA 2006, s 692).

There is no longer the requirement for the Articles of a private company to specifically state that a company may redeem or purchase shares, but the Articles may restrict or prohibit the company's ability to do this. The Articles of a public company do, however, still need to contain provisions in the absence of which the issue of redeemable shares and purchase of shares is not permitted.

There are different requirements for redeeming and purchasing shares:

- 'Redeemable' shares must be redeemed in accordance with the provisions of redemption determined before, or at the time they were issued, set out either in the Articles or in an ordinary resolution approved at that time. They will need to be set down in the Articles for a public company. These requirements in terms of the date, terms and manner of redemption and price to be paid for the shares must be observed for the redemption to take place but they may, for example, merely require approval by the board at a specific time.
- Purchase by a company of its own shares is not usually a pre-planned or anticipated event and a purchase contract, approved by special resolution of the members, is required before the purchase can proceed. This contract will determine the terms of the purchase (CA 2006, s 694). Purchase can only take place where the company will be left with some non-redeemable shares in issue after the purchase. It can be paid for by a transfer of assets (*BDG Roof-Bond Ltd v Douglas [2000] 1 BCLC 401*).

Where the purchase or redemption of shares by a private company is to be financed out of capital, there are additional tight statutory controls to protect creditors' interests, as a reduction of capital reduces funds available to creditors should the company be wound up. Directors therefore have a duty to ensure the following additional requirements are observed:

- The directors must make a statement confirming that the company will continue as a 'going concern' for at least a year after the payment from capital has been made (CA 2006, s 714). It is an offence for the directors to make such declaration without reasonable grounds, punishable by up to two years' imprisonment.
- The directors may also be personally liable to creditors where the company is wound up within a year of the redemption or purchase out of capital (IA 1986, s 76(2)(b)).
- Payment out of capital, as well as the purchase contract, must be approved by special resolution of the members.
- Payment out of capital can only be made when distributable profits and the proceeds of any new issue of shares have been exhausted (CA 2006, s 710).
- No capital can be applied to pay a premium on the shares.
- 'Relevant accounts' made up to a date less than three months before the proposed purchase are required to enable the directors to determine the amount of distributable profit and the permissible capital payment (CA 2006, s 710).
- The auditors must make a report confirming that they have not found anything to indicate that the directors' statement is unreasonable (CA 2006, s 712(6)).
- A notice about the purchase must appear in the London Gazette and either be published in a national newspaper or notified individually to all creditors.

Finally, should the purchase or redemption involve listed securities, the directors must also consult requirements for obtaining approval and making announcements in the relevant market's listing rules and ensure they are observed. Directors of listed companies should be aware that the Companies (Acquisition of Own Shares) (Treasury Shares) Regulations 2003 (SI 2003/1116) allow listed companies to hold qualifying shares bought back by the company in treasury. This means the shares can be held ready for resale at a later date.

General meetings

Directors have a duty to ensure that no decisions are made or actions taken on matters outside their authority. They must be aware of the limits of their authority and of the circumstances where members' approval must be sought in general meeting.

General meetings are meetings of the company's members. However, it is extremely unlikely that the members will be aware of requirements governing how such meetings are convened and held so they will rely heavily on the directors.

In practice, responsibility for ensuring all procedural requirements for general meetings are met is usually delegated to the company secretary (see Chapter 2). However, the board retains ultimate responsibility for general meetings and it is important the directors are aware of the basic requirements, set out below, and are able to ensure that everything all formalities are carried out correctly. Whilst convening and holding a general meeting is relatively straightforward there are many technical points that need to be observed which, if overlooked, could invalidate the meeting or some of the resolutions passed. It is therefore essential to have an organised approach to convening and holding such meetings, which might be assisted by having a list of matters that need to be addressed before, during and after the meeting, allocating responsibility to specific individuals for dealing with them. This is also an important review and control mechanism to ensure no detail has been overlooked.

i Convening the meeting

The directors of a company may call a general meeting as and when required and the board would normally hold its own meeting to discuss the matter and authorise the secretary or a director to issue notice of the meeting to members (CA 2006, s 302). In addition, CA 2006, s 336 requires a public company to hold an annual general meeting each year and, if the company fails to do so, the directors and officers will be liable to a fine (CA 2006, s 336(3) and (4)).

The directors should also be aware that the shareholders may:

- convene a general meeting at any time by requisition in writing deposited at the company's registered office (CA 2006, s 303);
- requisition the directors to circulate statements to the members of the company (CA 2006, s 314); and

- where the company is a public company, require the company to give notice of a resolution to be moved by the members at the annual general meeting (CA 2006, s 338).

In such instances, once the directors have checked and determined the validity of the requisition, they must comply with its requirements within the relevant time.

Directors should also note that when a listed company is convening a general meeting, the company is required by CA 2006, s 311A to make the following information available on its website:

- details of the matters set out in the notice;
- total number of issued shares over which shareholders can exercise voting rights;
- total voting rights that can be exercised at the meeting; and
- any statements, resolutions and matters of business received from members once the notice calling the meeting has been issued.

Save for the last point, this information needs to be put on the company's website before or at the same time the notice of meeting is issued to shareholders.

ii Types of meeting

The most frequent members' meetings are general meetings. However, where different classes of share have been issued, it may also be necessary to convene a class meeting where the resolutions would vary the rights of a class of shares (CA 2006, s 334).

AGM – public companies

Every public company must hold one AGM each year within six months of the day following its accounting reference date (CA 2006, s 336). Private companies are no longer required to hold an AGM, unless there is provision requiring that the company does so in its Articles.

The Articles of a public company will usually determine what routine business must be considered at the AGM, such as re-appointment of directors, receipt of the annual accounts, approval of any final dividend and re-appointment of the auditors. Public companies would also normally routinely include renewal of the directors' authority to allot shares and waiver of pre-emption rights on allotment of shares and listed companies would also regularly include approval of the directors' remuneration report and a resolution permitting general meetings, other than the AGM, to be held on 14 days' notice. Other 'special business' can be considered at the AGM where the timing is such that it is appropriate and possible for it to be included in the notice of the meeting, for example adoption of a Revenue approved share option or share incentive scheme.

The importance of the AGM (and other general meetings held in the year) as a forum and means for communicating with shareholders is discussed below.

General meetings

As only one AGM can be held by a public company each year, all other general meetings of the public company held in the year and all meetings of members of a private company are called general meetings. Such meetings are held where approval by members is required for a particular matter and timing is such that it cannot, for a public company, wait until the next AGM.

There are also a few instances where the CA 2006 specifically requires a matter to be considered at a general meeting, for example a public company reporting a serious loss of capital (CA 2006, s 656). The business to be conducted at the general meeting will be set out in the notice.

Class meetings

Where resolutions to be proposed at an AGM or general meeting include proposals to reorganise a company's share capital, change entitlement to dividends, alter voting rights or wind up the company, etc. and there is more than one class of share in issue, separate meetings of the holders of each class of shares may be necessary. Requirements for class meetings are contained in CA 2006, s 334 as well as the company's Articles and any shareholders' agreement that might be in place.

iii Notice of meeting

The directors, usually with assistance from the company secretary, are responsible for formulating and issuing notice of general meetings and class meetings to members (and, for a listed company, also to any persons nominated by members to enjoy information rights in accordance with

CA 2006, ss 146 and 147). They must ensure that all members who have a right to attend and vote at such meetings and all directors are sent the notice either by post or e-mail, or that it is displayed on a website (provided members have been notified of the latter).

Directors have a duty to ensure:

- the notice is correct and complies with statutory requirements as well as provisions in the company's Articles. For example, CA 2006, s 337(1) requires the notice to state the meeting is an AGM; the date, time, location and the general nature of business to be conducted must be included (CA 2006, ss 311 and 325); and details about the right to appoint a proxy also be included. The authority under which the notice is issued must be shown, and further notes about inspection of documents and 'cut-off' dates for members on the register may be required for companies with shares listed on the Official List, AIM or PLUS Market.

- the type of resolution proposed in the notice is correct. This is essential, to ensure the resolution is not invalidated by failure to secure the required percentage of votes for the resolution to be passed, being a simple majority for an ordinary resolution and a 75% majority for a special resolution.

- the length of notice given is sufficient in accordance with the statutory requirements shown below, and taking account of any longer period that may be required by provisions in the company's Articles.

TYPE OF MEETING	LENGTH OF NOTICE
AGM (public company)	21 days (CA 2006, s 307(2)(a))
General meetings (private company)	14 days (CA 2006, s 307(1))
General meeting (public company)	14 days (CA 2006, s 307(2)(b))
Class meeting	14 days (same as private company's general meeting)

The type of resolution proposed at the meeting no longer makes any difference to the length of the notice required.

Listed companies must also adhere to the UK Corporate Governance Code's requirement that notice be sent to shareholders at least 20 working days before the AGM.

The Articles usually also specify the number of days required for notice as 'clear days' (that is, they normally exclude the day of posting and day of the meeting and allow one or two days for postal delivery). The Articles may also now differentiate between notice requirements for hard copy documents, electronic notification and communication via the company's website.

Members can agree a shorter notice period where the need for urgent business decisions makes it necessary for the directors to convene and hold a general meeting or class meeting with less than the required period of notice (CA 2006, s 307). Such agreement must be obtained from members in the percentages set out below, provided no larger percentages are specified in the company's Articles.

TYPE OF MEETING	NUMBER OF MEMBERS REQUIRED TO AGREE SHORT NOTICE
AGM (public company)	All members entitled to attend and vote (CA 2006, s 337(2)).
General meeting (private company)	Members holding not less than 90% of shares having the right to vote (CA 2006, s 307(6)(a)).
General meeting (public company)	Members holding not less than 95% of shares having the right to vote (CA 2006, s 307(6)(b)).
Class meeting	Same as private company's general meeting.

In practical terms, the directors can only take advantage of these provisions where the company has a relatively small number of members as, although the Act does not specify it as a requirement, it is essential for evidential purposes that agreement to a meeting being held on short notice is obtained in writing. The directors must check the signed agreements to ensure that the necessary percentage approval has been obtained before they proceed and hold the general or class meeting. Failure to do this may invalidate the proceedings conducted at the meeting.

iv Holding the meeting

The directors' role of advising shareholders continues while general meetings and class meetings are being conducted. This is principally fulfilled by the chair of the meeting and company secretary, assisted by the other directors.

Together they need to ensure that business is conducted in a manner that complies with requirements in the company's Articles and any relevant statutory provisions, so that the validity of the meeting and resolutions passed cannot be questioned.

ICSA's publication *A Guide to Best Practice for Annual General Meetings* and the guidance notes *Polls – Chairman's Obligations* and *Proxy Instructions – Abstentions* provide more detailed information about these particular aspects of the meeting. Requirements for holding the meeting need to be determined before the meeting is held and, certainly for the larger private and public companies, this will involve a considerable amount of organising and planning. In advance of the meeting the following provisions need to be checked:

- *Chair of the meeting* – The Articles usually state that this shall be the chairman of the board or in the chairman's absence, another director. However, there may be other provisions set out in the Articles which, if they exist, must be observed.

- *Quorum* – The meeting cannot proceed until the requisite number of members ('quorum') is present. The quorum requirement is usually stated in the Articles. If the Articles do not state the quorum, CA 2006, s 318 requires two members to be present in person unless there is only one member of the company, in which case the sole member shall be a quorum.

- *Voting* – Shareholders' voting rights and the manner in which voting shall be conducted will be specified in the company's Articles and this should be established before the meeting. For example, if different classes of shares are in issue the holders of those shares may have different rights to vote. Additional points of note:
  - the vote may usually be conducted either by show of hands or on a poll (CA 2006, s 321 specifies who can call a poll);
  - 'best practice' requires the chair to call a poll where the chair knows proxy votes received will, on a poll, give a different result to the show of hands;
  - the UK Corporate Governance Code (as well as PIRC, NAPF and other shareholder action groups) requires the chairman of a listed company to announce what proxy votes have been received on each resolution, even where the resolution is approved on a show of hands;
  - CA 2006, s 341 requires listed companies to make the result of any poll taken at a general meeting available on a website and failure to do so may result in a director receiving a fine; and

- subject to certain conditions, CA 2006, s 342 gives members of a listed company the right to call an independent report on a poll taken at a general meeting.

- *Proxies* – The directors must check to ensure who at the meeting has been appointed a proxy to attend and vote on behalf of a member (CA 2006, s 324). Proxy forms usually have to be submitted 24 or 48 hours before the meeting, as determined in the Articles, which enables a summary of proxy votes received to be prepared in advance of the meeting. This is important as it gives an indication of how the votes would be cast on a poll. A proxy now has the same rights as the member to attend, speak and vote at a meeting.

- *Corporate representatives* – Companies such as institutional investors are entitled to appoint a 'corporate representative' to attend general meetings and vote on their behalf (CA 2006, s 323(1)). It is important to note that the Companies (Shareholder Rights) Regulations 2009 (SI 2009/1632) clarified that a corporate member can appoint multiple corporate representatives in respect of different shares.

Of particular note here is the need for directors to check whether the company's Articles include provisions enabling a member to nominate another person or persons to exercise all or any specified rights of the member in relation to the company and for the directors to determine whether this right has been exercised by any members (CA 2006, s 145). Where applicable, this needs to be considered when checking the above points.

To assist the chair of the meeting it is quite common for a chairman's script to be prepared to take the chair through the formal business of the meeting on a resolution-by-resolution basis. Technical procedural notes and question and answer sheets are also often prepared for the larger and listed companies and those companies that might be expecting challenging issues and questions to be raised at the meeting which benefit from consideration in advance.

v Minutes and resolutions

Once the meeting has been held, the directors must ensure that minutes recording business conducted at the general meeting are prepared, signed and placed in the company's minute book together with copies of all resolutions of members passed otherwise than in a general meeting (CA 2006, s 355(1)). These signed minutes and written resolutions are evidence of matters approved at the meeting and must be retained. In addition, where certain types of ordinary resolutions and all special resolutions are approved, signed copies of the resolutions will need to be submitted to Companies House, for which the directors will be responsible (see Chapter 6).

vi Written resolutions – private companies

It should also be noted that, except where the resolutions proposed are to remove a director or an auditor, members of private companies may approve resolutions in writing as an alternative to holding a general meeting (CA 2006, s 281). The written resolution procedure is a very valuable alternative for a private company as it means, in most instances, decisions can be made by this means without the need for a meeting.

A resolution may be proposed as a written resolution by the directors or by the members of the company (CA 2006, s 288(3)). The directors must ensure they observe the requirements to circulate a written resolution proposed by the members set out in CA 2006, ss 292 and 293 otherwise they may be liable to a fine for failure to comply.

The written resolution alternative is likely to be much more popular for private companies as the requirement for 'unanimous' consent has been repealed. Instead, if an ordinary resolution is proposed for approval by written resolution, it need only be approved by a simple majority of members and if a special resolution is proposed by this means it need only be approved by a majority of not less than 75% of members. Such approval must be obtained within 28 days of the circulation of the written resolution.

Minority interests

General meetings are an important part of the company process whereby shareholders with the right to vote are involved in decision making. However, directors must be aware that, whilst the general principle is that decisions are made by approval of the majority of members, where the directors themselves hold and control the majority of votes, they have a duty not to abuse their position.

Directors must ensure that they strike a balance in their recommendations and the need to protect minority shareholders' interests. For example, a recommendation to pay large and unjustified directors' bonuses may be considered detrimental to minority shareholders who are not also directors.

A member (or members) who consider the company's affairs to have been conducted in an unfairly prejudicial manner has a number of remedies available including:

- applying to the Secretary of State for an investigation of the company's affairs (CA 1985, s 431);
- application to the court for permission to bring a derivative claim against the directors for breach of duty (CA 2006, ss 260–269). More information on this is set out in Chapter 13;
- petitioning the court for a 'just and equitable' winding-up in situations where the management of a company has broken down or opposing parties have reached an irresolvable deadlock (IA 1986, s 122(1)(g));
- applying to the court for an order on the basis that the company's affairs have been conducted in such a way as to be 'unfairly prejudicial' to members generally or some part of them (CA 2006, s 994). The order may result in the court regulating the future conduct of the company's affairs; instructing that the act or omission considered prejudicial be stopped or carried out; a person being authorised to take civil proceedings for a wrongdoing in the name of the company; requiring the company not to amend its Articles without leave of the court to do so; or the member's shares being repurchased by the company or other members (CA 2006, s 996).

For example, in *Re Brenfield Squash Racquets Club Ltd [1996] 2 BCLC 184*, the majority shareholder caused the company to enter into arrangements, including giving a bank guarantee, which had no benefit to the company and was to the detriment of the minority shareholder. The court held that appropriate relief for the minority shareholder was the sale of shares by the majority shareholder to the minority shareholder in accordance with the pre-emption clause in the company's shareholders' agreement.

Directors should also note that, even where a company genuinely needs additional funds to be raised by a rights issue, a minority shareholder unable to participate in the rights issue may be able to restrain the issue on the basis that his or her interest would be diluted (*Hall v Gamut Technologies Ltd 1999 SLT 1276, OH*).

Communication

i Generally

An important principle for directors to remember is that they are appointed by members who have invested in a company to run the company for them. Directors must therefore be prepared and indeed, have a duty, to keep the members advised of the company's performance and progress. Given that members have ultimate control over who remains on the company's board, it is surely in the directors' own interests to establish good relations with shareholders through frequent, open communication.

In a small or even medium-sized company, where often the directors and shareholders are one and the same or there is a relatively small shareholder base, communication can be relatively informal and ad hoc. It is likely the shareholders will be quite close to the company's business and the nature of its operations already and merely need to be kept up to speed with developments which may, for example, be carried out in a much more personal way by holding informal gatherings and update sessions (eg by the chairman, CEO or other nominated director phoning or e-mailing the shareholders). Communication in this way is feasible where there are relatively small numbers of shareholders as the cost and time it takes will be more manageable.

However, in larger private, public and certainly listed companies, the sheer numbers of shareholders coupled with the complexity of operations and numbers of people involved makes such personal approach to communication with them unrealistic. Indeed, even the cost of convening and holding an AGM even once each year can be considerable, which means directors must look at other means of communicating with shareholders during the year. Obviously use of e-mail and the internet provide a very cost-effective means of communicating with a wide audience and the requirements in respect of these forms of communication are outlined in the paragraphs that follow.

Company law and the UK Listing Authority's regulations require that directors send certain compulsory information to shareholders (and any persons nominated to enjoy information rights), such as the annual report and accounts, interim statements (listed companies only), notice and details of any resolutions to be proposed in general meeting. This will ensure that shareholders are kept informed about the financial status and the company's progress and are aware of any proposed decisions that require their approval. Whilst traditionally these documents would have been sent in the post there is, as explained below, an ever- increasing move to electronic and website communication which is a much faster and cheaper way of reaching a wider audience.

Many company directors recognise the value of good member relations and have established member communication policies which extend beyond the limits of 'compulsory' information required to be sent to shareholders by the UK Listing Authority and statute. Such policies are supported and recommended as 'best practice' by professional bodies such as the ICSA and the additional communication may take the form of:

- a timely response to all shareholder enquiries by the executive who is best able to provide an answer;
- supply of quarterly financial reports;
- sending circulars to shareholders on plans, current developments and strategy;
- ensuring that market information and reports reach the financial press;
- holding briefing meetings with institutional investors and analysts;
- holding information face-to-face meetings with substantial share-holders, discussion forums and conducting surveys; and
- making information on the company's progress and development available through the internet and establishing this as a two-way channel of communication.

A company that has a shareholder communication policy will, generally, be more in touch and closer to shareholders and will be actively managing the two-way flow of information. This can be very beneficial, particularly where, for example, a company's short-term performance has not been good due to tough economic conditions and the strategic measures proposed by the directors to combat this and achieve success over the medium to long-term need support from shareholders. Managing a steady flow of information can save shareholders some unpleasant surprises, which might cause a 'knee-jerk' reaction from them if they have lost confidence in the board's ability to manage the company on their behalf.

Directors need to recognise the importance of actively engaging with shareholders to ensure they support the plans and actions being approved by the board. For example, discussing announced plans and strategies with the shareholders and explaining how some of the decisions were reached and the constraints within which the company operates, etc. will put shareholders in a more informed position when considering how the company and board are performing. Such a discussion might be held at the AGM, or in advance of the meeting.

In some instances it is important to seek shareholders' opinions, feedback and support for proposed strategy in advance, as the alternative might be confrontation and formal opposition at the annual general meeting where formal approval is required. This might take the form of meetings with major shareholders, institutions and analysts who, where necessary, would be made insiders to ensure no market abuse takes place. A prime example of this might be securing support for executive directors' remuneration packages, about which there has been a considerable amount of well-publicised unrest amongst the shareholders of large, high-profile, listed companies in recent years.

ii E-mail and websites

CA 2006, Schs 4 and 5 allow a company to send documents to a member's nominated electronic address; to permit the company to place company information on a website accessible to members; and to accept proxies sent to it by e-mail. Many companies have found that an increasing number of members are signing up to electronic communication, giving rise to large cost savings in terms of printing and mailing fees.

Subject to having authority in the company's Articles, or to approval by resolution of the members, a company may now communicate with members by posting documents on its website. Before doing so, they must seek consent from members individually but, if no response is received, consent is deemed to have been given. The company must still notify members when it posts new documents on its website and this can be done by post or, where they have provided an e-mail address, by electronic communication.

A listed company must also comply with the requirements for DTR 6.1.7 and 6.1.8 which, in addition to the requirements above, means the listed company must contact all shareholders with voting rights requesting their consent to use electronic communication. Where no reply is received, the shareholders concerned are deemed to have consented to this.

A member is also able to communicate electronically with a company, provided the company has agreed to that method of receipt. This can be done simply by including an e-mail address on the notice of the meeting or the proxy form.

More guidance can be found in the ICSA's *Guidance on Electronic Communications with Shareholders 2007.*

iii AGM

At the same time, many company directors have expanded the business conducted at the AGM well beyond the minimum statutory requirements. These directors recognise the value of the AGM not only as a forum through which to communicate details of the company's past performance, but also as a means of giving key messages about plans for the years ahead and of seeking shareholder engagement and feedback. Many companies now use their AGM to:

- explain items of business in the notice of the meeting clearly, minimising the use of legal terms which serve to confuse;
- ensure that accounts are not 'laid' before the meeting as a purely symbolic act, but are made part of the business of the meeting and discussed fully;
- make sure all members of the board attend the meeting, as far as possible, particularly the chairman, SINED, CEO, FD and chairs of the board committees;
- encourage constructive questions during the meeting;
- either as part of the meeting or before, giving oral, video or graphic presentations and reports on items such as the company's performance, market information and opportunities, new strategies and technological developments, etc which help to widen the shareholders' understanding of the company as a whole. It is also recommended that such presentations have a question and answer session to encourage shareholder engagement;
- provide information in an appropriate form to specialist shareholder groups, for example by the use of Braille in printed documents, audiotapes, large print, etc.

Directors of listed companies should also be aware that the UK Corporate Governance Code requires that:

- the board ensures a dialogue with shareholders takes place;
- the board uses the AGM to communicate with investors and encourages their participation;
- the chairman makes sure the board is made aware of major share-holders' views about the company and of their issues and concerns; and
- a 'senior independent director' is appointed from amongst the non-executive directors, part of whose role is to communicate with shareholders.

As set out in Chapter 2, the board has to comply with the requirements of the UK Corporate Governance Code or explain where they have not done so.

Although the directors' duty to impart any information at the AGM is not embodied in statute, given that their appointment is secured by the members and a vote to confirm reappointment of some of their number will doubtless form part of the business at the AGM, many would consider establishing good relations with shareholders vital.

iv Market abuse

Whilst not wanting to discourage communication, directors must be aware that a certain amount of caution needs to be exercised together with advance planning to ensure that no inside information is inadvertently communicated at the AGM without having been announced.

Directors need to ensure that communication with shareholders of a listed company, whether at the AGM, in writing, or otherwise, does not amount to 'market abuse' which is an offence under FSMA 2000, s 118. The FSA's Code of Market Conduct sets out three broad types of behaviour that amount to market abuse:

- *Misuse of information* – Behaviour based on information not generally available and which is relevant to an investor's dealings in an investment. This offence is similar to the existing offence of insider dealing and may occur, for example, following dissemi-nation of information at an AGM that has not been previously or simultaneously disclosed or announced.

- *Creating a false or misleading impression* – Behaviour likely to give
  a false or misleading impression about the price, value, supply or
  demand of an investment. Directors therefore need to ensure that
  all information they convey, whether verbally, in writing or via
  internet bulletin boards and chat sites, etc. is completely accurate
  and does not mislead the recipient.
- *Distorting the market* – Behaviour that manipulates the market
  value of an investment by interfering with the normal process of
  supply and demand.

More details about the standards required can be found in the FSA's Code
of Market Conduct (see www.fsa.gov.uk). Directors should be aware that
they could face unlimited financial penalties, be ordered to pay compensation to persons affected and be publicly censured for any breach.

Consequently it is very important to ensure that no price-sensitive
information is inadvertently communicated at the AGM, or otherwise
when communicating with shareholders, without having been
announced. It is therefore recommended that advance consideration be
given to likely questions the directors expect will be raised at the AGM
and to formulating appropriate, permissible answers. Arrangements
should be made for any inside information that is to be discussed at
the meeting to be included in an announcement at or before the time of
the meeting. This would usually take the form of a trading update or
statement.

Shareholder activism

Unrest or the expression of dissatisfaction amongst shareholders is
often referred to as 'shareholder activism'. The concept is not new and
'activism' may take many forms, ranging from communicating shareholder concerns in the hope the board will revise its proposals, voting
against a resolution or resolutions proposed at a general meeting,
requesting the circulation of written statements in an attempt to influence
other shareholders' voting decisions, requisitioning general meetings,
selling shares, commencing derivative action, to lobbying government, etc.

Whatever form the activism takes, it can be expected that once
the news reaches the public domain, it will receive considerable press
coverage. As well as putting the company's directors and management
under considerable pressure to address the issues whilst in the public eye

and under close scrutiny, the negative publicity created could damage the company's reputation in the market and discourage potential investors from acquiring shares.

Investors are increasingly exercising their rights to intervene in the management of listed public companies where they do not agree with the board's policies and decisions. Recent issues where shareholders have expressed concern about, and engaged with, companies include directors' remuneration, board composition, takeover bids and share buybacks. Some recent, high-profile, examples of shareholder activism at AGMs include:

- *Directors' remuneration* – Just under 27% of investors at Barclays voted against the remuneration report; at Thomas Cook more than 39% of voting investors voted against the resolution to approve the company's remuneration report in protest about the scale of bonus awards to the company's top 100 executives; easyJet where 45% of votes cast were against the remuneration report; and HSBC where 20% voted against the remuneration report.
- *Board composition* – F&C Asset Management where the chairman was voted off the board; at Prudential, 25% voted against the reappointment of the chairman.
- *Routine resolutions* – In protest about the boardroom pay settlement, 21% of investors at Barclays voted against the re-election of the director who chaired the remuneration committee.
- *Strategy* – HSBC, where Knight Vinke Asset Management were lobbying for changes to strategy and structure; and Vodafone where Efficient Capital Structures were also lobbying for a change in strategy.
- *Special interest groups* – Tesco, where shareholders were lobbying for an improvement in the working conditions of Tesco's clothes manufacturers in Asia.

Whatever the reason for activism, traditionally discussion with boards would have taken place behind closed doors out of the public domain. However, directors need to be aware that where they fail to engage, investors are often prepared to publicise their concerns as a means of escalating external pressure to create change. Directors are therefore well-advised to engage with their company's shareholders and to listen to and address their concerns. Engagement and dialogue with investors is recommended at an early stage so concerns and issues are fully understood. This will enable the directors to give a greater explanation of how a decision or strategy was derived and, where possible, to seek resolution and support from the investors. Often engagement is needed well in advance of the AGM or general meeting to ensure support for the resolutions that will be proposed.

Stewardship code

It fair to say that for some years listed companies in particular have been trying to communicate with shareholders at the AGM, but there has been a distinct lack of interest from the large institutional shareholders who rarely attend and, on some occasions, even fail to register their votes by proxy. It is hoped the FRC's Stewardship Code will encourage institutional investors to engage with companies, attend and participate at the AGM.

The Stewardship Code contains principles and supporting guidance which it is intended will enhance the quality of engagement between institutional investors and the companies in which they invest (see Appendix 8). By requiring institutional investors to comply with the principles of the Code or explain why they have not done so, institutional investors are being forced to recognise their responsibilities for engaging with and monitoring the workings of companies in which they are invested. It is believed their involvement will improve standards of governance in such companies which will need robust responses to what it is hoped will be stretching and challenging questions from institutional investors seeking to monitor performance of their investee companies (Principle 3, Stewardship Code). It is also hoped that the requirement for them to have a clear policy on voting and disclosure of voting activity will cause them to communicate and engage with the companies and ask questions of the directors.

From FRC statistics it is already evident that a considerable number of institutional investors support the Stewardship Code and have taken on board their responsibilities for stewardship of the companies in which they invest. There is also evidence from AGM statistics that shareholders' engagement is improving, evidenced in part by the percentage of shareholders casting votes at general meetings of FTSE 250 companies. This has increased from 50–60% to 80–90%.

9 Financial accounts

Directors must ensure detailed and comprehensive accounting records are maintained to fulfil their role as managers and custodians of a company's assets and to ensure they are aware of the company's true financial position at any given time and are able to make more informed decisions. They must also ensure that annual accounts are prepared and submitted to Companies House and presented to the shareholders for adoption.

To explain these duties further, this chapter covers:

- Accounting records
- Preparation of accounts
- Content of the accounts
- Notes to the accounts
- Approval of accounts
- Laying and delivering accounts
- Accounting exemptions
- Summary financial statements
- Audit exemptions
- Additional requirements for listed companies.

Accounting records

The directors are responsible for maintaining detailed accounting records so that, at any time, they are able to demonstrate and explain the company's financial position and determine what transactions have taken place (CA 2006, s 386). More specifically, directors have a duty to:

- keep accounting records which are sufficient to record and explain transactions and provide a reasonably accurate picture of the financial position of the company at any time;
- provide information from which to compile the balance sheet and profit and loss account for the annual accounts;
- keep records of all money received and paid out on a daily basis;
- maintain records of assets and liabilities;

- where applicable, carry out a year-end stock take and keep records of stock levels; and
- where goods are sold other than in the normal course of retail business, to keep details of the buyers and sellers so that they can be identified.

Failure to maintain adequate accounting records will cause every officer in default to be liable to a fine, imprisonment, or both (CA 2006, s 387).

The accounting records must be kept at the company's registered office or such other place as the directors consider appropriate and must be open for inspection by the company's officers at any time. They must be retained for a minimum statutory period of three years for a private company and six years for a public company. An officer found guilty of failing to take sufficient measures to ensure accounting records are retained, or of acting deliberately to defraud will be liable to a fine, imprisonment, or both (CA 2006, s 389(4)).

In most instances, the directors delegate responsibility for maintaining accounts to one executive director, usually called the 'finance director', who has the required accounting knowledge and experience to fulfil this function. Such a director will usually be responsible for managing the day-to-day accounting function and for compiling detailed accounting information and reports, such as monthly management accounts, cashflow statements, profit projections, forecasts and budgets for consideration by the board. The quality of the information provided is paramount, as it often forms the basis of key strategy decisions on how to manage and deploy the company's resources to best effect.

Preparation of accounts

CA 2006, s 396 requires the directors to prepare a profit and loss account for each financial year of the company, together with a balance sheet made up to the last day of that year. The basic accounting principles to be observed in preparing the accounts remain the same as they were under CA 1985, Sch 4. They prescribe in detail the form and content of the accounts. The five basic accounting principles which must be applied when preparing the accounts are:

- *Going concern* – as long as it is applicable, the company must be treated as if it will continue business and operations on the same scale for the foreseeable future.

- *Consistency* – accounting policies must be applied consistently from one financial year to the next to allow comparisons to be made.
- *Prudence* – the value of any item in the accounts must be determined on a 'prudent basis' by taking account of actual profit realised before the end of the financial year and any liabilities or losses that have arisen or are likely to arise in that period.
- *Accruals* – any income and charges must be taken into account in the financial period to which they relate, without regard to when they are paid or received.
- *Assets or liabilities* – their value in the balance sheet must be individually determined.

Directors should also be aware that additional provisions may apply, for example where the company is a banking or insurance company, or where it is part of a group that requires consolidated accounts for the group (CA 2006, s 399).

The finance director will usually draft the annual accounts in close association with the company's auditors to ensure the form and content is correct and relevant accounting standards and principles have been applied. Any departure from the prescribed format, or any change in the format used from one year to the next, can only be made where the directors consider there are special reasons for the change and they explain this in the notes to the accounts.

Contents of the accounts

As well as a profit and loss account and balance sheet, the accounts must include a directors' report, business review (save where the company is exempt as a small company), an auditors' report, and notes to the accounts. In addition the accounts for a listed company must also include a directors' responsibility statement, directors' remuneration report, separate corporate governance statement, going concern statement and management report. Whilst most of these requirements are covered in the paragraphs that follow immediately below, information on the going concern statement and management report is given towards the end of the chapter in the section covering additional requirements for listed companies.

Directors should be aware that they may be liable to compensate the company where false or misleading statements are made in the company directors' report, directors' remuneration report or (for listed companies) summary financial statements (CA 2006, s 463).

In certain circumstances, CA 2006, s 463 provides exemption from liability for statements in the directors' report, business review and directors' remuneration report. The exemption is subject to a director not knowing or not being reckless as to whether a statement is untrue or misleading and not dishonestly concealing a material fact. Its purpose is to give directors comfort that they cannot be sued for negligence by, for example, making forward-looking statements as to the prospects for the company in the directors' report.

It should also be noted that, to provide shareholders with more detailed information, many companies, especially those which are listed, include additional reports and information in the accounts. For example, the annual report and accounts will often contain a statement from the chairman providing an overview of performance and prospects for the company and may also contain detailed reports and information on employee, environmental and health and safety performance, etc.

Directors should also note that a number of fundamental changes are proposed to the form and content of narrative reporting in companies' accounts, which have been the subject of much discussion and formal consultation. The changes proposed will overhaul the way annual reports are prepared and presented and introduce a new, clearer, structure for reporting. Some of the current disclosures required in the annual report will fall away, as will the requirement for the directors' report, business review and remuneration report in their current form.

The proposed changes to the directors' report, business review and summary financial statement (SFS) are summarised below and, for the remuneration report, are set out in section v below.

Consensus from initial and further consultations issued by BIS on 'The Future of Narrative Reporting' and 'A Long-Term Focus for Corporate Britain' demonstrates widespread support by companies, shareholders, institutions and shareholder advisory bodies for changes to the reporting framework so that readers of companies' annual reports are able to find the information they require more easily without being overwhelmed by the sheer volume of information contained within them.

The FRC has issued discussion papers on the new framework and, whilst it was intended that the changes would become effective for accounting years starting 1 October 2012, BIS has already announced that they will be delayed until 2013.

It is proposed that the directors' report, business review and SFS (see below) will be replaced with a Strategic Report and an Annual Directors' Statement, which will be reviewed for consistency by the auditors. Broadly, the content and form of these reports will be as follows:

- *Strategic report* – A concise, high-level, forward-looking analysis and description of the company's strategy, risks, challenges and business model supported by key financial, environmental and social information. It will include much of the content from the existing business review. Listed companies will also need to include key information showing the link between company performance and the remuneration of directors and senior executives, cross-referring to other sections of the accounts and narrative where needed. A strategic report will not be required for a small company but, for all other companies where it is required, it will need to be signed by each director and the company secretary.

- *Annual directors' statement* – This will contain more detailed narrative disclosures in a structured and consistent format to allow comparisons between companies. It has also been proposed that the statement will include a report from the audit committee confirming how long the auditor has been in post, when the audit was last put out to tender and how long ago the auditors were last discussed with the shareholders. It is intended the statement will be suitable for online publishing.

Whilst for small companies these changes will largely involve the directors' report being re-named the Annual Directors' Statement, other non-quoted medium/large companies will need to re-name the business review and directors' report, simplify their content and remove any duplication. However, the changes for listed companies and the disclosures made will be more significant, as information will also need to be moved from the remuneration report; inclusion of additional information about diversity, the number of women on the board, human rights and pay will become mandatory.

Some of the disclosures around asset values, purchase by a company of its own shares and payment of creditors will cease to be required and other disclosures will be simplified to enhance the relevance of information included in the accounts.

Once finalised, the changes will be included in further updates of this book.

i Directors' report

All companies must prepare a directors' report to accompany the accounts each year. The directors' report must include the information required by CA 2006, s 416 as well as Sch 5 of the Small Companies and Groups (Accounts and Directors' Reports) Regulations 2008 (SI 2008/409) and Sch 7 of the Large and Medium-sized Companies and Groups (Accounts and Reports) Regulations 2008 (SI 2008/410). In brief, these require the following information to be included in the report:

- names of directors who held office during the year;*
- the principal activities of the company (and subsidiaries) during the year;*
- substantial differences between market value of land and the value stated in the balance sheet where the directors consider they need to be brought to the attention of members or debenture holders;
- the amount of any dividend, if any, recommended by the directors;
- political and charitable contributions which exceed £2,000 in any financial year;
- important post-balance sheet events for the company (and subsidiaries);
- mention of any likely future developments for the company (and subsidiaries);
- details of research and development by the company (and subsidiaries);
- particulars of any acquisitions of the company's own shares during the year; *
- a statement that, in so far as each director is aware, there is no relevant audit information of which the company's auditors are unaware and that each director has taken all steps necessary to make him or herself aware of any relevant audit information and to establish that the company's auditors have been made aware of that information;
- details of any branches of the company outside the UK;

- where the average number of employees exceeds 250 during the year:
  - the company's policy on employing and continuing to employ disabled people and on their training, career development and promotion;
  - a statement of employee involvement, including details of communication, procedures for consulting employees and arrangements to encourage involvement in the company's performance, such as an employee share scheme;
- where the company is a public company or subsidiary of a public company, its policy on payment of trade creditors;
- save where not material to determination of the company's financial position, the potential risks to the company and financial risk management objectives and policies for financial instruments;
- where the company is a listed company, certain information that could be relevant to a potential bidder (CA 2006, s 992 which amends Sch 7 to CA 1985). Such information might include rights and obligations attaching to shares, any restrictions on transfer, details of substantial shareholdings, restrictions on voting rights and any other concert party agreements known to the company, etc.

Where the directors fail to prepare a directors' report, or the contents do not comply with the requirements set out above, all directors who were in office immediately before the period for laying and delivering accounts shall be guilty of an offence and liable to a fine (CA 2006, s 415(5)).

Only those items marked with an asterisk (*) must be included in the directors' report of a small company.

Directors should note that if the accounts are group accounts, this must be stated in the directors' report.

Part 6 of Sch 7 to the Large and Medium-sized Companies and Groups (Accounts and Reports) Regulations 2008 (SI 2008/410) also requires that the directors' report for a listed company contains additional information as at the end of the year on the following matters:

- the structure of the company's capital, including the rights, obligations and percentage of total capital attributed to the shares;
- any restrictions on transfers;
- details of substantial shareholders;

- in the case of any person holding securities carrying special rights with regard to control of the company, the identity of the person, and the nature of the rights;
- where the company has an employee share scheme, and shares to which the scheme relates have rights with regard to control of the company that are not exercisable directly by the employees, how those rights are exercisable;
- restrictions on voting rights;
- agreements between holders of securities known to the company that may result in restrictions on the transfer of securities or on voting rights;
- any rules on appointment and replacement of directors or amendment of the company's Articles of Association;
- powers held by the directors to, in particular, issue or buy-back shares;
- any significant agreements to which the company is a party that take effect, alter or terminate upon a change of control of the company following a takeover bid, and the effects of any such agreements; and
- agreements between the company and its directors or employees providing compensation for loss of office of employment in the event of a takeover.

In addition, listed companies must also disclose information about directors' interests in shares and share options and changes from the beginning to the end of the year and this is often included in the directors' report.

ii Business review

CA 2006, s 417 requires that all companies, unless they are subject to the small companies' regime, include a business review in the directors' report.

The business review for such companies must include a fair review of the company's business and a description of the principal risks and uncertainties facing the company and be based upon a comprehensive and fair review of the performance and development of the company's business during the year and its position at the end of the year.

The review must, as far as necessary to facilitate understanding of the development and performance of the company's business, include analysis of 'key performance indicators' which, where appropriate, should extend to environmental and employee matters. Save where a company qualifies as 'medium-sized' for a financial year, key performance indicators must also be included for non-financial information.

iii Statement of directors' responsibilities for accounts

Directors of companies with a premium listing of securities are required by the Statement of Accounting Standards, Auditors' Reports on Financial Statements (SAS 600) and under provision C1.1 of the UK Corporate Governance Code to include a directors' responsibility statement in the annual accounts. Such report must detail the directors' responsibility to:

- prepare accounts that give a true and fair review of the company's state of affairs;
- select suitable accounting policies and apply them consistently;
- make judgments and estimates that are prudent and reasonable;
- state whether applicable accounting standards have been followed, subject to any material departures disclosed and explained in the notes;
- prepare accounts on a going concern basis, unless it is not appropriate (where there is no separate Going Concern Statement in the accounts);
- maintain proper accounting records, safeguard the company's assets and take reasonable steps to prevent and detect fraud or other irregularities.

This statement would usually be made by the directors after the company's report and accounts have been considered and approved. They should be positioned immediately before the auditors' report.

iv Separate corporate governance statement

All companies, whether quoted or unquoted, which do not qualify as small or medium-sized companies, are required by CA 2006, ss 446 and 447 to prepare a separate corporate governance statement (SCGS). However, CA 2006, s 472A makes it clear it is the statement required by rr 7.2.1 to 7.2.11 of the FSA's Disclosure and Transparency Rules and these only apply to companies with fully listed securities. Where required, the SCGS must be delivered to Companies House for each financial year.

The information required in the SCGS can either be included in the directors' report, set out in a separate report published together with the annual accounts or be made publicly available on the company's website, provided reference to the website and where the information can be found is made in the directors' report. The SCGS must include the following:

- a reference to the corporate governance code the company is obliged, or chooses voluntarily, to apply (for example the UK Corporate Governance Code) or information about corporate governance practices applied beyond the requirements of UK legislation;
- a statement as to where such corporate governance codes are available and the extent and reasons for any departure by the company from such Code;
- where the company has decided not to apply a provision of such Code, an explanation of the reasons for the decision must be given;
- a description of the main features of the company's internal control and risk management systems in relation to financial reporting;
- information on share capital, voting and other rights attaching to shares, significant shareholders, rules on appointment of directors, and rules on amendment of the company's Articles as required in the Large and Medium-Sized Companies and Groups (Accounts and Reports) Regulations 2008 (SI 2008/410), provided the company is subject to that part of those regulations; and
- details of the composition of the company's administrative, management and supervisory bodies and how they operate.

The SCGS comprises a narrative explanation of how the main principles of the UK Corporate Governance Code have been applied and a statement whether the company has complied with the best practice provisions of the UK Corporate Governance Code for the whole accounting period and reasons for any areas of non-compliance. This must be reviewed by the company's auditors, who must confirm whether they agree that the company has complied, be approved by the company's directors and signed by a director or the company secretary.

v Directors' remuneration report

Listed companies must prepare a directors' remuneration report for
each financial year under CA 2006, s 420. This report must include the
following information (in tabular form where appropriate) with such
narrative and explanation as is necessary to assist with interpretation and
understanding (Sch 8 of the Large and Medium-sized Companies and
Groups (Accounts and Reports) Regulations 2008 (SI 2008/410)):

- details naming each director who was, or has been, a member of
  the remuneration committee and any consultants who materially
  advised on remuneration and the nature of the services provided;
- a forward-looking statement of the company's policy on executive
  directors' remuneration including a summary of any performance conditions attaching to share options or, under a long-term
  incentive plan, an explanation as to why those criteria were
  selected, a summary of methods used to determine whether they
  have been satisfied, details of any external comparison figures
  required, details of any change in entitlement, an explanation of the
  absence of performance conditions (where applicable), an explanation of the importance of performance-linked elements of the
  remuneration package, and a statement on the company's policy on
  the duration of contracts with directors, notice periods and termination payments under such contracts;
- details (in a tabular format) of each element in the remuneration
  package for each director by name, together with any explanation
  notes as necessary – such information shall include basic salary and
  fees, bonuses, expenses allowance and benefits-in-kind, compensation for loss of office or early termination, and other non-cash
  benefits;
- total remuneration received by each director in the current and
  prior period;
- details (in a tabular format) of each director's share options
  (including SAYE options) as at the end of the year and up until
  not more than one month before circulation of the accounts – a
  distinction must be made between beneficial and non-beneficial
  interests and disclosure must include details of grants, exercises, and
  any variation to terms and conditions as well as the high/low market
  price for shares during the year and the price at the end of the year;

- a line graph to compare share price performance with that of comparable companies, with an explanation of why they have been chosen as comparators;
- details of any long-term incentive schemes including the interests of each director in such schemes at the beginning and end of the accounting period and any awards granted or commitments made during the period;
- an explanation and justification of any element of remuneration, other than basic salary, which is pensionable;
- details of any director's service contract with a notice period of more than one year or entitlement to compensation for loss of office of more than one year's salary and benefits and justification;
- details of directors' service contracts including the date, the unexpired term and notice period, and compensation payable on early termination (in particular the unexpired term for any director proposed for re-appointment at the AGM);
- a statement of the company's policy on granting options or awards under its employee share schemes or other long-term incentive schemes and explaining any departure from such policy during the period;
- details of, and any contributions paid in respect of, each director pursuant to any defined benefit scheme or money purchase scheme during the period;
- details of the aggregate of excess retirement benefits paid to directors, past directors or their nominees or dependants;
- disclosure of significant payments made to former directors during the year; and
- details of consideration paid to third parties for the services of any director.

Directors of AIM companies should note that, in addition, AIM Rule 19 has been expanded requiring companies with shares listed on AIM to disclose directors' remuneration in the companies' accounts. The disclosure must include details of all emoluments and compensation (including all cash and non-cash benefits), share options and long-term incentive plans and contributions paid by the company to the directors' pension schemes.

Parts of the remuneration report are required to be audited. These include the amount of each directors' emoluments and compensation for the financial year and details of any share options held by directors, long-term incentive schemes, directors' pensions, excess retirements benefits of directors (including past directors), any significant payment made to a past director for loss of office and information on any sums of money paid to third parties in respect of a directors' services. If, in the auditor's opinion, the company has not complied with the requirements to prepare a directors' remuneration report in any way, the areas of non-compliance must be reported.

The parts of the report which are not subject to audit include details of those persons on the remuneration committee, the company's policy in relation to directors' remuneration and the statement of what considerations on pay and employment conditions of employees were taken into account when determining directors' remuneration.

The directors' remuneration report must be approved and signed on behalf of the board by a director or the company secretary. Often the chairman of the remuneration committee will sign the report.

Where directors fail to prepare a directors' remuneration report, or the contents do not comply with the requirements set out above, all directors who were in office immediately before the period for laying and delivering accounts shall be guilty of an offence and liable to a fine (CA 2006, ss 420(2) and (3)).

Currently, the directors' remuneration report also needs to be approved by ordinary resolution of the listed company's members and is usually proposed for approval at the AGM as a routine item of business. Whilst this is an advisory process and the directors' entitlement to receive remuneration is not conditional upon the outcome of the vote (CA 2006, s 439 and LR 9.8.8), since it became a statutory requirement for the report to be put to the vote, a number of high-profile companies, including GlaxoSmithKline, Abbey National and Barclays have faced shareholder revolts where either a majority or significant number of shareholders voted down approval of the directors' remuneration report at the AGM.

Against this backdrop, there has been considerable debate about how best to address what appear to be excessive levels of remuneration paid to executive directors, improve transparency by requiring more information to be disclosed on directors' remuneration and increase the level of control that shareholders can exert over remuneration. To this end, BIS announced a package of measures to address these concerns on 20

June 2012. These measures are aimed at improving good pay practice and governance by increasing the level of transparency and strengthening shareholders' voting powers. It is currently proposed that they will take effect from October 2013. These changes are not intended to enable shareholders to micro-manage a company's decisions around pay.

On 5 July 2012, Revised Remuneration Reporting Regulations were published and consultation commenced on the proposals set out in the draft regulations, aimed specifically at improving transparency. Key changes proposed in the revised regulations include splitting the directors' remuneration report into two distinct parts:

- *Policy report* – comprising a forward-looking statement of the company's remuneration policy, detailing the key factors taken into account when setting the policy. This report will identify the key elements of pay, information on service contracts, the approach and principles applied when making exit payments and any other material factors taken into account when determining the pay policy. A table will be required setting out the key elements of remuneration including information on how the policy supports the company to achieve stated short and long-term strategy, the performance criteria, how all the elements of pay operate and what arrangements are in place for awarding over performance and clawing back remuneration for under-performance, and the maximum potential remuneration that can be achieved. It is also proposed that the policy contains explanation of whether, and if so why, the directors' remuneration is any different from that of other employees.

  It is proposed that there will be a binding shareholder vote on the forward-looking Policy Report every three years and that, once approved, payments to directors can only be made within the limits of the approved policy unless a new policy is approved by share-holders or their consent to a specific deviation is obtained.

  Where the Policy Report is not produced for a particular year, shareholders should be informed where they can obtain a copy of the last Policy Report approved by shareholders, which will normally be on the company's website. However, it is difficult to see companies not including their Policy Report in each annual report (even if approval is not formally required), since cross-referencing without it will be very difficult.

- *Implementation report* – detailing how the policy was implemented, what payments were made to directors and how they
were determined during the year. It is proposed that this report
will include information on actual payments made to directors and
a single total remuneration figure for each director, performance
conditions and how the company performed against annual targets,
pension entitlements, exit payments made, variable pay awards, a
comparison of the company's performance compared to the CEO's
pay, details of directors' shareholdings and details of how shareholders cast their votes on the Policy Report at the last AGM.

It is intended that the Implementation Report will be produced
and updated each year and that it will be subject to an annual
advisory vote.

It is also proposed in the revised regulations that the directors'
remuneration report will start with a statement or letter from the
chairman of the remuneration committee highlighting the key
messages and issues for the year.

These revised regulations aim to remove some of the complexity around
reporting directors' remuneration and to improve the quality of disclosures, making it much easier to see what directors are being paid overall
and to determine the rationale applied by the company and the link
between pay and performance.

Of particular note is inclusion of the provision that any pay or benefits
granted in breach of the legislation and approved Policy Report will be
recoverable either from the receiving director or from the directors who
authorised the relevant payments.

Consultation on the revised Remuneration Reporting Regulations
closed on 26 September 2012 and the final outcome is awaited. However,
directors should note that the proposal for a binding vote has been included
in the Enterprise and Regulatory Reform Bill laid before Parliament.

The aim of these changes is to create a robust framework for pay and
actively encourage long-term shareholder engagement

vi Auditors' report

Unless specifically exempt from the obligation to appoint auditors (see
pages 150 to 152), CA 2006, s 495 requires that the accounts include a
report from the auditors confirming whether, in their opinion:

- the balance sheet, profit and loss account and any group accounts give a true and fair view of the state of affairs of the company and profit and loss for the year;
- the accounts have been properly prepared in accordance with CA 2006 and the relevant reporting financial framework;
- the information in the directors' report is consistent with the accounts;
- if the company is listed, the audited part of the directors' remuneration report has been properly prepared; and
- the information in the separate corporate governance statement (see above), where required, complies with the Disclosure and Transparency Rules.

Where the company is listed, the auditors must also review the SCGS (see section iv above) and the company's internal controls, the outcome of which would usually form part of the auditors' report.

The directors must ensure the auditors have access to all books and records they require to audit the accounts fully and are provided with any information and answers to questions they raise. Should this not be the case, the auditors have a specific duty to disclose this fact in their report to the accounts.

The auditors' report must state the name of the auditor, and be signed and dated. Where the auditor is a firm, the report must be signed by the senior statutory auditor in his own name, on behalf of the firm. Directors should note that it is now acceptable for a copy of the auditors' report (rather than a version bearing an original signature) to be submitted to Companies House, the members and any other person entitled to receive the accounts (the Companies Act 2006 (Amendment) (Accounts and Reports) Regulations 2008 (SI 2008/393)).

The directors have a duty to ensure that the requirements concerning the auditors' report are met, as failure to do so could render the company and any officers in default liable to a fine (CA 2006, ss 505 and 507).

Notes to the accounts

Certain information must be set out in the notes to the accounts, which is explained below. However, the notes will also contain other information necessary to support and explain calculations and information shown elsewhere in the accounts.

CA 2006, ss 412 and 413 require disclosure of the following information about directors in the notes to the accounts, unless there is a specific reason for exemption:

- the aggregate amount of directors' emoluments (excluding company contributions to pension schemes);
- the aggregate amount of gains made on exercise of share options;
- the aggregate amount of money or other assets (excluding share options) paid to or received by directors under long-term incentive schemes;
- pensions of past and present directors (including entitlement to emoluments waived) and sums paid to third parties for directors' services;
- any advances, credits, guarantees or other dealings in favour of directors or connected persons and details of any agreements to enter into such arrangements or agreements;
- compensation paid to directors for loss of office, which now includes payments in respect of breach of directors' contracts; and
- consideration paid to third parties for providing the services of a director.

In addition, CA 2006, ss 409 to 411 require disclosure of information in the notes to the accounts about related undertakings, off-balance sheet arrangements and employee numbers and costs.

Any director, or past director, who ceased to be a director less than five years previously, has a duty to inform the company of personal information which must be disclosed in the accounts (CA 2006, s 412(5) and (6)), to ensure that the required disclosures are made. For example, it is the duty of any director, or a past director who ceased to be a director less than five years previously, to notify the company of matters relating to himself and his remuneration which need to be disclosed. Failure to fulfil this obligation is an offence, for which a fine may be imposed (CA 2006, s 412(5) and (6)).

Directors should also note that under CA 2006, the Secretary of State has the authority to make provision by regulations about information to be disclosed in the notes to the accounts. The information required to be inserted into the notes of the accounts is currently contained in the Small Companies and Groups (Accounts and Directors' Report) Regulations 2008 (SI 2008/409) and the Large and Medium-sized Companies and Groups (Accounts and Reports) Regulations 2008 (SI 2008/410). These regulations expand the requirements of CA 2006 and require disclosure of additional information either in the main body of the accounts or in notes, unless there is a reason for exemption. The required information for small companies and groups includes:

- the aggregate amount of dividends either liable to be paid or paid by the company together with amounts set aside or proposed to be set aside from the company's reserves;
- disclosure of accounting policies;
- the aggregate number and value of shares allotted and, if there is more than one class, details of each class and information if the shares are redeemable;
- the value of fixed assets at the beginning and end of the financial period and details of any acquisitions, disposals, transfers or revisions in value of fixed assets;
- details of any listed investments and the aggregate market value of those investments;
- where the company has any financial instruments and they have been valued to show their fair value (assets or liabilities) details must be given of the assumptions made, changes in value and any terms and conditions which may affect determination of value;
- where a company has any investment property or living animals and plants, details of the valuation models must be shown. Where the item is investment property, comparable amounts must be shown, using either historical cost accounting rules or the actual differences between those amounts and the amount shown in the balance sheet;
- where amounts have been transferred to or from reserves, to any provisions for liabilities or from any provision for liabilities other than the purpose for which it was established, the details of the amounts must be disclosed;
- details of any debts which are payable other than by instalments and fall due within the period of five years from the financial year end must be stated and, where debts are repayable in instalments, the amounts which fall due for payment after the current financial period. Details must also be provided of any fixed cumulative dividends which are in arrears;
- details must be given of any charge that exists over the company's assets;

- particulars of any asset where the purchase price of production cost has been determined for the first time;
- information to supplement the profit and loss account;
- particulars of turnover, expressed as a percentage of turnover, attributable to geographical markets outside the UK;
- particulars of extraordinary income or charges during the year; and
- the basis of any foreign currency translation into sterling.

Companies required to observe the Large and Medium-sized Companies and Groups (Accounts and Reports) Regulations 2008 (SI 2008/410) must observe additional requirements to those contained in the Small Companies and Groups (Accounts and Directors' Report) Regulations 2008 (SI 2008/409) listed above. Whilst the requirements listed in the bullet points above still apply, the required disclosures are generally more detailed and the following additional information is also required:

- the amount of any provision for deferred tax must be stated separately from any other tax provision;
- repayment details for all loans, advances and liabilities;
- details of all debt and other fixed-income securities;
- details of any subordinated liabilities that exceed 10% of liabilities;
- particulars of guarantees and other financial instruments;
- contingent liabilities of group undertakings;
- distinction between listed and unlisted transferable securities;
- aggregate amount of property (excluding land) leased by the company to other persons;
- explanation of any sundry assets and liabilities; and
- details of any unmatured/forward transactions outstanding at the balance sheet date.

Failure by directors to make the required disclosures should come to light during the audit and, if not rectified, these must be reported in the auditors' statement to the accounts (CA 2006, s 498).

Approval of accounts

When the accounts have been finalised, they must be approved by the board of directors and:

- the balance sheet must be signed by a director on behalf of the board (CA 2006, s 414);

- the directors' report must be signed by either a director or the company secretary (CA 2006, s 419).

The copy of the accounts submitted to Companies House must bear original signatures, whilst copies sent to members and others entitled to receive accounts must include the names of the signatories. Failure to comply with these requirements will render the company and any officer guilty of an offence and liable to a fine.

Circulating accounts

The directors of every company must ensure that copies of the company's annual report and accounts are sent to all members and persons entitled to receive notice of general meetings as well as any debenture holders, if there are any (CA 2006, s 423). The annual report and accounts must be circulated for a private limited company within nine months of the end of the accounting period or, if earlier, the date on which they are submitted to Companies House.

As set out below, the annual report and accounts of a public company have to be laid before the members and, given this is the case, CA 2006, s 424 requires that they are circulated at least 21 days before the date of the meeting at which this is to happen.

Failure to comply with these requirements is an offence for the company and every officer in default, punishable by fine (CA 2006, s 425).

Laying accounts before members

The directors of a public company have a duty to lay the annual report and accounts before the company in general meeting (CA 2006, s 437). Whilst this would normally be carried out at the AGM, accounts may be laid before the members at any general meeting convened for the purpose.

Directors should note that, unless a private company's Articles state otherwise, this requirement to lay accounts at a general meeting only extends to public companies. However, as set out above, private companies are still required to send copies of their annual accounts and reports for each financial year to every member and holder of debentures, without need for a meeting.

When a public company is convening the meeting and sending out copies of the annual report and accounts, directors should be aware that:

- copies of the company's annual accounts, the directors' report, the auditors report (and, for a listed company, the directors' remuneration report) which are usually all bound into one document commonly referred to as the 'annual report and accounts' must be laid before the company in general meeting;
- the general meeting must be convened with the appropriate period of notice, unless consent to a shorter notice period is approved by the members (see Chapter 8);
- every member, debenture holder and person entitled to receive notice of the general meeting must be sent a copy of the annual report and accounts (either by post or by electronic means) at least 21 days before the general meeting at which they are to be laid before the members (CA 2006, ss 423 and 424), although they may waive this requirement in favour of a shorter period (CA 2006, s 424(4));
- whilst a small or medium-sized company (see page 147) may be permitted to submit 'abbreviated' or 'modified' accounts to Companies House, the directors must ensure that full accounts are circulated to members and laid before them at the general meeting;
- where the company is a listed public company and has circulated a 'summary financial statement' to members, the full annual report and accounts must be laid before the members at the general meeting.

Delivering accounts to Companies House

The directors of every company, even where the company is dormant or has ceased trading, have a statutory duty to prepare and submit the annual report and accounts to Companies House within the periods set out below (CA 2006, s 442):

- *Private company* – nine months from the end of the accounting period.
- *Public company* – six months from the end of the accounting period.
- *New private company* – 21 months from the date of incorporation, or three months from the end of the accounting reference period (whichever is later).

- *New public company* – 18 months from the date of incorporation, or three months from the end of the accounting reference period (whichever is later).

In some instances these periods can be extended by making application to the Secretary of State (CA 2006, s 442(5)). This could be, for example, where there are extenuating circumstances such as the need to finalise a legal issue that has an important bearing on the accounts, which cannot be finalised until the outcome is known, or where there is a delay because the company carries on business or has interests outside the UK. Such application must be made before expiry of the period in which accounts are required to be filed.

Where the directors fail to ensure that the accounts are delivered to Companies House within the required period, they will be guilty of an offence and liable to a fine (CA 2006, s 451). In addition, the company is subject to a civil penalty, which falls due when the overdue accounts are submitted and is calculated as follows (CA 2006, s 453):

NUMBER OF MONTHS LATE	PUBLIC COMPANY	PRIVATE COMPANY
Not more than one month	£750	£150
More than one but less than three	£1,500	£375
More than three but less than six	£3,000	£750
More than six	£7,500	£1,500

The fines double where the accounts are submitted late one year and late again the next year. Where the accounts are not submitted within the required period, Companies House will notify the directors of their responsibilities and, if no response is received, will commence legal proceedings against the directors and the company.

It should also be noted that is a criminal offence for the directors to fail to file accounts and, even where a company has been dissolved and Companies House decides not to prosecute, a private prosecution could be brought by, for example, a creditor and the directors could be fined and ordered to pay costs for their failure to file accounts.

Directors should ensure the accounts submitted to Companies House are accepted for filing, particularly if they are submitted close to the filing deadline. With this in mind it is important to note that the accounts submitted to Companies House must state the company's number prominently in at least one of the required reports, be printed in black type or ink in portrait format on good quality A4 white paper, have a matt finish, bear original signatures and not have shaded areas or photographs. The senior statutory auditor of the company's audit firm must also sign the audit report in his own name (CA 2006, s 506).

If these requirements are not met, Companies House will reject the accounts as they cannot be easily microfilmed and scanned onto its image database.

Accounting exemptions

Subject to satisfying qualifying criteria set out below, 'small' or 'medium-sized' private companies and groups may qualify for exemptions in preparation of their accounts as will a company which is 'dormant'. It should be noted, however, that where abbreviated are permitted for the purposes of Companies House and the public record, full accounts still need to be prepared and delivered to the company's members.

To qualify for small or medium-sized company or group exemptions (discussed below), the company or group must satisfy at least two of the following criteria (CA 2006, ss 382(2), 383(3), 465(2) or 466(3) and Companies Act 2006 (Amendment) (Accounts and Reports) Regulations 2008).

	SMALL COMPANY/GROUP £M	MEDIUM-SIZED COMPANY/GROUP £M
Turnover not more than ...	6.5	25.9
Balance sheet total not more than ...	3.26	12.9
No of employees (monthly average) not more than ...	50	250

However, the special provisions and exemptions discussed in sections i to iii below do not apply to public companies, banking or insurance companies, authorised persons under FSA 1986, or members of an ineligible group (containing any one of these), even if the company satisfies the above criteria.

i Small companies

A small company does not have to deliver a profit and loss account, directors' report or full balance sheet to Companies House. It may instead submit abbreviated accounts comprising a modified balance sheet prepared in accordance with a 'special audit report' and modified notes to the accounts (the Small Companies and Groups (Accounts and Directors' Reports) Regulations 2008 (SI 2008/409) and CA 2006, s 444(7)). The requirement for a special audit report will be waived where the company is exempt from appointing auditors.

ii Medium-sized companies

A medium-sized company is permitted to file an abbreviated profit and loss account and does not have to disclose details of profit and turnover in the notes to the accounts (the Large and Medium-sized Companies and Groups (Accounts and Reports) Regulations 2008 (SI 2008/410)). A special audit report rather than a full audit report may be delivered.

iii Small and medium-sized groups

A parent company need not prepare group accounts where, for the financial year, the group qualifies as small or medium-sized and it is not an ineligible group (the Small Companies and Groups (Accounts and Directors' Reports) Regulations 2008 (SI 2008/409) and CA 2006, s 444(7) and the Large and Medium-sized Companies and Groups (Accounts and Reports) Regulations 2008 (SI 2008/410)). This said, a parent company subject to the small companies regime can opt to prepare group accounts as well as individual accounts if desired (CA 2006, s 398).

iv Group parent overseas

A company is exempt from the requirement to prepare group accounts where it is a subsidiary, the parent company is registered in an EEA State and the company's results are included in the parent's consolidated group accounts (CA 2006, s 400). This applies to wholly-owned subsidiaries and to those where the parent undertaking owns more than 50% of the allotted shares. Shareholders may request the preparation of group accounts by the holders of more than half the remaining allotted shares or of 5% of the total allotted shares making application to the company. (CA 2006, ss 400–401).

v Dormant companies

With the exception of banking or insurance companies and authorised persons under the FSA 1986, which are outside the scope of these provisions, a company may qualify as 'dormant' where there have been no significant accounting transactions entered in the company's accounting records during the period concerned (CA 2006, s 480) and where the company has been:

- dormant since incorporation; or
- dormant since the end of the previous accounting year, qualifies as a small company (or would qualify if it was not a member of an ineligible group) and is not required to prepare group accounts.

A company that qualifies as dormant is able to claim all accounting exemptions applicable to small companies (see above) and can also automatically dispense with the requirement to appoint auditors without the need for a special resolution. Companies House provides a very simple one-page format for dormant company accounts called 'DCA', which is available on request.

Public companies, previously excluded, may now qualify as dormant and claim dormant company exemptions when preparing their accounts.

Summary financial statements

Directors should be aware that all companies, subject to anything to the contrary in a company's Articles, are permitted to send (either by post or electronic means) a summary financial statement (SFS) rather than full accounts to shareholders, debenture holders and other persons entitled to receive copies of accounts and notice of meetings (including those nominated under CA 2006, s 146 to enjoy information rights) provided such persons have indicated that an SFS is sufficient or where they have not rejected proposals that it should be sent (CA 2006, s 426).

To determine which entitled persons would accept an SFS, the directors must either provide an opportunity for consultation with the entitled persons or send them written notice of the proposal. Either way, the shareholder must be provided with a pre-printed and postage-paid card or form (or an electronic address), circulated with the notice, on which they can indicate if they require full accounts. The notice may state that unless they indicate otherwise an SFS will be sent to them in future. At the same time, they must be sent a copy of the full accounts as well as the SFS with the notice of the proposal.

Directors should note that even where entitled persons have indicated their acceptance of an SFS, they may at any time request a copy of the full accounts and reports, which must be supplied free of charge. The directors must ensure that the SFS is approved and signed by a director on behalf of the board and that a copy is sent to entitled persons within the period required for delivering accounts.

The conditions for sending out a SFS, together with details of the form and content, are contained in the CA 2006, s 428 and the Companies (Summary Financial Statement) Regulations 2008 (SI 2008/374) and CA 2006, s 427.

Whilst the required content of the SFS varies according to whether the SFS is for an individual company, a banking or insurance company, a parent company of a group or a company preparing accounts under international accounting standards, essentially the information in the SFS must be derived from the company's annual accounts and directors' report, and the SFS must comprise:

- a summary profit and loss account;
- information on paid and proposed dividends;
- a summary balance sheet; and
- comparator figures for the preceding financial year.

In addition, the SFS must state:

- that it is only a summary of information derived from the annual accounts and that it does not contain sufficient information to allow a full understanding of the company's results and affairs;
- whether it contains information from the directors' report (and, where relevant for quoted companies, the directors' remuneration report) and whether or not it is the full text;
- how a full copy of the annual report and accounts can be obtained and how full accounts can be requested for future years;
- whether the auditor considers the SFS is consistent with the annual accounts and directors' report and complies with due requirements of CA 2006, s 417 and regulations made under it;

- whether the auditor's report on the annual accounts was qualified (in which case details need to be included) or unqualified and, where information is derived from the directors' report, whether it is consistent with the annual accounts;
- whether the auditor's report included statements about accounting records being inadequate or inaccurate or information and explanations not being provided when requested and, if so, full details must be given;
- the whole or a summary of the relevant notes to the accounts; and
- the name of the person who signed the SFS.

It is important for directors to ensure that requirements in CA 2006, ss 426–428 and related regulations are observed, as the directors could be held liable for any deficiencies in the SFS's form or content (CA 2006, s 429).

The SFS for a listed company must be prepared in accordance with CA 2006, s 428 and the Companies (Summary Financial Statement) Regulations 2008 (SI 2008/374). Whilst the requirements for listed companies are largely the same as those for all companies, information in the SFS must also be derived from the directors' remuneration report and include information on earnings per share during the period (LR 9.3.13).

Audit exemptions

At present, small and medium-sized companies which satisfy at least the balance sheet and turnover criteria as set out in CA 2006, ss 382, 383, 465 and 466 and the Companies Act 2006 (Amendment) (Accounts and Reports) Regulations 2008 (SI 2008/393) (see Appendix 12) may be entitled to claim exemption from having their accounts audited.

EU rules, however, only require companies to satisfy two of the balance sheet, turnover or maximum employee number criteria, which is much less onerous than the UK regime. As a result the government is considering altering the current qualification regime to the EU model, the consequence of which will be that a great many more companies will qualify for audit exemption. Responses to consultation on 'Audit Exemption and Change of the Accounting Framework' were issued in March 2012 and the government is now considering how to take the matter forward.

Another change currently being considered by the government is amendment of the audit exemption qualifying criteria so the majority of subsidiary companies will be exempt, provided their parent companies guarantee their debts and they are neither quoted nor in the financial services sector. In the meantime, the current regime applies.

Directors should note that public companies, banks, authorised insurance companies, emoney issuers, UCITS management companies, and companies that carries on insurance market activity are ineligible for exemption from audit.

Before the exemption is applied, the directors must ensure that provisions in the company's Articles permit it to take advantage of the audit exemption. For example, Table A in Sch 1 to CA 1948 requires the appointment of auditors and many companies have adopted detailed provisions for transfers of shares in their Articles that require independent valuation of the share price by the auditors. Where either of these provisions apply, the directors must ensure that a special resolution to amend provisions in the Articles is approved by the members before the company dispenses with the requirement to appoint auditors.

It is also important to note that, even where the company is not required to appoint auditors, the directors must ensure:

- proper accounting systems are maintained and adequate records are kept;
- the accounts prepared show a true and fair view and comply with CA 2006 provisions in terms of form and content;
- a directors' report is prepared as required by CA 2006; and
- the annual report and accounts are submitted to Companies House within the correct period.

i Qualifying criteria

For a company to qualify for exemption from audit it must:

- qualify as a 'small' company in accordance with provisions of CA 2006, s 382 (see page 146);
- have an annual turnover not exceeding £6.5 million net (CA 2006, s 477 and the Companies Act 2006 (Amendment) (Accounts and Reports) Regulations 2008 (SI 2008/393)). (The requirement for a report from a 'reporting accountant' has been repealed except where the small company is a charitable company with gross income of between £90,000 and £250,000);

- have a balance sheet total of not more than £3.26m net. If the company is a parent company or subsidiary, it will be exempt if the group qualifies as a small group (CA 2006, s 383), is not ineligible and the group's aggregate turnover and aggregate balance sheet totals do not exceed the stated limits.

In addition, companies which are dormant may claim exemption from audit (CA 2006, s 480).

ii Form of accounts

The form of the accounts must comply with provisions relating to small companies (except that no audit report is required) and will comprise an abbreviated balance sheet and modified notes to the accounts. Requirements for the form and content of the accounts are set out in the Small Companies and Groups (Accounts and Directors' Reports) Regulations 2008 (SI 2008/409).

Where a company takes advantage of the audit exemption, the directors are required to include statements on the balance sheet that:

- the company was entitled to claim exemption under CA 2006, s 477(1);
- no notice has been received from the holders of 10% or more of the issued share capital (of any class) requiring an audit to be conducted (CA 2006, s 477(5));
- the directors acknowledge their responsibilities to keep proper accounting records and prepare accounts that show a true and fair account of the state of affairs of the company (in accordance with requirements of CA 2006, ss 386 and 394); and
- advantage has been taken of exemptions conferred by CA 2006, ss 382 and 383 and the Companies Act 2006 (Amendment) (Accounts and Reports) Regulations 2008 (SI 2008/393) relating to small companies and that the company, in the opinion of the directors, is entitled to those exemptions.

These statements must be signed by a director on behalf of the board.

Additional requirements for AIM, PLUS Market and listed companies

In addition to the requirements to prepare, lay and deliver accounts set out above, there are a number of other accounting requirements that directors of listed companies must ensure are observed. The need for directors of listed companies to ensure that information in the company's annual half-yearly or quarterly results is accurate, true and not misleading has been brought home by FSMA 2000, s 90a which makes the company liable to compensate investors who reasonably rely upon untrue or misleading results where the directors have been dishonest or reckless.

i Preliminary announcement of results

The Listing Rules no longer require premium listed companies to make a preliminary announcement of financial results but where a company chooses still to make this announcement, the company must comply with the requirements of LR 9.7A.

Where a listed company prepares a preliminary announcement of results, it must ensure:

- the preliminary results are notified to the RIS as soon as possible after approval by the board;
- the statement has been agreed with the auditors prior to publication;
- it is in table format consistent with the layout of the annual accounts, including the items in the half-year report;
- it gives details of any qualification or modification likely to be made by the auditors in the annual accounts; and
- it includes any additional information necessary for shareholders and others to assess the accounts.

Where a company decides not to issue a preliminary announcement of results, consideration will need to be given how otherwise to address the DTR's requirement to notify the market of inside information as soon as possible.

ii Annual accounts

Directors of listed public companies must ensure that the annual accounts are made public as soon as possible after approval and, in any event, not more than four months after the end of the accounting period to which they relate (DTR 4.1.3). Two copies of the accounts must be sent within this period to the FSA's National Storage Mechanism and a copy should also be placed on the company's website.

An AIM company must publish annual audited accounts which must be sent to shareholders without delay and, in any event, no later than six months after the end of the accounting year to which they relate. These accounts must be prepared in accordance with International Accounting Standards.

A PLUS company must announce final results as soon as possible and no later than five months after the end of the period to which they relate.

LR 9.8. 4 and LR 9.8.6 require that the annual accounts of a listed company contain the following additional information, much of which needs to be audited:

- An explanation of any difference of 10% or more on previously forecast results.
- A statement of the amount of interest capitalised, if any, and details of any related tax relief.
- Details of any waiver by directors of their emoluments in the current or future accounting periods.
- Details of any waiver of dividends by shareholders relating to the current or future accounting periods.
- Details of the interests (distinguishing between beneficial and non-beneficial interests of any person who has been a director during the period under review and of all changes between the beginning and end of the period and of any right to subscribe for shares or debentures). This information must be updated to within one month of the date of the notice of the AGM.
- A statement of information concerning major interests in shares (CA 2006, Part 22 and LR 9.8.6(2)) or a statement that there are no such interests. As above, this information must be as at a date no more than one month prior to the date of the notice of the AGM.
- Details of any shareholder approval given for purchase of the company's own shares and of any purchases made during the period.
- Subject to certain exemptions (that is, through the market or for an employees share scheme), particulars of the names of the purchasers of such shares.
- Details of allotments for cash (other than to existing shareholders pro rata to their shareholdings), including the class of shares, number issued, nominal value, name of allottees, consideration paid and market price of shares at the time of issue. These same details

must also be given for any major, unlisted subsidiary undertaking of the company.

- Details of any undertaking given by the parent company (if any) where a placing was made during the period.
- Particulars of any significant contracts in which a director is or was materially interested by the company or a subsidiary undertaking.
- Particulars of any significant contracts made with a controlling shareholder during the period by the company or a subsidiary undertaking.
- Subject to certain exemptions, details of any contract for the provision of services to the company by a controlling shareholder in the period under review.
- Details of any small related party transactions during the period.
- Details of long-term incentive schemes (if any).
- A statement made by the directors and reviewed by the auditors that the company is a going concern. This may be included as a separate 'Going Concern Statement' or form part of the directors' report.

In addition, LR9.8.6(5) and (6) require the annual accounts of a listed company to contain a statement, reviewed by the auditors, reporting on the extent of compliance with the corporate governance principles in the UK Corporate Governance Code and on effectiveness of the company's internal controls. Where the company has not complied, the provisions not complied with must be stated together with the length of the period of non-compliance and the reasons for non-compliance.

Furthermore the accounts of a listed company must comply with the requirements of DTR 4.1.5 to 4.1.13 which means that the annual financial report must include:

- Audited financial statements comprising, where applicable, consolidated accounts prepared in accordance with IFRS and accounts of the parent company prepared in accordance with the national law which, for a parent company incorporated in England and Wales, means UK GAAP.
- A management report including a fair review of the company's business at the beginning and end of the year and a description of the principal risks and uncertainties facing the company. The review must be balanced, comprehensive and consistent with the size and complexity of the company's business and involve the use of key

performance indicators (KPIs) including those on environmental and employee matters. The management report also needs to include details of any important events since the end of the financial year, likely future developments, research and development activity and the existence of any branches of the company and of any financial instruments. This requirement is mirrored in CA 2006, s 417(5) which applies to listed companies, specifying that KPIs must also cover social and community issues and for the review to be forward-looking, analysing the main trends and factors likely to affect the company's business. Save where such information could be commercially prejudicial, CA 2006 also requires a listed company to include information about persons with whom the company has important contractual or other arrangements essential to its business.

- Responsibility statements from persons, usually the directors, stating that to the best of their knowledge the financial statements, prepared in accordance with applicable accounting standards, give a true and fair view of the assets, liabilities, financial position and profit and loss and the management report includes a fair review of the development and performance of the business and of the principal risks and uncertainties faced.

iii Interim report

As well as the annual report and accounts, directors of listed companies must also prepare an interim report (also referred to as a 'half yearly statement') detailing the activities and profit or loss made by the company in the first six months of the financial year. The interim report must be made public as soon as possible and no later than two months after the end of the half-year period to which it relates (DTR 4.2.2).

DTR 4.2.3 to 4.2.10 require that the interim report comprises, essentially, a condensed profit and loss account, balance sheet and explanatory notes, together with sufficient explanation to enable understanding of performance, provide comparison with previous years and identify future prospects. It must also include an interim management report and responsibility statements, prepared along the same lines as required in the annual accounts.

An AIM company must also prepare a half-yearly report which must be notified without delay and, in any event, not later than three months after the end of the relevant half-year period.

The half-yearly report for an AIM company must include at least a balance sheet, profit and loss account and cashflow statement with comparative figures for the same period the previous year and be in a format consistent with the company's annual accounts. Whilst a PLUS Market company is required to prepare and announce interim results within the same timescales as an AIM company, the announcement as a minimum need only contain a statement by the board, profit and loss account and a statement whether the information has been reviewed by the company's auditors.

Whilst there is no requirement for the interim report to be audited, it is recommended by the Auditing Practices Board. Where the report is not audited a statement needs to be made to this effect and, where it is, the audit report must be reproduced in full.

iv Interim management statements

A listed company whose home state is in the UK must make a public statement by its management during the first six-month period of the financial year and a further statement in the second six months of the year (DTR 4.3.2). These public statements must be made between ten weeks after the beginning and six weeks before the end of the relevant six-month period (DTR 4.3.3).

The interim management statement must include an explanation of any material events and transactions during the relevant period and the impact on the company and its undertakings as well as a general description of the financial position and performance during the period.

However, where a listed company produces quarterly financial reports it will be taken to have satisfied the requirements of DTR 4.3.2.

10 Health and safety

All companies have a duty to ensure the health, safety and welfare of their employees whilst at work. This emanates from requirements of common law, legislative provisions contained in the Health and Safety at Work etc. Act 1974 (HSWA 1974), numerous regulations made under the HSWA 1974 and the HSE's approved codes of practice (ACOPs). The company also has responsibility for the health and safety of:

- contractors whilst on the company's premises or carrying out work for the company (*Andrews v Initial Cleaning Services [2000] ICR 166*);
- third parties using the company's goods or services, who should not be exposed to risks caused by an employee's negligence or lack of skill, experience or training (*R v Nelson Group Services (Maintenance) Ltd [1999] IRLR 646, CA*);
- visitors, the general public and emergency services (HSWA 1974, ss 2 and 3).

Strong leadership for health and safety at board level is essential and this chapter explains what directors must do to ensure the company fulfils its responsibilities in terms of health and safety, covering:

- General duty
- Managing health and safety
- Risk assessment
- Health and safety policy
- Costs and penalties for breaches
- Legislative review.

General duty

All employers must provide employees with safe conditions and systems of work and with appropriate training and supervision to enable them to perform their work safely (HSWA 1974, s 2).

Because directors direct and control the company, they must make sure procedures are in place to address the requirements of HSWA 1974 and ensure that:

- safe equipment, plant and systems of work are provided and suitably maintained;
- articles and hazardous substances are safely used, handled, stored, transported and disposed of;
- appropriate instructions are given on how to carry out work safely, supported by additional information, training and supervision where necessary;
- risks in the workplace are periodically assessed and employees are encouraged to engage and be involved in health and safety;
- the working environment is safe at all times; and
- a written health and safety policy is prepared where the company has five or more employees.

There are numerous other regulations made under HSWA 1974 which impose duties on directors and the companies for which they act. Whilst application of these other regulations largely depends on the company's activities and the facilities and equipment provided to employees, a number have wide application and need to be observed by most businesses. By way of example:

- Health and Safety (First Aid) Regulations 1981 (SI 1974/2013) – require provision of first-aid equipment and trained persons;
- Reporting of Injuries, Diseases and Dangerous Occurences Regulations 1995 (SI 1995/3163) – require accidents to be recorded, investigated and, where necessary, reported to the enforcing authority;
- Regulatory Reform (Fire Safety) Order 2005 (SI 2005/1541) – requires businesses to carry out their own fire safety risk assessments and implement a fire risk management plan;
- Provision and Use of Work Equipment Regulations 1998 (SI 1998/2306) – require equipment provided to be safe, suitable, inspected and manaintained and for those using it to be appropriately trained in how to do so safely;
- Workplace (Health, Safety and Welfare) Regulations 1992 (SI 1992/3004) – set out requirements for a wide range of issues such as lighting, heating, ventilation, seating and washroom facilities provided, etc.;

- Health and Safety Information for Employees (Amendment) Regulations 2009 (SI 2009/606) – require employees to be provided with certain, minimum, health and safety information;
- Health and Safety (Training for Employment) Regulations 1990 (SI 1990/1380) – require provision of such information, instruction and training as necessary to protect employees' health and safety; and
- Smoke-free (Premises and Enforcement) Regulations 2006 (SI 2006/3368) – prohibit smoking in enclosed or substantially enclosed workplaces and public areas.

This list is by no means exhaustive, but gives an indication of the volume of regulations applicable to most businesses, each of which needs to be observed.

In addition there will be regulations that are specific to the company's activities addressing requirements such as noise at work, manual handling, use of display screens, provision of personal protective equipment, storage and use of hazardous substances, working at height and lifting operations to name but a few. It is important for directors to ensure that all relevant regulations and their specific requirements are identified prior to commencement of the activities affected to ensure compliance.

Many of the HSWA 1974 regulations require employers to implement 'reasonably practicable' measures to address risk and what is expected of this requirement can be confusing. To address the lack of clarity the HSE have issued a number of Guidance Notes and ACOPs containing practical advice on how to comply with the law. They give practical advice and illustrations of what is necessary and what might be considered 'reasonable'. Observance of requirements set out in the ACOPs is important as failure to do so where an accident or injury has occurred is likely to result in a finding of default unless compliance with the regulations was secured by some other suitable means.

Managing health and safety

Whilst most companies are aware of their general health and safety duties, many have traditionally addressed and managed health and safety at an operational management level with very little consideration or involvement from the board. This level of delegation can have serious limitations and strong leadership for health and safety at board level is considered essential for developing a positive culture and approach towards health and safety within a company. Individual directors and the board need to lead by example to demonstrate the seriousness with which health and safety is treated. By involving the board, the health and safety implications of strategic and other decisions will be identified and assessed at an early stage, in the same way as issues concerning finance, resource allocation and technical requirements, etc. and will be taken into account when options are evaluated and decisions made. Similarly, periodic review of the company's health and safety performance by the board will help ensure the importance of good health and safety practice is recognised and followed throughout the company.

To help directors understand their responsibilities, the Health and Safety Commission (HSC) issued guidance entitled Directors' Responsibilities for Health and Safety which emphasised the benefits of:

- *Appointing a health and safety director* – By delegating responsibility for health and safety to one member of the board, that person will ensure the board always considers the health and safety issues arising, in the same way that the finance director mentions finance restrictions or the operations director raises concerns over business interruption.

- *Directors providing leadership and support* – It is very important for people both inside and outside the company to see from individual director's actions and decisions that they are actively promoting good health and safety practice and that this is the culture to be followed within the company.

- *Consulting and involving employees* – Active employee participation with health and safety matters should be encouraged. This will help generate greater commitment amongst employees to achieving objectives and adhering to policies and procedures, improve their understanding of issues that affect them and utilise their often valuable experience and knowledge when determining what procedures, means of communication, reporting and training will work best in practice.

- *Reviewing health and safety performance* – To keep the board informed of relevant health and safety risk management issues implementing a system of control is recommended, comprising a regular review of performance to identify any problems,

investigating and reporting the causes and ensuring that
preventative measures for managing the risks remain effective.

- *Reporting* – The HSC considers it good practice to report on
corporate risk and health and safety issues in annual company
reports and has issued guidance on how to do so (Health and
Safety in Annual Reports: Guidance from the Health and Safety
Commission – available from www.hse.gov.uk).

More recently, the HSC and the Institute of Directors jointly published
guidelines on *Leading Health and Safety at Work: Leadership Actions
for Directors and Board Members* (available from www.hse.gov.uk/
leadership). The guidelines reinforce the HCSs earlier recommendations
and identify three essential principles for successful health and safety
leadership and performance, namely: strong and active leadership from
the top; the need for worker involvement; and for periodic assessment
and review.

The guidelines suggest these principles can be achieved by:

- *Board planning to set the direction for health and safety
management* – The board should set the direction for effective
health and safety management. Board members need to understand and recognise the significant risks faced by their company
and establish a health and safety policy that is an integral part of
the organisation's culture, values and performance standards. The
board's own role and that of individual board members leading on
health and safety should be set out in the policy. Health and safety
should, as a matter of good practice, be a regular agenda item at
board meetings.

- *Delivering results through an effective management system* – There
needs to be an effective management system in order to ensure, so
far as is reasonably practicable, the health and safety of employees,
customers and members of the public. To achieve this, the board
must ensure that health and safety arrangements are adequately
resourced, competent advice is obtained when needed, risk assessments are carried out and employee involvement is encouraged.

- *Putting in place processes for monitoring and reporting* –
Monitoring and reporting are vital parts of a good health and safety
culture and management systems must allow the board to receive
both routine reports on health and safety performance and reports
on particular incidents. Reporting of information to the board is

paramount and must be given sufficient weight and recognition. Periodic audits should be carried out and reported, as should the impact of any proposed changes in the workplace.

- *A formal, annual review of health and safety performance by the board* – A formal boardroom review of health and safety performance is essential. The board should review health and safety performance, at least on an annual basis and ensure that appropriate action is taken when any weaknesses or necessary improvements are identified.

Directors need to consider these guidelines and whether to adopt them. There is a strong argument for doing so in that it demonstrates that the board is actively seeking to keep informed about current health and safety issues and developments, maintain high standards, monitor health and safety performance and make improvements where necessary.

Risk assessment

Regulations 3 and 4 of the Management of Health and Safety at Work Regulations 1999 require all employers formally to assess risks to employees whilst at work and implement arrangements for protective or preventative measures to reduce risks identified by the assessment. In addition, where five or more people are employed, the findings of the risk assessments must be recorded in writing.

Risk assessment is carefully examining what in a workplace could cause harm to people, following which the board can decide whether sufficient precautions have been taken to minimise the risk of injury or illness. Essentially the risk assessment process involves the following.

STAGE	PURPOSE
1. Examine characteristics of the workplace and activities being carried out.	To identify hazards that could cause harm.
2. Identify who could be effected or injured and how.	To establish the likelihood of an injury occurring and quantify the severity of the risk and how many people could be affected.
3. Evaluate the risks in light of existing precautions.	To determine whether more could be done to remove or reduce the risks that injury may occur.

STAGE	PURPOSE
4. Record the findings and outcome.	To demonstrate that a proper check was carried out, problems were identified and appropriate action was taken. Inform employees of the corrective action taken.
5. Review and revise the assessment.	To ensure that recommended precautions have been implemented and are working effectively and to ensure that risks are assessed when new processes or equipment are implemented.

The sort of matters that would be examined in a risk assessment include what is involved in the employee's work activity, who is carrying out the work, the physical characteristics of the work area and environment, fire safety measures and evacuation procedures, first aid provisions and arrangements for maintenance and servicing of equipment and security measures.

Numerous other regulations require employers to carry out specific risk assessments, the need for which is determined by the employee's work activity. For example:

- Control of Substances Hazardous to Health Regulations 2002 (as amended by SI 2004/3386) – where employees are exposed to risks presented by hazardous substances.
- Health and Safety (Display Screen Equipment) Regulations 1992 (SI 1992/2792) – where employees are working at a VDU workstation.
- Personal Protective Equipment at Work Regulations 1992 (SI 1992/2966) – where personal protective equipment is needed to carry out work safely.
- Manual Handling Operations Regulations 1992 (SI 1992/2793) – where employees' work involves manual handling.
- Control of Noise at Work Regulations 2005 (SI 2005/1643) – where employees are exposed to noise at work.

The company's operations and employees' work activities will determine what additional risk assessments are needed, depending on which specific regulations apply. Many of the regulations include recommendations for 'best practice' and minimum performance standards which should be observed.

Directors must ensure that an assessment of risks is carried out, as described above, to make sure no harm is caused to employees or others affected by the company's activities. There have been numerous successful cases brought against companies for failing to carry out risk assessments resulting in harm to employees. For example, *Alexander v Midland Bank plc [1999] IRLR 723, CA* where employees suffered work-related upper limb disorders attributed to their work activity and working practices; *Lancaster v Birmingham City Council [1999] CLY 1438* where the employer failed to carry out an assessment of risks and breached its duty of care by moving an employee, already suffering from stress, to a new job without providing training or support resulting in stress-related psychiatric damage; and *Hardman v Mallon [2002] IRLR 516* for failing to carry out a risk assessment for a pregnant woman before offering her alternative employment.

Directors should be aware that assessment of the risks to health and safety is important in many decisions that are made, for example before making changes to production methods, opening a factory in an overseas jurisdiction, changing distribution methods etc. This will be familiar to boards that have adopted Turnbull's recommendations for a risk-based approach to internal control.

Directors should also ensure this assessment of risks is carried out when decisions are made about doing business with other companies or employing sub-contractors. Whilst the initial cost of engaging certain companies may be attractive, where they are known to have a poor health and safety record and little or no means of managing health and safety risks there is a strong likelihood that this would undermine the company's good health and safety practice, potentially put the company's own employees at risk and ultimately damage the company's reputation. These factors should all be borne in mind.

Health and safety policy

Directors must be aware that where their company employs five or more people it has a statutory obligation to prepare and periodically review a formal written statement of the company's health and safety policy (HSWA 1974, s 2(3)). The directors can be personally liable for failing to prepare and implement such a policy.

The policy must be communicated to employees via notice boards, posters, training and briefing sessions and during induction training for new recruits and, whilst they vary considerably in size and complexity from company to company, they must contain the following information:

- a general statement of the company's policy on health and safety, outlining the company's overall philosophy on health and safety and the broad responsibilities of management and the workforce;
- organisation for health and safety matters, detailing how responsibility is allocated to individuals for particular aspects of health and safety; and
- a statement of arrangements and procedures for implementing the policy.

Directors must be aware that it is not enough merely to prepare this statement. They must ensure that arrangements are made to communicate the policy to employees and that activities are monitored on an ongoing basis to ensure that the manner in which work is carried out complies with the policy.

To adopt the HSC's recommended action points in respect of the health and safety policy, the directors must ensure that:

- they clearly and publicly explain the board's responsibilities and commitment to achieving health and safety objectives in the health and safety policy and demonstrate how they will be achieved through organisation and procedures put into effect;
- the policy is not left to sit on the shelf gathering dust, but is a living document referred to as decisions are being made. It must be periodically updated to reflect changes within the company such as technology, processes and staff; and
- employees are consulted when devising the health and safety policy.

A further point for directors to note is that it is becoming increasingly common for customers and suppliers to ask to review a company's health and safety policy before deciding to engage in business. A well-drawn-up policy can in itself give the company a competitive advantage sufficient to secure new business.

From the content of the health and safety policy it can be seen that it is the ideal means through which to publicly explain the board's responsibilities and commitment to health and safety and to demonstrate how this will be achieved.

Costs and penalties for breaches

According to HSE statistics in 2010/11, 171 people were killed in work-related accidents; 1.2 million suffered work-related illnesses (500,000 of which were new cases occurring in that year); there were 200,000 other injuries resulting in over three days away from work were reported by employers; and 26.4 million days were taken off work due to work-related illness and injury.

Many employers misguidedly believe that most incidents will be covered by insurance. Whilst employer's liability insurance will (subject to any excess) meet the cost of serious injury to an employee (see Chapter 6), it would not usually cover costs incurred through:

- time away from work and loss of the injured person's production;
- payment of sick pay;
- damage and/or loss of products, stock and raw material;
- delays to production;
- arranging temporary cover;
- repairing plant and equipment;
- investigating the incident;
- imposition of fines;
- legal costs;
- loss of contracts; and
- damage to business reputation.

Such uninsured costs can be substantial. Furthermore, employers with a poor record for health and safety claims may find that insurance premiums are substantially increased or, in some instances, that insurance cover is actually refused.

As well as avoiding the hidden costs of rectifying health and safety failures, many companies with high standards for health and safety have benefited from lower insurance premiums, improved levels of productivity and efficiency, improved quality of work, fewer staff absences and lower staff turnover. This is particularly important where investors, suppliers and customers are taking an increasing interest in the company's health and safety performance.

i Enforcement action

Under HSWA 1974, enforcing authorities (primarily the HSE and local authorities) have the power to investigate suspected health and safety offences. This power includes the right to make enquiries, search premises, take measurements and photographs, test equipment and order disclosure of information. If the investigation shows that a company has failed to comply with the requirements of health and safety legislation, the HSE inspector may issue an enforcement or improvement notice or, where the breach may involve serious risk of personal injury, a prohibition notice. Where an improvement notice is issued a date will be given by which the contravention must be remedied. The HSE is also able to apply to the court for a remedy notice and to seize and render harmless articles and substances where deemed necessary.

Failure to comply with a notice or order is an offence for which the offender is liable for imprisonment, a fine, or both (HSWA 1974, s 33). To give some idea of the likelihood of enforcement action being taken, there were 18,290 enforcement notices issued by the HSE and local authorities in 2010/11 and details are now published on the internet, which can be very damaging for a company's reputation.

Directors need to be aware of the HSE's intention to introduce a scheme to charge employers for the cost of enforcement action (the 'Fee For Intervention' or 'FFI' scheme). Whilst implementation has been delayed, it is likely to include an hourly charge for an inspector's time dealing with the contravention which, it is hoped, will act as a further deterrent.

ii Breach of HSWA and subsequent regulations

A breach of duty and failure to provide for the health, safety and welfare of employees constitutes a criminal offence giving rise to civil liability for breach of the statutory requirements of HSWA 1974 and subsequent regulations and, in more severe cases, risk of imprisonment. The scale of the financial penalty imposed and whether imprisonment is considered will reflect the seriousness of harm caused and how far short the employer's performance was of the appropriate standard. Maximum penalties for each offence are detailed in Schedule 3A to HSWA 1974, as inserted by the Health and Safety (Offences) Act 2008 which also specifies the mode of trial. Where action is brought through the magistrates' court there is a maximum fine of £20,000 and a 12-month limit on imprisonment, but the fine is unlimited and maximum prison term extended to two years where the case is brought thorough the Crown Court.

In 2010/11, HSE statistics show that 912 offences were prosecuted by the HSE and 294 by local authorities in Great Britain, resulting in them imposing total fines of £18.6m and £2.2m. Average fines were £24,005 and £8,154 respectively.

Where a company is found guilty of a breach of duty under HSWA 1974 and subsequent regulations, a director, officer or manager of that company may also be criminally responsible and be liable personally for the offence where it occurred with their consent, connivance or was due to their negligence. If convicted, the same scale of fine will apply as for companies and the director, officer or manager found guilty may also face a prison term and be disqualified as a director for up to two years. Such a prison term would be restricted to 12 months where action is taken through the magistrates' court. However, where the contravention is more severe, for example involving a breach of licence requirements or obstructing an inspection and action is taken through the Crown Court, the term of imprisonment could be for up to two years.

A simple scan through press releases, the HSE website and information readily available on the public domain will demonstrate the prevalence of health and safety offences and scale of fines being imposed. For illustration, a few sizable examples are set out below:

- Network Rail was fined £1m and ordered to pay costs of £60,000 for failing to assess risks and control corrective measures properly at a railway crossing in Essex, resulting in two deaths.
- Electrical Waste Recycling Group were fined £140,000 and ordered to pay costs of £35,000 and a director was fined £5,000 for exposing workers to toxic mercury fumes at a site in Huddersfield.
- The Co-operative Group was fined £210,000 at one of its sites for locking emergency exits, obscuring fire alarm call points, failing to test the fire alarm and not having any persons with fire safety training. Five companies were fined a total of £9.5m for the Buncefield Oil Storage Depot explosion for breaches of HSWA 1974, failing to limit the effects of a major incident and causing water pollution.

iii Corporate manslaughter

Whilst it has been possible for some years to convict a company of 'corporate manslaughter', convictions have been difficult to secure given the need to first find one of the company's officers guilty of manslaughter and then demonstrate that the person was the 'controlling mind' of the company.

This was established in *R v Kite, Stoddart and OLL Ltd, Winchester Crown Court, (8 December 1994, unreported)*, which involved a small company owned and run by the managing director, whose actions were found to be criminally negligent in the face of obvious risks. The company was fined £60,000 for the offence and personal prosecution under HSWA 1974, s 37 was also pursued, by which directors, or any person involved in the management of the company, may be prosecuted where they are believed to have commissioned the offence, or where it can be proven to be attributable to their negligence. In the *OLL* case, above, the director was found guilty of manslaughter and jailed for three years. In *R v Rollco Screw and Rivet Co Ltd [1999] IRLR 439, CA* penalties were imposed on the company and the responsible directors personally for failing to remove asbestos from a building safely and breaching HSWA 1974, ss 2(1) and 3(1).

It has, however, been difficult in cases involving larger companies to establish existence of a 'controlling interest', necessary if a case for corporate manslaughter is to be pursued. This was certainly a problem following the Zeebrugge ferry disaster, the King's Cross fire in 1987, the Clapham rail crash in 1988, the Piper Alpha oil platform disaster in 1988, the sinking of the Marchioness in 1989, the Southall rail crash in 1998 and the Ladbroke Grove rail crash in 1999. Whilst each of these incidents involved a large number of deaths and casualties, attributed largely to management failings and allowing dangerous working practices to continue, no conviction for manslaughter proved possible because the existence of a 'controlling interest' could not be established.

However, this changed when the Corporate Manslaughter and Corporate Homicide Act 2007 came into effect. This created a new statutory offence of corporate manslaughter where a fatality is caused by the 'gross breach' of a duty of care, and where the actions of the company's senior management played a 'substantial' part in the breach. 'Gross breach' will occur where there has been a failure to comply with health and safety law and where an organisation's conduct falls far below what can reasonably be expected.

This makes it easier for prosecutions to succeed, particularly against large organisations, as the prosecution will not have to identify the controlling mind behind the organisation's activities. Instead, the prosecution will focus on the conduct of the senior management, both individually and collectively.

The new offence is directed at the company itself and an organisation convicted under the Act will face an unlimited fine. The Sentencing Guidelines Council has issued guidance on the level of fine to be imposed, indicating that fines for organisations and companies found guilty of corporate manslaughter should seldom be less than £500,000 and could run into millions. In determining the appropriate level of fine, account will be taken of a company's turnover and profit, whether risk of serious injury could be foreseen, whether the non-compliance was widespread and a common occurrence and at what levels in the organisation the breach occurred.

Three cases have been brought under the Act to date for corporate manslaughter:

- *R v Cotswold Geotechnical Holdings Limited [2011] All ER (D) 100 (May)* in which the company was successfully charged with corporate manslaughter for the death of an employee killed when the unsupported sides of a pit in which he was taking soil samples collapsed. The company was fined £385,000, representing 115% of annual turnover and, whilst the sole director was also initially charged with manslaughter by gross negligence, these charges were not pursued given his ill health;
- *R v JMW Farms Limited* On 8 May 2012, JMW Farms Limited was successfully prosecuted for corporate manslaughter in Northern Ireland, fined £187,500 and ordered to pay costs of £13,000 where serious management failings caused the death of an employee who was struck by an unsecured bin as it fell from a forklift driven by a company director; and
- *R v Lion Steel Limited* On 3 July 2012, Lion Steel Limited was found guilty of corporate manslaughter, fined £480,000 and ordered to pay prosecution costs of £80,000 following death of an employee who fell through a fragile roof panel.

The Act also provides for courts to impose a Publicity Order requiring the organisation to publicise details of the conviction and fine. Commercially, this could be very damaging for a company's reputation and should serve as a significant deterrent. Indeed, the Sentencing Advisory Panel has recommended that Publicity Orders should be imposed in virtually all cases – this has been made possible by the Corporate Manslaughter and Corporate

Homicide Act 2007 (Commencement No 2) Order 2010. The court may also issue a remedial order, requiring action to be taken to address failures in the organisation that contributed to the employee's death.

Although the Act creates a new offence, it does not impose any new obligations on employers. The principal duties of employers are contained in the Health and Safety at Work Act 1974 and subsequent regulations and these remain unchanged.

However, individual managers and directors cannot be prosecuted under the Act and the court cannot impose a custodial sentence, although individuals who commit a serious breach of a duty of care leading to a person's death may still face prosecution and possible imprisonment for the common law offence of gross negligence manslaughter.

iv Individual penalties

As mentioned above, an individual director, officer or manager of a company can be criminally responsible for health and safety offences where the company has been found guilty of an offence by breach of HSWA 1974, ss 2 to 6 and the offence was committed with their consent or connivance, or where it can be proven to be attributable to their negligence (HSWA 1974, s 37). Where convicted, the same scale of penalties as for companies will apply and a director found guilty of a breach of HSWA 1974, s 37 may also be disqualified for up to two years.

An individual might be found guilty of manslaughter where his or her gross negligence caused a death. To be found guilty it must be established that:

- the defendant owed a duty of care to the deceased;
- this duty of care had been breached; and
- the breach had caused the death and was so grossly negligent as to be criminal and deserving of punishment.

Directors can be prosecuted personally where they are believed to have committed a health and safety offence, or where the offence can be attributed to their negligence. Historically, personal prosecutions for health and safety breaches were rare, but it is now clear from HSE figures that many more prosecutions have been successfully brought against directors and managers in recent years. One such example is the conviction, imprisonment and disqualification for three years of a director of IC Roofing Limited, who breached HSWA 1974, s 37(1). A worker died when he fell through the roof of an industrial unit. He was not wearing a harness and had not been given adequate training.

The forms of action which may now be taken for a breach of health and safety requirements emphasise the importance to directors of observing health and safety provisions on behalf of the company. Not only is the company now liable to criminal prosecution for a breach, but the directors are also personally liable and, in this context, it is important to note that directors cannot be protected from their own criminal liability by a company's limited liability.

Legislative review

There have been a number of health and safety reviews in recent years amidst concern that regulation has become overly complex and confusing and has caused a move towards demonstrating and documenting compliance without improving actual health and safety performance.

Lord Young's report *Common Sense, Common Safety* was published on 15 October 2010. It recommended that:

- the law should be updated, and made more accessible by bringing it into one place;
- a move away from a 'compliance-driven' approach should be encouraged; and
- requirements for small and medium-sized businesses carrying out low-risk operations should be simplified.

Lord Young's recommendations were largely endorsed by the government in their plans for reform entitled *Good Health and Safety, Good for Everyone* heralding a new start for health and safety regulation for Britain's businesses. The plans for reform recognise the need to shift legislative focus back towards high-risk areas and to address serious breaches of health and safety requirements.

In March 2011, the government established an independent review of health and safety legislation chaired by Professor Löfstedt to determine how existing legislation and guidance (comprising some 200 regulations and 53 ACOPs) might be improved and simplified, whilst at the same time easing the burden on small businesses carrying out low-risk activities.

Professor Löfstedt's report *Reclaiming Health and Safety for All: An Independent Review of Health and Safety Regulation* was published on 28 November 2011, from which it is evident that:

- whilst Professor Löfstedt does not consider there is a case for radical reform, he is concerned about the sheer volume of regulation and confusion amongst businesses about how they are to be interpreted and applied;
- all too often, reams of paperwork and lengthy risk assessment documents are generated to demonstrate compliance; these fail to identify and focus on key risks and do not achieve any real benefit or improve health and safety outcomes;
- enforcement action is inconsistent, partly as a result of the division of responsibility between the HSE and local authorities; and
- employers are confused by the obligation expressed in much of the legislation for them to take steps to address health and safety issues 'as far as is reasonably practicable', especially given that strict liability often placed upon the employer by the civil justice system.

As a consequence, Professor Löfstedt recommends a number of changes to ensure that the regulatory and legal systems are aligned and focus on addressing risk and achieving proper management of health and safety. These include:

- The HSE streamlining and consolidating sector-specific regulations, thereby reducing the amount of regulation by up to 35% by April 2015. It is anticipated this will involve revoking some regulations and amending many others including (as identified in Professor Löfstedt's report) those covering first aid, electricity at work, reporting of injuries and dangerous occurrences, working at height, construction and design management, etc, which will be familiar to most readers.
- Clarifying regulatory requirements, particularly the distinction between specific duties as opposed to administration concerns, to improve understanding of what is meant by doing what is 'reasonably practicable'.
- Improving consistency of enforcement action by one body, the HSE, directing all inspection and enforcement activity.
- Re-directing enforcement activity towards businesses with the greatest risk of injury or ill-health.
- Reviewing regulatory provisions that impose 'strict liability' on employers and clarifying the content and status of pre-action protocols, to address inconsistency with 'reasonably practicable' requirements by June 2013.

The government has also announced its intention to address the excessive health and safety burden faced by small, low-risk businesses. Changes are therefore expected in the coming years and will be included in future editions of this book.

11 Stakeholders

In addition to duties dictated by common law, those contained in CA 2006 and related company legislation covered earlier, directors also have an extensive range of duties imposed by other statutes concerned with protecting the wider interests of company 'stakeholders'.

As well as shareholders, the term 'stakeholder' also covers employees, customers, creditors and the environment, all of which are affected by, and have an interest in, the company's activities and how its business is conducted. This is endorsed by their inclusion in the statutory statement of a director's duties in CA 2006 (see Chapter 4).

Whilst directors' responsibilities towards stakeholders have been embedded in statutes for many years, awareness about them has perhaps not been as good as it should, largely because the duties are set out in an extensive range of the statutes and regulations and it has not been readily accessible. For example, many directors are surprised about the extent of their statutory liability for offences relating to environmental, employment and ethical matters.

More recently, directors' awareness of wider stakeholder interests and the need to communicate the company's performance in these areas has improved. This is partly as a result of numerous non-statutory developments and initiatives such as:

- introduction of the Turnbull Report's recommendations for a risk-based approach to internal control, extending beyond mere financial controls to encompass areas such as environmental, health and safety, community and social risks;
- appointment by the government of a Minister for Corporate and Social Responsibility;
- the requirement for occupational pension fund trustees to issue a statement of their investment policy, which involves obtaining information from the companies in which they invest about their performance with regard to social, environmental and ethical matters;

- developments in financial reporting standards, such as FRS 12, which requires the financial impact of certain environmental liabilities to be disclosed in the accounts;
- launch of the 'FTSE4Good Index Series' to measure listed companies' performance in meeting globally recognised corporate responsibility standards to identify those which are socially and environmentally responsible;
- the Tyson Report which, amongst other things, recommended that non-executive directors be recruited from more diverse backgrounds to widen the board's perspective, knowledge and understanding of stakeholder issues;
- the requirement for listed companies to identify non-financial key performance indicators and report on achieving performance targets in respect of them; and
- the increased tendency by government bodies, such as the HSE, Department of Energy and Climate Change, the Environment Agency, etc. to publicly 'name and shame' those companies that commit offences by making lists of offenders available on the internet.

As well as statutory provisions that may impose a direct personal liability on directors to observe their duties to stakeholders, directors should also be aware that ignoring the interests of stakeholders may have a more indirect effect on the company's performance. This could include high staff turnover and poor productivity, reduced sales turnover as a result of bad publicity about products, or poor environmental performance, discouraging investors. Eventually this might also have an effect on the length of directors' service where the shareholders lose confidence in the directors' ability to run the company effectively and decide to take action to replace all or some of the board.

This chapter addresses directors' duties to stakeholders by covering basic duties towards:

- Employees
- The environment
- Customers
- Creditors.

In many cases the company's size will mean that directors delegate day-to-day responsibility for these matters to senior managers with specialist knowledge and experience. However, the directors must consider the implications for stakeholders when making policy and strategy decisions.

They must also ensure that appropriate policies, procedures and controls are put in place to guide and monitor performance and that those people dealing with these matters on a daily basis have the requisite knowledge, experience, training and information.

Employees

Essentially, employees sell their labour to companies in exchange for a salary and other benefits included in a contract. However, employees' rights contained in employment protection legislation now go well beyond the limits of this contractual relationship.

The directors are responsible for ensuring that the company complies with the requirements of employment legislation. If they fail to do so, the aggrieved employee can make a claim against the company, not the directors. However, where the directors have acted fraudulently or have been negligent, the company may in turn make a claim against them for failure to act in the best interests of the company and to attend diligently to the company's affairs. Such counterclaim may be for a contribution to, or an indemnity against, the financial penalty incurred by the company.

Provisions in CA 2006, s 172(1) place a general duty on directors to take regard of employees' interests in their management of the company. In practice it would be difficult not to observe this if the company is to attract and secure a workforce.

CA 2006 also requires that unless a company is entitled to the 'small company' exemption, the business review in the company's annual accounts must contain a fair review of the company's business and description of the main risks and uncertainties. This might, for example, include employment matters. Furthermore, a quoted company must include information about a company's employees where it is relevant and necessary in order to understand issues concerning the development, performance and future of the company. This might include information on the company's employment, training, promotion and advancement of disabled persons policies with analysis of whether they are effective, linked to measured key performance indicators.

If the necessary disclosures are not made in the business review in the annual accounts, the directors in office immediately before the end of the relevant accounting period will be guilty of an offence and be liable to a fine (CA 2006, s 419).

To observe their general duties to the company (set out in the statutory statement, see Chapter 4) the directors must ensure that they treat employees in a way that is likely to 'promote the success of the company', which means that they must ensure:

- an employment contract or written particulars of employment are provided and the terms are observed;
- there is no discrimination in the workplace on any grounds;
- employees are treated fairly and their statutory rights are observed;
- a safe and healthy work environment is provided (see Chapter 10);
- required insurance policies are effected and maintained (see Chapter 6);
- data protection principles are observed in keeping of employment records;
- illegal immigrants are not employed; and
- employees are of a legal age.

Failure to meet the requirements of legislation in these areas may result in claims against the company for unfair dismissal, injury arising from work, or breach of contract terms, etc, all of which would be likely to involve direct or indirect costs to the company in the form of damages or by attracting bad publicity and damaging the company's reputation. Although a considerable number of claims for unfair dismissal, for example, are often subsequently withdrawn or settled through ACAS, dealing with them in the first instance can take up significant amounts of management time which could be much better spent on directing and managing the company's operations.

In addition, the majority of directors and those in managerial positions recognise that by treating employees fairly and rewarding them with fair pay, job security and good working conditions, the company is more likely to achieve a high level of productivity coupled with harmonious employee relations, both of which are desirable from a commercial perspective. Many companies have adopted government-supported staff motivation and training schemes such as 'Investors in People' in recognition of the benefits such initiatives can provide.

From a practical perspective, directors need to ensure that employees know what is expected of them in terms of performance and behaviour and what they can expect from the company in return. A great many employment problems stem from a lack of understanding and difference in expectations, which can be avoided by good, clear, written communication. Even a small company will benefit from a concise employment handbook setting out what an employee must do when they are sick or would like to take holiday, what form performance reviews will take, how training and development needs will be addressed, and how the company will support equal opportunities, etc. The handbook might be longer and more complex in a larger company and be supported by numerous other stand-alone policies such as those addressing use of e-mail and the internet, anti-bribery and corruption, whistle-blowing, equal opportunities, etc., each of which will help ensure employees know what behaviour is expected of them and the consequences of breaching these requirements. In addition, it is important the handbook or supporting policies identify the channels an aggrieved employee can use to raise a complaint and what the employer will do to try and resolve matters.

Directors of large companies are likely to have the benefit of expertise of employment professionals within their organisation who can advise on human resources, personnel and employment matters. They will be able to delegate day-to-day responsibility for employment matters to these specialists, whilst retaining overall responsibility for the company's treatment of employees. However, directors in smaller companies are unlikely to have the luxury of such internal resources and may need to consult outside specialists, such as the Advisory Conciliation and Arbitration Service (ACAS) and employment lawyers, to help them deal with more complex employment issues.

The directors must, therefore, have regard to the following.

i The contract of employment

All employees working eight or more hours per week must receive a written statement of basic terms and conditions of employment (see Appendix 13) within two months of the start of their employment (ERA 1996, s 1, as amended by the Employment Act 2002). This must include details of the company's disciplinary and grievance procedures.

Additional provisions in the employment contract need to be carefully worded as they often increase the employee's benefits and at the same time increase the employee's obligations to the company. They may, for example, include requirements in relation to confidentiality of information, restrictive covenants, mobility and travel requirements, 'garden leave', extra benefits and ownership of intellectual property.

Once the terms of the contract have been agreed, the directors must ensure they are observed; if not the employee could make a claim for breach of contract.

The directors need to arrange for employment contracts to be periodically reviewed to ensure they remain consistent with current legislative requirements and best practice.

ii Discrimination

Discrimination, victimisation and harassment, whether direct or indirect, against any person or any less favourable treatment of employees on the grounds of sex, race, religion, disability, spent convictions or whether they are part-time, fixed term or agency workers is unlawful where it occurs at any time during the employment relationship. Given the potential for an Employment Tribunal to impose financial penalties on companies (including vicarious liability for other employees' discriminatory acts) as well as the potential for bad publicity, companies will be keen to avoid such proceedings.

A company must try to prevent discriminatory acts. It is therefore important that directors are aware of the legal requirements and make sure that the company's policies, procedures and employment practices are regularly reviewed to ensure measures to address and discourage discrimination are implemented and communicated to employees. Such policies may include a code of practice to eliminate racial discrimination (recommended by the Commission for Racial Equality – see www.cre. gov.uk), an equal opportunities policy (recommended by the Equal Opportunities Commission – see www.eoc.org.uk), a discrimination and harassment policy and an appeals and grievance procedure.

iii Dismissal

Where there is a valid reason, directors may dismiss an employee from working for the company. For example in *Denco Ltd v Joinson (1991) IRLR 63 EAT*, dismissal of an employee for unauthorised use of a restricted computer file was considered gross misconduct and was deemed to have been fair. Similarly, an employer may dismiss an employee for reasons relating to capability, qualifications, conduct and redundancy.

However, unless the dismissal is for gross misconduct (other examples include theft and violence) and the employee is summarily dismissed, the employee must be made aware of the problem and be given the opportunity to improve before being dismissed. It is important that in each case employees are treated consistently and, to achieve this, directors are recommended to implement a formal disciplinary procedure, identifying clear rules and steps to be taken that could lead up to dismissal. The ACAS Code of Practice on handling disciplinary and grievance matters in the workplace provides guidance on how to draw up disciplinary rules and procedures and operate them effectively. It can be downloaded from www.acas.org.uk. Whilst failure to observe the ACAS Code of Practice will not necessarily render a dismissal unfair or the employer's actions unreasonable, observing its recommendations could present a strong defence against a claim of unfair dismissal.

It is advisable for the directors to implement and communicate the company's disciplinary and grievance procedures to employees in writing and to ensure they are applied in the same manner to all employees, equally and without any discrimination.

Employees have statutory rights protecting them from 'unfair' dismissal (ERA 1996, s 94) and an employee who has been employed for at least two years and considers him or herself to have been unfairly dismissed may make application to an employment tribunal disclosing details of the complaint for consideration (the Unfair Dismissal and Statement of Reasons for Dismissal (Variation of Qualifying Period) Order 2012 (SI 2012/989)), save that a one-year qualifying period applies to employees engaged prior to 6 April 2012. Notwithstanding this qualifying period, dismissal will be considered automatically unfair where it:

- is connected with maternity;
- followed the employee seeking to assert an employment right, such as the right to receive the minimum wage or a request for flexible working arrangements;
- arises when an employee attempts to take action on health and safety grounds;
- follows a transfer of undertaking;
- arises by the employee refusing to work on Sundays or to waive any other restriction under the Working Time Regulations;
- follows a 'protected disclosure' by the employee on wrongdoing at work;
- occurs due to an employee's membership or non-membership of a trade union;

- follows proceedings brought against the employer by a part-time employee refusing to accept less favourable treatment than a full-time employee.

Where an employee's claim is successful and dismissal is judged to have been unfair, from February 2013 the employee may be awarded up to £74,200 as compensation for dismissal (ERA 1999, ss 33 to 37). This award may be even higher where the employer refuses to reinstate the employee. Where the dismissal followed a protected disclosure by the employee, ('whistleblowing') under the Public Interest Disclosure Act 1998, the award is uncapped.

Directors must be aware of the overall constraints on dismissal of employees and ensure that a formal disciplinary policy is implemented and followed. They should also be aware that in an attempt to reduce the number of vexatious claims and to encourage more mediation and settlement, the government has announced its intention to introduce fees for employees lodging a claim for unfair dismissal. Consultation on details of the scheme and how it will work is still underway, although it was intended it would take effect in December 2013.

iv Data protection

The structured and personal nature of a company's employment records means that they come within the scope of the DPA 1998. The directors must ensure that notification about processing made to the Information Commissioner includes employment records, and that the eight data protection principles (set out in Appendix 10) are observed at all times.

To help employers understand the impact of data protection requirements on processing of an employee's personal data, the Information Commissioner issued the Employment Practices Data Protection Code as well as Supplementary Guidance and a brief guide setting out recommendations for how organisations can adhere to the requirements of the DPA 1998. These are available from www.ico.gov.uk and help employers to understand data protection requirements in respect of personal information that is gathered during the employment relationship from recruitment to termination and, beyond these, by setting out standards in relation to:

- managing data protection;
- recruitment;

- employment records;
- access and disclosure of information, including references;
- contract and agency staff;
- employee monitoring (including monitoring telephone, e-mail and internet use);
- medical testing (including for alcohol and substance abuse);
- discipline and dismissal; and
- retention of records of former employees.

The Code comprises four parts:

- Part 1 – recruitment and selection and employment practices;
- Part 2 – management of employment records;
- Part 3 – monitoring at work; and
- Part 4 – medical information.

In each section, the Code sets out 'benchmarks' to help businesses to comply with the requirements of DPA 1998 and directors would be well advised to ensure the recommendations made by the Information Commissioner are observed, as they provide a marker against which alleged breaches of the DPA 1998 will be judged.

There are, then, many practical measures that directors must ensure are implemented including, for example, restricting access to employees' personal data, periodic reviews to keep records up-to-date, ensuring only information relevant to the employment relationship is collected, processed and retained and that controls are in place over to whom and how the information is released. Also, employees have a right to see information being held about them within 40 days of their request and a formal process should be in place to deal with such 'data subject' requests.

Where a data protection offence has been committed by the company with the consent or connivance of the directors, or it has occurred as a result of their neglect, the directors will be guilty of the offence alongside the company and be liable on summary conviction to a fine (DPA 1998, ss 60 and 61). It is also a criminal offence to process personal data without notification, and a person may be entitled to claim compensation for damage caused as a result of breach of the DPA 1998.

v Restrictions on who can be employed

Directors should be aware that there are some restrictions which must be observed over who is employed. For example, it is an offence to employ a person who is not entitled to work in the UK (Asylum and Immigration Act 1996, s 8). A fine of up to £5,000 may be imposed on the company or its directors and officers where they were complicit in the offence, or it arose as a result of their neglect. Prosecution directors must ensure that, as part of the usual recruitment process, no person is allowed to start work without providing evidence of their entitlement to work in the UK, such as a P45, passport confirming citizenship, birth certificate or Home Office letter confirming their right to work.

Subject to certain exceptions and restrictions, the employment of children under 14 is prohibited, and the employment of young people between school-leaving age and 18 years is subject to restrictions, for example in terms of hours and suitable work (Children and Young Persons Act 1933, as amended by SI 1998/276 and SI 2000/1333).

In other instances, such as a bank or financial institution, it is likely that, before the person is engaged, approval must be sought from the Financial Services Authority where they will be carrying out a regulated activity.

It might also be a requirement of the company, particularly larger organisations, or of its relevant regulatory body (if applicable), that all employees go through a pre-vetting process carried out by the Criminal Records Bureau. Where applicable, this needs to be observed.

v Other statutory rights

Directors should note that the matters set out above cover only a small proportion of the requirements in relation to employment issues. Consideration must also be given to levels of pay, minimum wage requirements, statutory maternity rights, parental leave, paternity leave, statutory sick pay, restrictions on working time, flexible working and requests for time off for dependents and training, the need to provide information to employees and consult with them in certain situations, whistleblowing, preserving employment rights on transfer of undertakings, pension provisions and redundancy, to name but a few. Whilst this list only touches on the range of other statutory employments rights, it does help illustrate and emphasise the need for directors to ensure their companies have put in place carefully considered policies and procedures to deal with employment matters. ACAS and BIS have very useful advisory handbooks, booklets and information which will assist with this process.

The environment

It is widely recognised that good environmental performance makes sense for business as environmental factors and the continued availability of natural resources are significant factors in their long-term sustainability. Poor environmental performance or the occurrence of a large scale, high-profile disaster can damage a company's reputation so badly that it is difficult to recover and continue into the future. The expression 'bad news travels fast' has never been more true given the speed with which messages and images can be communicated through mobile phones and the internet, especially where disasters and catastrophes are concerned.

It is therefore important for a company to fully assess and understand the impact of its operations on the environment and to measure, manage and communicate its performance in this respect. This is necessary not only to ensure that the company does not fall foul of regulatory requirements or have its reputation damaged by environmental incidents, but also to capitalise on the benefits that demonstrating high standards of environmental performance can bring in terms of the positive influence it can have on consumer behaviour and investment decisions.

An expansive range of 'green' legislation has extended a company's responsibility to avoid pollution and protect the environment well beyond civil liability for environmental damage (established in common law by *Rylands v Fletcher [1861–73] All ER Rep 1*). It imposes criminal liability on the company for infringement, as well as making directors personally liable for offences committed with their consent or connivance, or resulting from their neglect.

Statutory provisions are now largely consolidated in the Environmental Protection Act 1990, the Environment Act 1995 and, more recently, the Pollution Prevention and Control (England and Wales) Regulations 2000 (SI 2000/1973). They set down requirements for 'preventing' pollution, which encompass emissions into the air, water quality and effluent waste, solid waste (including toxic and radioactive substances), smoke, dust, steam, gas, and fume emissions, noise pollution, litter, and disposal of waste, etc. Directors should also be aware that other legislation, such as the COSHH Regulations 2002 (SI 2002/2677) governing the supply, use, storage and disposal of hazardous substances, and COMAH Regulations 1999 (as amended by COMAH Regulations 2005, 2008 and 2009) on the prevention and limitation of the effects of major accidents, are intrinsically linked to environmental protection.

In addition to this targeted 'green' legislation, one of the general duties of directors stated in CA 2006, s 172 is to have regard to the impact of any decisions they make on the community and the environment.

Directors, therefore, need to consider the company's operations and the risks and impact its activities might have on the environment and thereby determine the full extent of statutory provisions that apply. This assessment would usually form part of the company's overall risk management process, as not only could damage to the environment expose the company to heavy financial penalties, including costs for cleaning up contaminated land (EPA 1990, Part IIA), but it may also attract bad publicity and damage the company's reputation, result in a ban on the company's activities and discourage potential investors and customers from dealing with the company.

Whilst directors of, say, an industrial or manufacturing company will undoubtedly be aware of the importance of environmental protection and implications for their companies, it may not be so apparent for the directors of a lower risk, office-based non-manufacturing company. However, even in the last instance there are environmental protection matters that need consideration, for example:

- disposal of paper waste as, if there are no arrangements for recycling or recovery, the company has to make suitable waste disposal arrangements and pay landfill tax; and
- how much and what type of packaging is used, as many companies have an obligation to reduce the amount of packaging waste sent to landfill sites (Producer Responsibility Obligations (Packaging Waste) Regulations 1997 (SI 1997/648)) and to minimise the use of noxious or hazardous substances in packing and improve recycling, re-use or recoverability of packaging (the Packaging (Essential Requirements) Regulations 1998 (SI 1998/1165)).

Given that, in varying degrees, all companies must consider the need for protection of the environment, key practical issues for directors include the following.

i Planning

EA 1995, s 5 requires companies to assess levels of pollution arising from their activities and to pre-determine measures that will be implemented where it becomes apparent they need to prevent, minimise, remedy or mitigate pollution. Again this would usually form an important part of a company's formal risk management and internal controls process.

In addition, ongoing assessment of environmental impact and risks would be expected by the board when they are making decisions on strategy and the company's activities, for example, the opening of a new factory or changing production processes, etc.

ii Authorisation

There are certain processes with an inherent risk of harm to the environment that require authorisation, and the company must obtain a licence before such activities commence (EPA 1990, s 2(1)). Where such authorisation is obtained, the company's activities will be regulated and emissions will need to be monitored. Should the company then breach the conditions of authorisation, an enforcement, or prohibition, notice may be issued (EPA 1990, ss 13 and 14).

In other circumstances an environmental permit might be required before commencing operations (Environmental Permitting (England & Wales) Regulations 2007, SI 2007/3538).

It is an offence to fail to obtain authorisation where required or to exceed maximum omission limits and in such cases action may be taken against the directors as well as or instead of the company (EPA 1990, ss 157(1) and 158 and other relevant environmental legislation). For example, the managing director of Pharmacos was disqualified from acting as a director for four years (CDDA 1986) and was personally fined £2,500 and ordered to pay costs of £3,500 for unlawfully operating a prescribed process under EPA 1990, Part I (Environmental Data Services Report 299, December 1999). More recently, on 23 February 2012, the Environment Agency reported that two businesses, B W Riddle and Chungs UK Limited, and one of the partners of B W Riddle had been fined a total of £9,000 and ordered to pay costs of £6,500 for exporting containers of mixed waste to China illegally and without observing regulatory requirements.

iii Setting standards and monitoring performance

The Environment Agency has statutory powers to regulate and control pollution, inspect premises and impose bans where it finds operating methods need to be changed or where further controls are necessary to prevent or minimise the risk of pollution.

It is therefore important for the directors to ensure that standards for environmental performance are set, appropriate measures to achieve them are implemented and actual performance is measured against the targets to identify potential problems at the earliest opportunity. Many companies aim to achieve this by implementing:

- *Environmental policies* – these vary enormously, from a single-page statement of intent to basic guidelines and voluminous policy manuals. Often there are multiple stand-alone policies, each setting targets and objectives for specific aspects of environmental performance such as disposal of waste, energy conservation and air and water pollution;
- *Environmental management systems* – this is a more integrated approach to environmental management, based on the environmental policy but extending further to address the organisation of personnel and management, details of statutory requirements, clear objectives and targets, operational controls, record systems, audits and reviews.
- Whilst there is no legal requirement to have an environmental policy or environmental management system in place, companies are increasingly under pressure to assess the impact of their operations on the environment and to formalise the steps it will take to protect the environment in a policy statement. Surveys have shown the companies that have done this have benefited from improvements in corporate image, lower insurance premiums, improved relations with environmental regulators who can see that the company is committed to minimising damage to the environment and better employee, customer, community and investor relations.
- Indeed customers and suppliers increasingly ask to see evidence of a company's environmental policy, production of which may be a condition of business.

iv Reporting

Whilst listed companies are required by CA 2006 to report on significant environmental matters in the business review (see Chapter 9), there is no other statutory requirement at present. Nevertheless, directors and those involved in the management of companies are under increasing pressure to account and demonstrate to shareholders, investors, pressure groups, customers, employees and regulators that the company is taking steps to protect the environment. For example, a number of shareholder pressure groups and pension fund managers have indicated that they will vote against receipt of the annual accounts of any FTSE 100 company that does not contain an environmental report. This pressure is largely a result of initiatives such as those described in the opening paragraphs of this chapter, including the Turnbull Code (also see Chapter 2); occupational pension fund trustees being required to issue a statement of investment policy setting out their approach to social, environmental and ethical matters; the 'FTSE4Good Series Index', particularly the 'FTSE4Good Environmental Leaders Europe 40 Index' which identifies and rates companies on how they manage the risks and impacts of their activities on the environment and measures being taken to reduce their environmental impact; and financial reporting standard FRS 12 which requires the financial impact of certain environmental liabilities to be disclosed in a company's accounts.

Parliament is currently considering a report from DEFRA on reporting by companies on greenhouse gas emissions to address a requirement in the Climate Change Act 2008 to determine whether mandatory reporting and disclosure in the directors' report is appropriate.

A survey carried out by the Environment Agency on the 2009/2010 reporting period found that whilst environmental disclosures by FTSE All-share companies have improved over the last five years in terms of qualitative information provided, more quantitative data is needed. This is borne out by the statistics which showed that although 99% made a qualitative disclosure, only 67% made any quantitative disclosures of performance against key performance indicators and a much smaller number provided statistics in line with government recommendations. The disclosures made were in a variety of locations in the annual reports including the business review and operating and financial review. Whilst 79% of companies in the survey reported on pollution and the most common disclosures were on climate change and energy consumption. It is also important for directors to note that environmental procurement was referred to and considered important by 33% of companies, up from 10% in 2004, demonstrating a sizeable shift of awareness about the needs and requirements of those further along the supply chain. It is believed that further improvements in environmental disclosures will be made as customers, shareholders and investors ultimately attribute greater importance to this information.

However, it should be noted that the government has expressed concern that the level of reporting is still not higher and, unless more companies with over 250 employees voluntarily make their environmental policies public and report progress against them, consideration will be given to introducing a mandatory standard.

Customers

Directors will be aware that they have extensive duties to a company's customers which must be observed, not only to reduce the potential for litigation but also to preserve the company's corporate image and obtain new and repeat sales. Duties to customers include the following.

i Product safety

It is a fundamental requirement that all products placed on the market are safe. Therefore extensive product research and testing needs to be carried out before products are placed on sale.

The ramifications and costs of contravening this requirement can be substantial. Not only will the goods need to be withdrawn from sale and those already sold be recalled, but also a penalty of up to £5,000, three months' imprisonment, or both may be imposed (General Product Safety Regulations 2005 (SI 2005/1803)). The company as the producer, supplier or importer of the goods will have strict criminal liability for damage caused by the defect.

Directors should also be aware that prohibition and suspension notices can be issued to prevent the supply and sale of defective goods (CPA 1987, ss 13 and 14) and action can be taken where goods are sub-standard or of a lower quality that expected (Sale of Goods Act 1979 and Sale and Supply of Goods Act 1994 amongst others).

In addition, the Sale and Supply of Goods to Consumers Regulations 2002 (SI 2002/3045) provide consumers who have purchased faulty goods, with the right to rely on a statement made by any business in the supply chain, a guarantee whether or not it was intended to be legally binding, and to request that the goods be repaired or replaced or that a full refund be given.

ii Accurate trade descriptions

All advertising – on packaging, in sales literature and in statements made by sales staff – must describe goods accurately in terms of their physical characteristics, price, quantities, weights, composition and sizes, fitness for purpose, etc. (TDA 1968 and CPA 1987, Part III).

The company has criminal liability where a false description of goods has been given. The directors may also be held personally liable where the offence was committed with their knowledge or consent, or was due to their negligence, and may face a fine of up to £2,000, two years' imprisonment, or both (TDA 1968, s 20 and CPA 1987, s 2).

Directors should note that trade description requirements apply to both large and small businesses. By way of an example, in October 2005, Swansea Magistrates Court fined Mr O'Connell, trading as Roofseal, £1,250 for falsely claiming membership of the Confederation of Roofing Contractors.

Directors, therefore, need to ensure that formal procedures are in place with regard to sales literature and advertisements and that they are reviewed in detail to ensure accuracy before publication. Statements made on, or about, the company's goods should be checked to ensure they remain accurate and that the company's employees are giving the correct information to customers.

iii Fair contract terms

The Unfair Terms in Consumer Contracts Regulations 1999 (SI 1999/2083) require contracts to be fair and invalidate any unfair terms in contracts that have not been individually negotiated, such as a clause allowing the supplier not to fulfil his or her obligations fully. Directors should therefore ensure that wording of the company's standard contracts is clear and easy to understand, and does not contain clauses that would be considered unfair. For example, the FSA recently issued a statement requiring the term 'consequential loss' in insurance contracts to be more clearly explained to assist consumer understanding.

Regulation 15 of the Sale and Supply of Goods Regulations 2002 also states that where goods are sold or otherwise supplied to a consumer with a guarantee, the guarantee shall take effect as a contractual obligation.

Having read what is required, directors would therefore be well advised to carry out a full legal audit of all existing agreements with customers, suppliers and competitors to ensure they comply. They must also ensure that those responsible for negotiating contract terms are aware of and observe these requirements.

iv Commercial practice

Misleading, aggressive or unfair commercial practices by companies to consumers, whether exercised directly or indirectly are prohibited by the Consumer Protection from Unfair Trading Regulations 2008 (SI 2008/1277). These contain a wide-ranging general prohibition which requires that no act, omission, conduct, representation or commercial communication (including marketing and advertising) aimed at promoting, selling or supplying a product to a consumer is unfair (Reg 2). This includes all practices before, during and after the sale transaction which are unfair, but not necessarily misleading or aggressive. It would, for example, include a practice that falls below the standard a buyer could reasonably expect a seller to demonstrate when acting honestly and in good faith. It also includes any practice that distorts the consumer's economic behaviour, causing them to make a decision about the product and transaction that would not otherwise have been made.

As well as the general prohibition, Regulations 5 and 6 prohibit misleading practices (including both actions and omissions) like the giving of false information or deceptive messages or the omission of important information causing, or likely to cause, a consumer to make a different decision about the transaction than would otherwise have been made.

In addition, Regulation 7 prohibits the use of aggressive commercial practices which intimidate consumers. These might, for example, include attempting to harass, coerce or unduly pressurise a consumer to purchase something which they would not have done otherwise.

There is also a list of other, specific prohibited commercial practices in Schedule 1 to the regulations which a company must avoid. For example, claiming a quality or trust mark without having obtained authorisation, claiming without any foundation that a product or trader has been endorsed, or inviting to consumers to buy a product at a low price but not taking orders for it with the intention of promoting a different product. These are just three of the 31 commercial practices listed in Schedule 1 which are in all circumstances considered unfair.

Should a company fail to comply with the regulations and carry out unfair commercial practices, Part 8 of the EA 2002 permits enforcers to take enforcement action. This would involve making an application to a court for an enforcement order, any breach of which could lead to imprisonment for up to two years or an unlimited fine.

The regulations also contain criminal offences, which can be prosecuted by the OFT or trading standards services (not consumers or competitors), the penalties for which are a fine not exceeding the statutory maximum (currently £5,000) on summary conviction or, on conviction on indictment, an unlimited fine or imprisonment for up to two years, or both.

It is important for directors to note that where an unfair commercial practice has been carried out by a company, the regulations provide that the officers of that company (which includes the directors) with whose consent or connivance the practice was carried out or where the practice was attributable to his or her neglect shall be liable to prosecution as well as the company (Reg 15).

The enforcement authorities have investigative powers and may make a test purchase of a product, inspect goods and enter premises (with or without a warrant), inspect and take copies of relevant documents and, where they have reasonable grounds to believe a breach of the regulations has been committed, seize and obtain products and documents.

Directors will need to ensure that there is complete compliance with any requests or instructions received from the enforcement authorities as it is a criminal offence to intentionally obstruct them or to make any false statements. Any person who does not comply or intentionally obstructs them will be guilty of an offence and, on summary conviction, be liable to a fine (Reg 23).

v Competition and consumer protection

Provisions protecting consumers against unfair trading practices and anti-competitive behaviour are mainly embodied in the Enterprise Act 2002 (which largely replaced the Fair Trading Act 1973) and the Competition Act 1998. Particular practices which directors must ensure are avoided include:

- *anti-competitive agreements* – prohibited by the Competition Act 1998, which permits the Office of Fair Trading (OFT) to impose a financial penalty of up to 10% of an offending company's turnover for three years. In addition, competitors and customers may seek compensation for damages and, where directors obstruct investigations, they themselves may face unlimited fines or up to two years' imprisonment;

- *abuse of a dominant market position* – the Competition Act 1998 prohibits monopolies limiting production, markets or technical development to the detriment of the consumer. For example, Napp Pharmaceuticals Limited of Cambridge was fined £3.21m for abusing its dominant market position in its pricing practices;

- *criminalisation of cartels* – in addition to the imposition on the company of civil sanctions permitted by the Competition Act 1998 for the operation of cartels and anti-competitive agreements, the Enterprise Act 2002 now makes it a criminal offence for an individual to dishonestly engage in cartel agreements. Directors face personal liability where they or their undertakings engage in price-fixing, limitations of supply or production, market sharing or bid-rigging. By way of example, in January 2011, RBS agreed to pay a fine of £28.59m after admitting breaches of competition law requirements by disclosing confidential future pricing information about loan products for professional services firms to Barclays Bank which was taken into account by Barclays to determine its own pricing; and

- *offering bribes to secure business* – this has long been an offence in the UK and, in addition to prohibitions established through common law, the Bribery Act 2010 creates two general offences: bribing another person ('active bribery', s 1) and being bribed ('passive bribery', s 2). It also creates the offence of bribing a foreign official (s 6), an offence for a commercial organisation to fail to prevent bribery by persons working for or associated with them (s 7), although implementation of 'adequate procedures' may prove sufficient defence (s 7(2)) and the ability to prosecute bribery committed abroad in the UK (s 12).

A breach of the requirements of the Bribery Act carries a maximum penalty of 10 years' imprisonment or an unlimited fine for any individuals convicted and an unlimited fine for commercial organisations, including companies (s 11). In addition, the directors and senior managers of a company may be prosecuted if an offence was committed by the company with their consent or connivance (s 14).

It is therefore important for directors to review the company's anti-bribery procedures and internal control and risk management processes to prevent the giving or receiving of bribes by those within, associated with, or working for the company.

Directors should note that the OFT and trading standards authorities have the power to enforce consumer legislation and to require a trader to stop a course of conduct which is unlawful and detrimental to consumers. The OFT must first consult with the offending business to get them to stop the infringing conduct. Where this is not successful, application can be made to the court for an Enforcement Order (EO). Should a person breach the requirements of an EO, he or she will be in contempt of court and liable to a fine and imprisonment. For example, EOs can be issued where a business is required to change its practice and has failed to do so in respect of advertising, use of unfair contract terms, or the way it sells and supplies its goods.

As mentioned in Chapter 13, the OFT has the power to seek disqualification of a director where serious breaches of competition law are established. Alternatively, the OFT may accept a competition disqualification undertaking from a director.

Directors must ensure that policies, procedures, management systems and codes of conduct are implemented to discourage and prevent unfair trading practices. Should they fail in prevention, they could be facing not only personal liability and penalties for anti-competitive behaviour, but also a successful conviction could seriously damage a company's reputation for integrity and fair trading and, either directly or indirectly, lead to a loss of customers and quality staff and make it difficult for the company to raise capital from the investment community.

The OFT recently published statistics demonstrating that although knowledge of competition law held by businesses has increased significantly in the last four years there is still room for improvement in awareness, particularly amongst smaller businesses which remain less able to identify competition law breaches. The OFT's survey of approximately 2,000 businesses recorded that just 25% of survey participants felt they knew a considerable or fair amount about competition law, although this proportion did increase to 45% in the larger businesses included in the survey.

To further improve understanding and help businesses and company directors comply with competition law, in July 2011 the OFT issued practical guidance on what is required to ensure compliance. The OFT worked with business groups and consulted on two guidance documents.

The first of these OFT guidance documents – *How Your Business Can Achieve Compliance* – suggests a four-step risk-based approach to help companies achieve a compliance culture in relation to competition law matters. Central to this is the board and senior management demonstrating their commitment to competition law compliance, so it becomes embedded in the company's culture. Once this is demonstrated, the company must:

- *Identify risks*: Identification of the company's actual competition law risks, which will vary according to the size and nature of business;
- *Assess those risks*: Determine how serious the risks are, what the high, medium and low risks are and which employees are in high-risk areas;
- *Mitigate risks*: Establish, implement and periodically review the policies, procedures and training to ensure the risks identified do not materialise, or are reported and addressed at the earliest opportunity if they do occur;
- *Review the process at appropriate intervals, often annually*: There might also be a need for interim reviews based on corporate transactions, operating in new markets, changes in legislation and best practice recommendations, etc.

The board also needs to demonstrate what practical measures are being implemented. The OFT suggests that, whilst it is for individual boards and companies to determine what is appropriate, it might be achieved through one director being made responsible for driving compliance, monitoring and reporting to the board (or, in some instances, audit committee); the board periodically reviewing and challenging effectiveness of the company's compliance measures; regular communication

amongst directors and senior managers about competition law requirements and the need to identify and address any potential infringement
concerns; regular training and information updates; and making clear to
employees that a competition law infringement will constitute a breach of
the company's code of conduct and a disciplinary offence for which they
could face dismissal.

Where a company can demonstrate that it has taken 'adequate steps'
to ensure a competition law infringement does not occur, then this may
help to mitigate any penalty imposed by the OFT where an offence still
occurs. Adopting the OFT's four-step process may help to establish that
appropriate steps were taken by the company.

The OFT's second guidance document *Company Directors and
Competition Law* has been issued to help directors understand their
responsibilities for ensuring their companies do not infringe competition law requirements and the sorts of matters the OFT will take into
account when determining the extent of a director's responsibility if an
infringement has occurred. It is clear from the guidance document that
these would include, amongst other things:

- the level of knowledge the director had of the infringement and
  whether he or she was directly involved;
- the directors' commitment to competition law compliance and how
  this can be demonstrated by practical compliance measures and the
  company's competition law compliance culture;
- what steps had been taken to prevent, detect and address potential
  infringements, with particular attention to whether the directors
  have implemented 'adequate procedures' possibly involving the
  OFT's four-step process outlined above;
- consideration of the director's role, in particular whether executive
  or non-executive, any specific executive responsibilities within the
  company (e.g. for contract negotiations, sales or compliance) and
  the size of the company or group of companies. The OFT considers
  these relevant when determining what level of understanding
  it is reasonable to expect the director to demonstrate and what
  practical steps he or she could have taken to detect or address the
  infringement; and
- how frequently and vigorously the directors reviewed and
  challenged measures implemented to detect and prevent
  infringements.

In general, all directors are expected to be committed to complying with competition law requirements, to understand what the most serious forms of infringement are and that an offence could have serious consequences for both the company and for them personally (see Chapter 13 for information on competition disqualification orders).

The OFT expects all directors to know that:

- cartel activity (bid rigging, price fixing, production restrictions and market sharing) is a serious offence; and
- abuse of a dominant position constitutes infringement.

Those directors with specific executive duties involving compliance and commercial agreements, etc. would be expected to have greater, more in depth knowledge of the sorts of activity and agreements that might cause infringement.

Another point for directors to note is that BIS published the much-awaited Enterprises and Regulatory Reform Bill (ERRB) on 27 May 2012 making important changes to the competition regime in the UK, principally the creation of an overarching Competition and Markets Authority (CMA) to replace and carry out all the functions of the Competition Commission and the competition functions of the OFT, both of which are to be abolished. Amongst other things, the CMA will carry out whole market studies and investigations of market practices, investigate potential breaches of competition rules, investigate cartel offences, possibly with enhanced powers in respect of price-fixing and investigate all other competition concerns and issues which are in the 'public interest' but not necessarily competition issues.

Directors should note that whilst, at present, conviction of a cartel offence currently requires a finding of 'dishonesty', the ERRB proposal is that this be removed and an agreement where 'relevant information' is not publicised could be subject to the offence. This in itself might lead to increased levels of criminal enforcement. Whilst no timetable for these changes has been announced, it is intended that the new regime will be implemented by April 2014.

vi Marketing and advertising

Directors must be aware that, as well as needing to observe the requirements of regulations in terms of how products are described in marketing material produced, consideration also needs to be given to the manner in which this information is communicated and how marketing activities are carried out in an attempt to attract new business or to increase the volume of existing business.

Whilst marketing carried out by post is covered by data protection requirements, the Privacy and Electronic Communications (EC Directive) Regulations 2003 (amended in 2004) and the Privacy and Electronic Communications (EC Directive) (Amendment) Regulations 2011 (the 2011 Regulations) apply where direct marketing messages are sent by electronic means including telephone, fax, e-mail, text and video messages and marketing by automated calling systems. The different rules and requirements that apply to the various methods of marketing are as follows:

- *Electronic mail:* this includes any electronic message that consists of text, voice, sound or images (such as SMS, messages transmitted in WAP, voicemail and answerphone messages). It is an offence to send unsolicited marketing material by electronic mail to an individual without first obtaining consent from them confirming that they agree to you doing this. This is known as 'opt-in' consent and an individual must have positively indicated their desire to 'opt-in' and receive marketing material in this way.

  However, where an individual is already a customer and his or her details have been obtained in the course of business, you do not have to obtain their consent before marketing the company's own products and services to them ('soft opt-in') provided the individual is given the opportunity to 'opt-out' should they so wish. Such requests must be promptly complied with.

  Consent is not needed before marketing material is sent to an organisation by electronic mail, but the organisation does need to be given the opportunity to 'opt-out' and a valid address where such request can be sent.

- *Website:* when information about goods or services is given on a company's website and ordering is facilitated via the website, regulations governing the use of internet 'cookies' must be observed. Cookies enable websites to keep track of visitors by storing information about a site visitor and his or her preferences (often so customised web pages can be presented next time he or she visits the site). The 2011 Regulations require all websites using cookies to obtain actual, positive consent from a user prior to the cookie being downloaded. The request must be prominently displayed and the user be made aware of the purpose of the cookie and why it is being used.

- *Telephone marketing and telesales*: unsolicited telephone calls cannot be made to individuals or organisations where they have either directly notified the company that they do not want to receive such calls or they have registered with the Telephone Preference Service (or Corporate Telephone Service for companies);
- *Automated calls*: where pre-recorded phone messages are used to make automated calls, prior consent must be obtained from individuals and organisations before marketing is carried out in this way;
- *Faxes*: a company must not send an unsolicited marketing fax to an individual unless his or her prior consent has been obtained and the individual may withdraw consent at any time and can register on the Fax Preference Services so as not to receive marketing faxes. However, prior consent is not required before sending marketing material to an organisation by fax, although the organisation can request that the company does not send marketing material by fax in the future or it can register with the Fax Preference Service giving a blanket ban.

These regulations have had a profound effect on how companies promote themselves through direct marketing as individuals have a statutory right to opt out of receiving marketing faxes and calls, and companies can opt-out of receiving unsolicited faxes and such opt-out requests must be observed. It is important to ensure that marketing material is not sent to any numbers on the Telephone or Fax Preference Services' lists, which must be checked before a marketing campaign commences, or it could result in a fine.

The Consumer Protection (Distance Selling) Regulations 2000 (SI 2000/2334) place further restrictions on the way companies sell goods by phone, the internet, mail order, e-mail, etc. without any personal contact with the customer. These restrictions must be observed and, in brief, include requirements to provide clear information, confirm the information in writing, allow a seven-day 'cooling off' period in which the order can be cancelled and supply the goods within 30 days.

There are also around 100 UK statutes, orders and regulations, including the Consumer Protection from Unfair Trading Regulations

2008, setting out requirements for advertising and promotions that must be observed, as a breach may give rise to criminal prosecution or civil action. Directors should ensure that those responsible for marketing and advertising are aware of the restrictions placed upon them and that appropriate controls are in place to ensure all advertisements and promotions are accurate, ethical, do not mislead, offend or contain unacceptable comparisons and meet all requirements of legislation and the Advertising Standards Authority's code of practice. Having to amend or withdraw advertisements is not only costly but can also attract damaging publicity.

For example, the OFT's investigation of MyCityDeal Limited's (trading as Groupon) commercial practices following the occurrence of nearly 50 breaches of advertising regulations in a year concluded in June 2012. The OFT identified possible breaches of the Consumer Protection from Unfair Trading Regulations 2008, the Unfair Terms in Consumer Contracts Regulations 1999 and the Consumer Protection (Distance Selling) Regulations 2000 by Groupon in how they conduct promotions, fail to provide evidence of the availability of offers and exaggerate claims of savings. Information about this investigation and the undertaking that Groupon has given is now freely available on the internet, which cannot help the company's reputation.

vii Protection of personal data

Personal data about individuals who are customers needs to be protected in the same way as data about employees and others who have dealings with the company, and principles of the DPA 1998 (see Appendix 10) must be observed.

For example, if an individual has provided personal details to receive a brochure about a company's products, that information should not be used for another purpose such as cross-selling by other companies in the group, unless the individual has given consent.

The need to observe data protection principles such as keeping the information up-to-date and secure makes sound sense from a commercial point of view. Not only will information be sent to the right address, but a company's client list is a valuable asset that needs protection from third parties and competitors. Consequently, as well as the need to avoid an offence being committed under the DPA 1998, good management of data can have very positive benefits for the company.

viii Selling goods on credit

Most businesses that offer goods or services on credit or lend money to consumers must obtain a credit licence (Consumer Credit Act 1974, as amended by the Consumer Credit Act 2006). A company is likely to need a licence where, for example, it sells goods on credit or allow customers time to pay, offers hire purchase terms, leases goods for more than three months, lends money, or arranges consumer credit for others, etc.

Not only is it a criminal offence to make such transactions without a licence, punishable by fine, imprisonment or both, but the company may also be left exposed as the unlicensed agreement may be unenforceable.

The Consumer Credit Act also sets out certain requirements covering the form and content of credit agreements and the directors must ensure the company complies with these requirements and ensure that, in all cases, credit arrangements are clearly and adequately explained so each borrower understands the key facts of the arrangement, the amount of credit being given, the contract period, what payments will need to be made, the costs and consequences of missing a payment or withdrawing, the rate of interest and any other fees payable.

Depending on the nature of the company's operations and credit being offered, other consumer credit regulations may also need to be observed including, for example, the Financial Services (Distance Marketing) Regulations 2004 (SI 2004/2095).

ix Health and safety

As detailed in Chapter 10, the company has a duty to those who are not its employees, but who may be affected by the way it conducts its undertakings. The duty extends to the general public, and may include customers and contractors. The company must ensure that their health and safety is not at risk (HSWA 1974, s 3(1) and (2)). Directors should note that action may be taken against the company and the directors for a breach of this duty.

Creditors

A company must be able to pay for the goods and services it acquires and meet its debts as they fall due. If at any time this is not the case, or there is a change in the conditions under which the creditor agreed to do business with the company, the directors must inform the creditors. To protect the interests of creditors, directors therefore have a duty to:

- enter into contracts for goods or services only when there is a reasonable prospect that the company will be able to pay for them; and
- inform creditors of any payment out of capital for purchase by the company of its own shares as, in the event of a winding up, this will reduce the company's ability to repay amounts owing to creditors.

Two important developments for creditors in recent years include:

- the requirement for a company to include a statement about the company's practice, policy and performance on payment of creditors in the directors' report to the annual accounts (CA 2006, s 416 and Sch 5 of the Small Companies and Groups (Accounts and Directors' Reports) Regulations 2008 (SI 2008/409) and Sch 7 of the Large and Medium-Sized Companies and Groups (Accounts and Reports) Regulations 2008)(SI 2008/410) (unless exempt – see Chapter 9); and
- the Late Payment of Commercial Debts (Interest) Act 1998 allowing all companies, businesses and the public sector, irrespective of size, to charge interest on overdue payments and claim reasonable debt recovery costs.

Both developments have important implications for directors. In the first instance, information on payment performance disclosed in the accounts may influence a supplier's decision on whether to do business with the company and, in the second, a company may need to review its payment policy to keep the cost of supplies to a minimum by avoiding interest and recovery costs on late payments.

12 The struggling company

Provisions have been introduced into the IA 1986 to deter improper activities by directors when a company is struggling as a going concern and faces the possibility of liquidation. Damage to creditors can be extensive and duties contained in the IA 1986 are devised to encourage directors to take early action to minimise the loss. To focus the directors' attention, the IA 1986 also introduced personal liability by requiring directors to contribute to the assets of a company on winding up where they have committed certain statutory offences (see Chapter 13). In addition, the Enterprise Act 2002 introduced new Schedule B1 to replace existing provisions in Part II of the IA 1986 on administration in its entirety.

This chapter covers directors' duties in relation to:

- Voluntary arrangement
- Administration
- Liquidation.

Voluntary arrangement

If a company is experiencing difficult trading conditions and the directors reasonably believe that, with 'breathing space', changes could be implemented to allow the company to continue trading, the company could enter into a voluntary arrangement with its creditors (IA 1986, s 1). This may, for example include reaching agreement with creditors on the proportion of debts they will be paid, followed by a scheme of arrangement for the company's affairs by, say, selling off part of the business to allow it to continue trading. Once a voluntary arrangement has been agreed the company's trading can continue and each party to the agreement must abide by the terms.

The proposal would usually be put by the directors to the company's shareholders and its creditors for approval based upon representations and proposals from the directors (IA 1986, ss 1 and 3). If any director or officer makes false representations to obtain approval of the voluntary arrangement, he or she will be liable to imprisonment, a fine, or both (IA 1986, s 6a(4)).

Small companies may take advantage of the voluntary arrangement 'moratorium' procedure available under IA 2000, s 1A as a means of obtaining valuable breathing space and protection at a difficult and vulnerable time. Whilst a moratorium is in place no petition may be made for the company to be wound up, or placed into administration or receivership, nor can any action be taken to enforce security over assets.

Administration

Part 10 of the Enterprise Act 2002 changed IA 1986 by substituting a new Part II on administration and introducing new Schedule B1. These changes have been made to facilitate the rescue of struggling companies wherever possible and to restrict the use of administrative receivership and encourage the use of administration which collectively takes account of the interests of all creditors rather than just one.

Entry into administration is now possible by appointment of an administrator by the:

- court, on application by the company, its directors, one or more creditor, or a magistrate's court (IA 1986, Sch B1, paras 11–13). This may well remain the preferred route into administration for larger and more complex cases;
- holder of a floating charge (IA 1986, Sch B1, para 14); or
- company or its directors (IA 1986, Sch B1, para 22).

In each case there are procedures that must be followed and information that must be provided for the administration to take effect. The last two means of entry described above do not require a court application or hearing, making them a quicker and less costly alternative.

Once the administrator has been appointed, the administration process is the same for all classes and the administrator has the duty to act in the interests of all creditors.

Directors should note that the Enterprise Act 2002 introduced the requirement that, unless an extension has been arranged, administration will cease automatically at the end of one year from the date it took effect (IA 1986, Sch B1, para 76).

In each of the above instances the directors will be required to provide a true and accurate statement of the company's affairs to the administrator, containing details of assets, debts and liabilities, creditors' names and addresses, securities held by creditors and any other information relevant to administration (IA 1986, Sch B1, para 47(1)). Failure to provide information requested, to conceal any information, or make a false statement is an offence giving rise to imposition of a fine (IA 1986, Sch B1, para 48(4)).

Furthermore, the directors must ensure that every invoice, order for goods, business letter and other document on which the company's name appears clearly states that the company is in administration (IA 1986, Sch B1, para 45(1)). The Companies (Trading Disclosures) (Insolvency) Regulation 2008, para 4 also requires this information to be placed on the company's website. Failure to show this information is an offence for which the directors, as well as the administrator, will be liable to pay a fine.

Liquidation

Where a company, for whatever reason, is not able or permitted to continue in operation, application may be made to the court for the company to be placed in liquidation and be wound up.

The company may be wound up voluntarily by the members, where the directors can declare that the company is solvent and will remain so for at least 12 months, or by the court or the creditors, where it is not solvent.

As well as needing to follow set procedures leading up to the appointment of a liquidator, once the liquidator has been appointed directors have certain duties to co-operate with them and supply information (as detailed in Appendix 14), but otherwise in all other respects the powers of the directors cease (IA 1986, s 91). The directors must fulfil these duties to avoid claims that they have acted against the interests of creditors. In addition, case law has established that directors must co-operate pro-actively rather than reactively with liquidators by, for example supplying information they know to be relevant rather than waiting to be asked to supply it (*R v McCredie [2000] 2 BCLC 438*).

Importantly, once the company is placed in liquidation the actions of the directors will be subject to close scrutiny, especially where the company is insolvent and unable to pay its debts. Matters that will receive particular attention include whether there is evidence that the directors:

- gave preferential treatment to particular creditors when settling their debts (IA 1986, s 239);
- entered into any transactions at an undervalue and did not receive adequate consideration for the company at a time when it was unable to pay its debts (IA 1986, s 238);
- misappropriated any of the company's money or property or were guilty of any misfeasance or breach of duty (IA 1986, s 212);
- conducted the business of the company with a dishonest intent to defraud creditors or for any other fraudulent purpose (fraudulent trading); and
- allowed the company to continue to trade where they knew, or ought to have known, that the company had no reasonable prospect of avoiding insolvent liquidation (wrongful trading) and did not take every step necessary to minimise the potential loss to creditors (IA 1986, s 21).

Where directors are found to have committed any of these offences, depending on the offence, they may be personally liable to contribute to the company's assets, be fined, imprisoned or both, or be disqualified from acting as a director (see Chapter 13).

Whilst these penalties alone are quite severe, the Enterprise Act 2002 further increases penalties on reckless and culpable bankrupts who fail to give consideration to a company's creditors by imposing 'bankruptcy restriction orders' to last for two to 15 years. During this time, the person may not act as a director of a company or take part in its management.

It should also be noted that directors of a company placed in insolvent liquidation are generally prohibited from trading through a company or business with the same, or a similar, name for a period of five years (IA 1986, s 216). The restriction applies to anyone who was a director or shadow director at any time during the 12 months prior to liquidation. Breach of this prohibition is a criminal offence, and the directors may be personally liable for the debts of the company, be imprisoned for up to two years or be required to carry out community service as was the order in *R v McCredie [2000] 2 BCLC 438*. Furthermore, misuse by a director of a liquidated company's name may also be taken into account when determining whether to disqualify a director for unfitness (*Re Migration Services International Ltd [2000] 1 BCLC 666*).

Directors should be aware that, even though they themselves may not have been involved with the insolvent company and are not committing an offence under s 216, they may be personally liable for the company's debts where they take instructions from, or act with, persons they know to be in contravention (IA 1986, s 217). This liability extends to anyone involved in the management of the company who acts on instructions given by a person prohibited from using the name. Furthermore, the offence is one of strict liability whether or not there was any intent to deceive or defraud (*R v Cole [1998] 2 BCLC 234*). These provisions are designed primarily to prevent directors defaulting on obligations to creditors of one company but immediately setting up a 'phoenix' company of a similar name to carry on the business, exploiting the goodwill and often using the old company's assets.

13   Penalties for breach of duty

A director who fails in his duties to the company may be liable for any loss suffered by the company as a result of his acts or omissions, even if he himself has not made any personal gain. Similarly, a director may be personally accountable to third parties for any loss or damage they have suffered as a result of the director's actions, omissions or defective information supplied by them.

A director or directors who have breached their statutory duties may also face removal from the board by the company's members, imposition of civil and criminal penalties or, to protect the public interest, they may be disqualified from holding office as a director. Each of these, as well as the possibility of giving a voluntary disqualification undertaking and of being granted relief by the court are discussed in the following paragraphs and together serve to emphasise the importance to directors of fulfilling their duties.

- Dismissal
- Consequences of breaching general duties
- Consequences of breaching statutory duties
- Personal liability
- Disqualification
- Voluntary disqualification undertakings
- Ratification of breach
- Derivative claims.

A particular point for directors to note is that courts will not accept a director's ignorance of duties as a defence for a breach of duties and expect a director to have full understanding of what is expected and required. Indeed in *Grupo Torras SA v Al Sabah (No 5)* [2001] 1 CL 75, the court clarified that foreign individuals who accept directorships in UK companies must familiarise themselves with the obligations arising from such appointments.

Dismissal

If members of the company become aware and are concerned that a director is not carrying out his or her duties in relation to the company and its affairs effectively, is not acting in the best interests of the company, or is in some way damaging the company's reputation or prospects, they may consider it necessary to remove the director from office to protect the company. Whatever the circumstances, the members have the power to remove a director by ordinary resolution, as set out in Chapter 3 (CA 2006, s 168).

Consequences of breaching general duties

Where a director breaches the requirements of the statutory statement of general duties (see Chapter 4), CA 2006, s 178 states that the consequences of such breach are the same as would apply if the corresponding rule or equitable principle that applied under common law had been breached. This means that, save for a breach of s 174 (see below) the general duties are enforceable through civil action for any loss suffered, undisclosed profit made or advantage taken. Such action will be brought by the party to whom the duty is owed, most often the company. Action might be taken by the company to obtain:

- an injunction to restrain the director and prevent him or her from carrying out or continuing with the actions or behaviour that constitute a breach of duty;
- damages by way of compensation where the director's action is considered negligent;
- restoration of the company's property, provided it does not prejudice an innocent third party, where the director's fiduciary duty has been broken and assets have been misappropriated;
- an account of profits made by the director;
- rescindment of a contract in which the director has an undisclosed interest; or
- the director's dismissal.

For example in *Item Software (UK) Ltd v Fashini [2002] EWHC 3116 (Ch), [2003] 2 BCLC 1, (Ch)*, the director failed to disclose his interest in an arrangement as he was trying to divert business to his own company for his own benefit. The company successfully pursued an action for payment of damages by the director in respect of the lost contract. Similarly, in *CMS Dolphin Ltd v Simonet [2001] 2 BCLC 704*, a director who persuaded former clients to transfer their business to a new company after his resignation was in breach of his fiduciary duty and was held personally liable to account for the resulting profits.

Where a director is believed to have breached his duty to exercise reasonable care, skill and diligence in respect of the company (CA 2006, s 174), the remedy would be for the injured party to seek an award of damages to be paid by the director. A director's duty to exercise skill and care is commonly called into question in respect of statements and information issued on behalf of the company to third parties, for example in brochures, accounts, circulars, prospectuses and offer documents. Where these statements are found to contain inaccurate, misleading, false or unsubstantiated information the directors may be liable for breach of their duty under s 174 and face:

- a civil claim for negligence if the misstatements are made as a result of careless omission or neglect; or
- criminal penalties where there is evidence of intentional fraud or recklessness.

Where a director is found to have abused his or her position as 'trustee' of the company's assets and has misapplied them in any way, the provisions of IA 1986, s 212 permit the liquidator to pursue the director for restoration of the company's property and for payment of the money involved or compensation. Furthermore, where, in the course of winding up it transpires that the company's business has been conducted with intent to defraud creditors – itself considered as misapplication of funds – the court may impose personal liability on those directors party to the fraud for all debts and liabilities of the company, without limitation.

Consequences of breaching statutory duties

Many statutes impose duties on directors, each of which includes provisions detailing the criminal or civil consequences for a breach of such duties. In the CA 2006 alone there are some 250 offences, the majority of which are summary offences meaning that action would be brought through the magistrates' court and result in a fine.

Unless specifically stated in the relevant statute, criminal liability for acts of the company rests with the company and not the directors. However, directors should be aware that:

- many sub-sections of CA 2006 make 'every officer of the company who is in default' accountable for the offence (including 'shadow' and 'de facto' directors) and often the directors will be first in line when action is being considered because of their position in the company. The nature of accountability will be specified in the relevant section and may be a fine, imprisonment or both; and

- some requirements of the CA 2006 are the directors' responsibility, not the responsibility of the company. For example, delivering annual accounts to Companies House (CA 2006, s 451) and disclosing their own interests in contracts to be made with the company (CA 2006, s 183). As a result the directors are personally responsible for ensuring compliance and directly liable for their failure to comply. As above, the nature of accountability will be stated in the relevant section of CA 2006.

Many other statutes and regulations also place duties on directors and contain sanctions for offences committed by them. For example, the Bribery Act 2010, the Proceeds of Crime Act 2002, the Theft Act 1968, the Health and Safety at Work, etc. Act 1974, the Trade Descriptions Act (TDA) 1968 and the Consumer Protection for Unfair Trading Regulations 2008 (SI 2008/1277).

Directors should be aware that the courts are now enforcing severe penalties on directors who fail to meet their statutory obligations and, should their conduct be called in to question as well as a fine or imprisonment as stated in the relevant statute (outlined above), the director might also be personally liable for the breach or face disqualification proceedings as explained below.

Personal liability

As illustrated in the table below, there are many circumstances in which directors may find themselves personally liable to third parties for loss resulting from their acts or omissions in managing the company and for statutory offences committed by them.

OFFENCE COMMITTED	STATUTORY PROVISION/ CASE EXAMPLE
Making false or misleading statements or omitting information from listing particulars or a prospectus	FSMA 2000, s 90(1) for any resultant loss
Irregularities in allotments	CA 2006, s 579(3)
Fraudulent trading	CA 2006, s 993
Failing to show the company name clearly on bills of exchange, promissory notes, endorsements, cheques or orders for money (the director is liable to the third party where the company fails to pay)	CA 2006, s 84
Failure to observe shareholders' rights of pre-emption	CA 2006, s 563(2) and s 568(4)
Failure to obtain a trading certificate for a public company before entering into a transaction with a third party	CA 2006, s 767
Where, in winding up the business of the company, it becomes apparent that it has been conducted with intent to defraud	IA 1986, s 213 and CA 2006, s 993
Where guilty of 'wrongful trading'	IA 1986, s 214 *(Official Receiver v Doshi (2001) 2 BCLC 235* where a director responsible for wrongful trading was ordered to make an appropriate contribution to the company's assets)
Where a director of an insolvent company carries on business using a prohibited name	IA 1986, ss 216 and 217 *(Archer Structures Ltd v Griffiths [2003] All ER (D) 172 (May), ChD)*
Non-payment of betting or gaming duties by the company	Betting and Gaming Duties Act 1981 *(Customs and Excise Comrs v Hedon Alpha Ltd [1981] QB 818, [1981] 2 All ER 697 CA)*

OFFENCE COMMITTED	STATUTORY PROVISION/ CASE EXAMPLE
Fraudulent evasion of VAT	FA 1986, s 14 *(Customs and Excise Comrs v Bassimeh [1995] STC 910)*
Making a dishonest declaration or failing to register for VAT	FA 1986, s 13(1) *(Stevenson and Telford Building and Design Ltd v Customs and Excise Comrs [1996] STC 1096, CA)*
Employing illegal immigrants and overstayers	Asylum and Immigration Act 1996 (fine of up to £5,000)
Deliberately driving the company into liquidation to avoid NI debts	Criminal Justice Act 1988 (Confiscation Orders) Order 1996 (SI 1996/1716)
Failure to pay NI	Criminal Justice Act 1988 (SI 1996/1716) under which an order can be made to freeze the assets of officers of a company which intentionally failed to pay NI and the Social Security Act 1998
Knowingly giving preference to a creditor on a winding up	IA 1986, ss 238 to 240 *(Re Living Images Ltd [1996] 1 BCLC 348, [1996] BCC 112)*
Acting as a director whilst disqualified	CDDA 1986, s 15
Health and safety offences	Health and Safety at Work, etc. Act 1974 *(R v Rollco Screw and Rivet Co Ltd [1999] 2 Cr App Rep (S) 436, CA* where directors were fined for asbestos contamination)
Authorising payment of an illegal dividend	*Bairstow v Queens Moat Houses plc, [2000]1 BCLC 549*
Giving a loan to a director without disclosing it to the shareholders and obtaining their approval	CA 2006, s 213
Bribing, being bribed or bribing a foreign official	Bribery Act 2010, ss 2 and 10

As well as the statutory offences listed above, directors should be also aware of the following instances where they may also be held personally liable to third parties:

- where they fail to make their capacity as an 'agent' for the company clear when contracting with a third party, they may find themselves liable where the company defaults or breaches the contract;
- where they have personally guaranteed the company's obligations under a contract or arrangement, such as a bank overdraft;
- where they know, or ought to know, that the company is insolvent, but give representations that the company will be able to pay for goods in the future, they could be liable to pay damages for the deceit (*Drouzhba v Wiseman [2007] EWCA Civ 1201*);
- they have made false statements on behalf of the company, for example confirming incorrect dates on bills of lading in order to secure payment (*Standard Chartered Bank v Pakistan National Shipping Corp (No 2) [2002] UKHL 43, [2002] 2 All ER (Comm) 931*).
- Directors may also be fined personally by industry regulators, such as the HSE, the Environment Agency, the Pensions Regulator and the FSA where their actions or inactions fall short of what is required by relevant statutes and regulations. There are many examples of where regulators have fined the directors as well as the companies for which they act, just a few of which are set out below in illustration:
  - *R v Dhaliwal [2008] EWCA Crim 1275* where the company's sole director was fined £25,000 for dumping large amounts of waste without a waste management licence;
  - In March 2012, the finance director of Cattles plc was fined £400,000 by the FSA for publishing misleading information to investors (enforcement section, FSA website);
  - On 16 August 2011, the FSA fined Sir Ken Morrison £210,000 for failing to notify the market of his own transactions in shares.

In addition, a director may also be required to account to the company for any loss or damage as a result of their failure to observe their duties to the company. For example, where the directors authorise a loan to a director contrary to provisions of CA 2006, s 213, they can face civil action for restitution of money (*Currencies Direct Limited v Ellis [2002]*

1 BCLC 193). Similarly, the directors would be held liable to repay monies to the company for substantial property transactions with the company in which they failed to disclose their interest and obtain prior approval from the members (CA 2006, s 190) and to compensate the company where, in the course of a winding up, it is apparent that they have misappropriated any of the company's money or property (IA 1986, s 212). A further case worth considering is *Safeway Stores Ltd v Twigger [2010] EWHC 11 (Comm), [2010] ALL ER(D) 90 (Jan)*, QBD where a company was fined for anti-competitive practices and then took action against the directors on the grounds they had breached their contracts and their fiduciary duties to the company.

A recent case outside the UK serves to further illustrate that, regardless of jurisdiction, directors must play an active role in overseeing and controlling how the companies to which they are appointed are run. Judgment handed down by the Grand Court of the Cayman Islands in the *Weavering Macro Fixed Income fund (in liquidation) v Stefan Peterson and Hans Ekstrom* case involved awards for damages totalling $111m against two non-executive directors for failing to fulfil their duty to supervise the hedge fund. Another case worth noting is the Federal Court of Australia's judgment in *Australian Securities and Investments Commission v Healey (No. 2) [2011] FCA 1003* in which the CEO was ordered to pay AUS$30,000 plus a share of costs; the CFO was disqualified for two years; and six non-executive directors were ordered to share the costs of the case for breaching their duties by failing to exercise the level of care and diligence expected of a reasonable person when reviewing and approving Centro Group's financial reports.

Directors should note that any provision that claims to exempt a director from liability for negligence, default, breach of duty or trust in relation to a company, whether expressed in the Articles or a contract with the director, is void (CA 2006, s 232). Furthermore, any provision by which a company directly or indirectly provides indemnity to a director from liability for any other of these matters is also void save that, subject to certain restrictions, the following are permitted (CA 2006, ss 232 to 235):

- provision of insurance (CA 2006, s 233);
- a qualifying third-party indemnity provision which must, if given, be disclosed in the directors' report to the accounts (CA 2006, ss 234 to 238); and

- a qualifying pension scheme indemnity provision which, if given, must also be disclosed in the directors' report to the accounts and be available for inspection (CA 2006, ss 235 to 238).

However, where there has been a breach of duty, the court has power pursuant to CA 2006, s 1157 to exempt a director from action for negligence, default, breach of duty or breach of trust where it considers the director acted honestly and reasonably having regard to all the circumstances. However, relief is not always forthcoming. For example, in *Globalink Telecommunications Ltd v Wilmbury Ltd [2002] EWHC 1988 (QB), [2002] BCC 958*, a nominee director on instruction from his principal, who was an undischarged bankrupt, negotiated an agreement to sell the company's assets whilst the other directors and shareholders were out of the country. The nominee director applied for relief under CA 1985, s 727 (now repealed and replaced by CA 2006, s 1157) but it was not granted as it was considered that he had not acted honestly and reasonably, as he did not have authority to negotiate agreements without his fellow directors.

Disqualification

Provisions enabling courts to disqualify persons from acting as directors have been in force for many years, and each year a significant number of directors continue to be disqualified. As courts are now imposing increasingly severe penalties on directors for failing to meet their obligations and, indeed, directors' behaviour and actions are under ever-closer inspection, directors must be fully aware of their obligations to ensure their conduct in managing the company cannot be called into question and lead to disqualification.

The law regarding disqualification of directors is consolidated in CDDA 1986 and allows for:
- automatic disqualification as an outcome of defined events or occurrences; and
- application to be made to the court for a disqualification order. Where a director has failed to meet obligations required by other legislation, such as CA 2006, FSMA 2000, IA 1986, EnA 2002, or HSWA 1974, an application may be made for a disqualification order under the relevant section of CDDA 1986.

i Implications of disqualification order

Once disqualified, the person who is the subject of the disqualification order may not, without leave of the court, be a director of a company, act as receiver of a company's property or as an insolvency practitioner, or directly or indirectly be concerned with, or take part in, the promotion, formation or management of a company (CDDA 1986, s 1). These same restrictions apply where a person has given a voluntary disqualification undertaking (CDDA 1986, s 1(a)).

It is a criminal offence to act in contravention of a disqualification order, punishable by legal process with up to two years' imprisonment or an unlimited fine.

The name of anyone disqualified will appear on the 'register of disqualified directors' maintained by Companies House on its website (www.companieshouse.gov.uk). This has been made available in an attempt to 'name and shame' offenders. In addition, to enforce disqualification orders, the Insolvency Service operates a 'disqualified directors' hotline', encouraging members of the public to name disqualified directors who are blatantly continuing to act despite disqualification orders made against them.

ii Grounds for disqualification

There are many grounds for disqualification under CDDA 1986, but these normally involve culpable mismanagement. Application for disqualification is made under the relevant section of CDDA 1986 and, depending on which section applies, may be automatic, an outcome of certain defined events, or discretionary:

- *Disqualification for unfitness* (CDDA 1986, s 6) – Where a company is, or has been, insolvent, the court is obliged to make a disqualification order against a director, for between two and 15 years, where it is satisfied that the director's conduct makes him or her 'unfit' to be involved in management of a company. The court will consider the matters set out in Sch 1, Parts I and II to the CDDA 1986 when determining whether there has been a breach of duty (see Appendix 15).

  For example, in *Official Receiver v Doshi (2001) 2 BCLC 235*, a director of an insolvent company was disqualified for 12 years for unfitness resulting from false invoicing and evading VAT.

Furthermore, in *Structural Concrete Ltd, ChD (Blackburne J) [2000] 26 LS Gaz R 35*, the deliberate policy of withholding crown debts to finance the company's business was considered misconduct for which directors were disqualified for two and five years. A director can also be found unfit for failing to act. In *Re Bradcrown; Official Receiver v Ireland [2002] BCC 428*, a director who exercised no independent judgement and relied solely on professional advice and the controller of the company when a complex demerger was considered, resulting in liquidation of the company, was found unfit and disqualified for two years.

- *Conviction of an indictable offence* (CDDA 1986, s 2) – The court may make a disqualification order against someone who has been convicted of an indictable offence in connection with the promotion, formation, management or liquidation of a company or with the receivership or management of a company's property. The offence must have some bearing on the management of a company and, where the director is convicted summarily, the maximum period of disqualification is five years – in other cases it is 15 years. Such occurrences might involve insider dealing (*R v Goodman [1993] 2 All ER 789*) or carrying on insurance or financial services without the required authorisation.

- *Persistent breaches of statutory obligations* (CDDA 1986, s 3) – A disqualification order may be made against a person for a maximum of five years for persistent breaches of statutory obligations, such as failure to prepare and submit annual accounts, returns or other documents to the Registrar of Companies. For example, in *Secretary of State for Trade and Industry v Ettinger [1993] BCLC 896*, CA, two directors were disqualified, one for two years, the other for five, based on their persistent failure to comply with requirements to file annual audited accounts. Furthermore, in *R v Victory [1999] 2 Cr App Rep (S) 102*, CA a director was disqualified for one year for failing to keep proper accounting records and fined £1,000.

- *Fraudulent trading* (CDDA 1986, s 4) – A disqualification order for a maximum of 15 years may be made against a person who, in the course of winding up a company, is found to be guilty of an offence for fraudulent trading (CA 2006, s 993) or has committed some other fraud or breach of duty whilst an officer of the company.

For example, on 21 December 2011, Mr Yaqub, a director of property company Maple Grow Limited, was disqualified as a director for 15 years by Birmingham City Court and four other directors gave voluntary disqualification undertakings totalling 32 years for involvement in a fraudulent property scam whereby mortgage loans of £3.8m were obtained on six properties when Mr Yaqub and other directors knew they were worth less than £1m (Insolvency Service announcement, 21 December 2011). In *Re Funtime Ltd [2000] 1 BCLC 247*, an unfit director of an insolvent company was disqualified for five years for permitting transactions constituting preferences and in *Morphites v Bernasconi [2001] 2 BCLC 1*, directors who made dishonest representations to creditors about payment of the company's rental obligations on leases when they had no intention of paying were found guilty of fraudulent trading.

- *Conviction of a summary offence* (CDDA 1986, s 5) – The court may make a disqualification order against someone who has been convicted of a summary offence as a consequence of continuous failure to meet statutory obligations to file returns, accounts or other documents. At least three default orders have to have been made against the person, and the disqualification order will be for a maximum period of five years.

- *Public interest* (CDDA 1986, s 8) – The Secretary of State has power to apply to the court for a disqualification order where such an order appears to be in the public interest, even where the company is still solvent. This may occur following a report by BIS inspectors or from information or documents obtained under the CA 2006 or FSA 1986. Consideration may be given to Sch 1 to the CDDA 1986 (see Appendix 15) when determining whether the director's conduct makes him or her 'unfit'. The maximum period for disqualification is 15 years.

- For example, in *Re Looe Fish Ltd [1993] BCLC 1160*, an investigation by the DTI revealed that a director had used his power to allot shares in the company to keep control of the company. The director was disqualified for two-and-a-half years as use of his authority to allot shares in this manner was a clear breach of his duty. The mis-selling of financial investments and failure to keep proper records were considered to demonstrate a lack of commercial probity against which the public needed protection by disqualifying the directors in *Secretary of State for Business, Innovation and Skills v Aaron [2009] EWHC 3263 (Ch)*.

- *Competition infringements* (CDDA 1986, ss 9a to 9e) – The court must make a 'competition disqualification order' against a person where the company of which he is a director commits a breach of competition law and the court considers the director's conduct makes him unfit to be concerned in the management of a company. The maximum period for disqualification is 15 years. A director may face disqualification where he or she had reasonable grounds to suspect a breach of competition law but did nothing about it.

  Application may be made by the OFT or a specified regulator and, whilst at present application tends to be made where the director is involved or responsible for the contravention, the OFT is considering exercising its powers to situations where the director should have known about the breaches and taken action to prevent them.

- *Wrongful trading* (CDDA 1986, s 10) – A disqualification order may be made for a maximum of 15 years against a director of a company in insolvent liquidation where the director is required to make a contribution to the company's assets for insolvent trading under IA 1986, ss 213 and 214.

The Court of Appeal clarified in *Secretary of State for Trade and Industry v Cregan (2002) 1 BCLC 99*, that both elements of the 'wrongful trading' test, namely that a company is trading whilst insolvent and there is no reasonable prospect that it will be able to meet creditors' claims, must be present to constitute unfitness for the purposes of disqualification.

'Shadow' and de facto directors can also be liable for disqualification. Disqualification orders have been successfully brought against shadow directors where their conduct rendered them unfit and they exercised real influence over the affairs of the companies; for example, *Secretary of Trade and Industry v Deverill [2001] Ch 340*. Similarly, a management consultant found unfit and considered a de facto director was subject to disqualification in *Secretary of State for Trade and Industry v Jones [1999] BCC 336*. More recently, in *Secretary of State for Trade and Industry v Hall and Nuttall [2000] EWHC 1995 (Ch)* two de facto directors were found guilty of misfeasance and breach of their duties as directors for unlawfully paying dividends totalling £13m.

Directors should also note that, whilst under the CA 2006 a non-executive director has the same statutory duties and obligations as any other director, past cases of disqualification have shown that, in some instances, the court expects a different, often lower, standard of skill and care from them. For example, in *Re Stephenson Cobbold Ltd [2001] BCC 38*, the court refused to disqualify a non-executive director who, whilst he signed cheques, was not involved in deciding who was to be paid where preferential treatment was given to creditors.

iii Obtaining leave of the court to act (CDDA 1986, s 17)

A director who is subject to a disqualification order may apply to the court for leave to act as a director or to be involved in the management of a company. Whether the court grants leave to act depends on the director's behaviour and the circumstances giving rise to the disqualification, as well as the overriding need to protect the public interest.

A wealth of cases concerning leave of the court to act continues to develop, a very small sample of which are set out below to illustrate how the court makes its decision:

- *Re China Jazz Worldwide plc [2003] All ER (D) 66 (Jun)*, a director was granted leave to act as a director of another company on the basis that he had not acted dishonestly and the other company had appropriate procedures in place to ensure proper accountability.
- *Secretary of State for Trade and Industry v Barnett [1998] 2 BCLC 64*, in which it was held that, whilst the director had not acted dishonestly, two of the companies in which he was involved had collapsed at the expense of creditors. It was not considered appropriate for the court to grant leave to act.
- *Re Barings plc [1999] 1 BCLC 262*, leave of the court to act as an unpaid non-executive director was granted where fellow directors submitted affidavits to the court stating that they valued the director's advice and expertise in company management. The court decided that the need for the director to act was balanced by the need to protect the public. Leave was granted on the condition that the director continued in a non-executive capacity and did not enter into an employment contract or receive director's fees from the company concerned.
- In *Secretary of State for Trade and Industry v Rosenfield [1999] BCC 413*, leave of the court to act was granted as failure to do so

may have resulted in serious consequences for employees of the company concerned. In granting leave to act, the court required the production of quarterly accounts and the appointment of a person with financial expertise to the board.

- In *Shuttleworth v Secretary of State for Trade and Industry [2000] BCC 204*, the High Court granted leave for a disqualified director to take part in the management of a company in circumstances where the disqualification resulted from inadequate management rather than dishonesty or a lack of probity, and the new company to which the individual was seeking appointment as a director was unlimited.

Voluntary disqualification undertaking

Provisions contained in the IA 2000, ss 5 to 8 permit a director of an insolvent company who recognises and accepts that there are grounds for his or her disqualification to give a voluntary undertaking to the Secretary of State not to act as a director or be involved in the management of a company. A disqualification undertaking may be given for between two and 15 years.

If the Secretary of State considers the director's conduct in relation to the company makes him or her unfit to be involved in management of a company, the director may accept the undertaking if he or she feels that to do so would be in the public interest (CDDA 1986, s 7(2)(a)). Account will be taken of the matters for determining unfitness, detailed in Sch 1 of the CDDA 1986 (see Appendix 15), when the Secretary of State is considering whether to accept the undertaking.

As well as giving a voluntary disqualification undertaking, directors who consider themselves unfit must also provide a 'statement of unfitness', setting out their own admission of events and conduct (clarified in *Secretary of State for Trade and Industry v Davies [2001] All ER (D) 96, (May) following Secretary of State for Trade and Industry v Davies All ER (D) 27 (Sept), CA*).

A recent example of where the voluntary disqualification undertaking was successfully applied was in Northern Ireland where Mr Dougan, a director of Eurotec Fire & Safety Limited, gave a voluntary disqualification undertaking for nine years in respect of his conduct as a director which was unfit on account of the misappropriation of company monies, retention of monies due to the Crown in respect of PAYE, VAT and NIC, failing to fully co-operate with the liquidator by not delivering up all books and records and causing and permitting the company to fail to file Annual Returns (reported Northern Ireland Executive, 11 July 2012).

The voluntary undertaking has the same legal effect as a disqualification order, but is intended to save time and money. This is particularly important where the company is insolvent and funds are to be recovered from directors for payment to creditors. Benefits include the speed with which a voluntary undertaking can be agreed, making the Disqualification Unit's time, money and resource available for other cases, the disqualification taking effect sooner and there is, possibly, less potential for adverse publicity than were protracted court action to commence.

Ratification of breach

In certain circumstances the company has power, within a reasonable period, by resolution of the director or members, to ratify a director's breach of duty after the event, for example where:

- shares were allotted for an improper purpose;
- the director failed to disclose his or her interest in a contract;
- a substantial property transaction was entered into between a company and a director without approval of the members (CA 2006, s 196);
- a loan was made to a director without the members' approval (CA 2006, s 214);
- the director's duty of skill and care was not exercised, provided it was not fraudulent; and
- the act was outside the company's powers.

Furthermore, CA 2006, s 239 permits a company to ratify a director's actions where they amount to negligence, default, breach of duty or trust in relation to the company. Such approval to the ratification must be obtained only from members excluding the director and any persons connected with him.

In addition, there is the common law principle that members of the company may, by unanimous resolution, ratify a director's actions which still remains.

However, breaches cannot be ratified where they infringe shareholders' rights, are fraudulent or dishonest, or involve a secret profit being made by a director at the direct expense of the company.

Derivative claims

Prior to 1 October 2007, where a wrong was done to a company by its directors only the company itself, not the shareholders, could bring an action for damages or other remedy. This meant that, in many instances, no claim was pursued, save where the shareholders were able to direct the board by special resolution to do so or the board was replaced and the newly appointed directors took action on behalf of the company against the outgoing directors. Whilst in certain circumstances (principally where a director was negligent and benefited from his negligence) the courts allowed minority shareholders to apply to bring a derivative action, it could only be done so at the discretion of the court and provided a majority of independent shareholders did not object.

In response to these difficulties and the obstacles to bringing a claim, CA 2006, ss 260 to 264 contain provisions to facilitate derivative claims and proceedings by a member or members of a company.

Directors should therefore be aware that, from now on, a derivative action can be brought against a director (including former and shadow directors) by a member of the company in respect of an actual or proposed act or omission involving negligence, default, breach of duty or breach of trust (CA 2006, s 260). Such claims can be brought by a single member (with no minimum shareholding requirement) even if they were not a member at the time the act or omission took place.

Initially these provisions caused concern, given their potential to increase the volume of vexatious claims against directors for negligence or breach of duty. This was, in part, anticipated by CA 2006, s 261 which requires that once an application has been made to the court it can only proceed where the applicant is able to show a *prima facie* case against the defendant and permission of the court is granted to proceed.

Where it appears to the court that the application and evidence filed by the applicant demonstrate a *prima facie* case, the claim will be allowed to proceed. Where not, the court may dismiss it or require more evidence be produced.

The court will not grant permission for the derivative action to proceed where it determines that a person acting in accordance with the duty to promote the success of the company (CA 2006, s 172) would not seek to continue the claim or where the act or omission has been authorised or subsequently ratified by the company (CA 2006, s 263(2)).

In all other situations the court will consider the following factors when deciding whether to give permission of the action to proceed:

- whether the member is acting in good faith;
- the importance of the claim to the person seeking to promote the success of the company;
- whether the act or omission is likely to be authorised or subsequently ratified by the company;
- whether the company has decided not to pursue the claim; and
- whether the member could pursue the claim in his own right.

Obviously the risk for any director is that a claim might be allowed to proceed, although case evidence to date suggests that the court is adopting a restrictive approach when considering whether permission to proceed should be granted. For example:

- *Mission Capital plc v Sinclair [2010] 1 BCLC 304 (Ch),* heard in March 2008 – The court exercised its discretion and refused permission for a derivative claim by two dismissed executive directors against the continuing directors to proceed. The basis of the refusal by the court was that a notional director seeking to promote the success of the company would not continue the claim and that the two directors could instead pursue action in their own right for unfair prejudice.
- *Franbar Holdings v Patel [2009] 1 BCLC 1 (Ch),* heard in July 2008 – Whilst the court did not consider permission should be withheld based on the mandatory factors, permission was refused on the grounds that it was questionable whether the member was acting in good faith and that claims could be pursued in the member's own right.
- *Parry v Bartlett [2011] EWHC 3146 (Ch)* – Permission was granted for a shareholder to continue a derivative claim as there was strong evidence of a breach of duty in relation to distribution of the proceeds of sale of the company's only asset to the other 50% shareholder and the company was deadlocked making it impossible for the breach to be ratified.

Directors should also be aware that, whilst CA 2006, s 261 allows the court to make cost and civil restraint orders against an applicant, the court may also order the company to pay the costs of an unsuccessful claim where it was reasonably brought by a member.

Appendix 1

THE UK CORPORATE GOVERNANCE CODE
September 2012

THE MAIN PRINCIPLES OF THE CODE

Section A: Leadership

Every company should be headed by an effective board which is collectively responsible for the long-term success of the company.

There should be a clear division of responsibilities at the head of the company between the running of the board and the executive responsibility for the running of the company's business. No one individual should have unfettered powers of decision.

The chairman is responsible for leadership of the board and ensuring its effectiveness on all aspects of its role.

As part of their role as members of a unitary board, non-executive directors should constructively challenge and help develop proposals on strategy.

Section B: Effectiveness

The board and its committees should have the appropriate balance of skills, experience, independence and knowledge of the company to enable them to discharge their respective duties and responsibilities effectively.

There should be a formal, rigorous and transparent procedure for the appointment of new directors to the board.

All directors should be able to allocate sufficient time to the company to discharge their responsibilities effectively.

All directors should receive induction on joining the board and should regularly update and refresh their skills and knowledge.

The board should be supplied in a timely manner with information in a form and of a quality appropriate to enable it to discharge its duties.

The board should undertake a formal and rigorous annual evaluation of its own performance and that of its committees and individual directors.

All directors should be submitted for re-election at regular intervals, subject to continued satisfactory performance.

Section C: Accountability

The board should present a fair, balanced and understandable assessment of the company's position and prospects.

The board is responsible for determining the nature and extent of the significant risks it is willing to take in achieving its strategic objectives. The board should maintain sound risk management and internal control systems.

The board should establish formal and transparent arrangements for considering how they should apply the corporate reporting, risk management and internal control principles and for maintaining an appropriate relationship with the company's auditors.

Section D: Remuneration

Levels of remuneration should be sufficient to attract, retain and motivate directors of the quality required to run the company successfully, but a company should avoid paying more than is necessary for this purpose.

A significant proportion of executive directors' remuneration should be structured so as to link rewards to corporate and individual performance.

There should be a formal and transparent procedure for developing policy on executive remuneration and for fixing the remuneration packages of individual directors. No director should be involved in deciding his or her own remuneration.

Section E: Relations with Shareholders

There should be a dialogue with shareholders based on the mutual understanding of objectives. The board as a whole has responsibility for ensuring that a satisfactory dialogue with shareholders takes place.

The board should use the AGM to communicate with investors and to encourage their participation.

SECTION A: LEADERSHIP

A.1 The Role of the Board

Main Principle

Every company should be headed by an effective board which is collectively responsible for the long-term success of the company.

Supporting Principles

The board's role is to provide entrepreneurial leadership of the company within a framework of prudent and effective controls which enables risk to be assessed and managed. The board should set the company's strategic aims, ensure that the necessary financial and human resources are in place for the company to meet its objectives and review management performance. The board should set the company's values and standards and ensure that its obligations to its shareholders and others are understood and met.

All directors must act in what they consider to be the best interests of the company, consistent with their statutory duties.[1]

Code Provisions

A.1.1. The board should meet sufficiently regularly to discharge its duties effectively. There should be a formal schedule of matters specifically reserved for its decision. The annual report should include a statement of how the board operates, including a high level statement of which types of decisions are to be taken by the board and which are to be delegated to management.

A.1.2. The annual report should identify the chairman, the deputy chairman (where there is one), the chief executive, the senior independent director and the chairmen and members of the board committees.[2] It should also set out the number of meetings of the board and those committees and individual attendance by directors.

A.1.3. The company should arrange appropriate insurance cover in respect of legal action against its directors.

A.2 Division of Responsibilities

Main Principle

There should be a clear division of responsibilities at the head of the company between the running of the board and the executive responsibility for the running of the company's business. No one individual should have unfettered powers of decision.

Code Provision

A.2.1 The roles of chairman and chief executive should not be exercised by the same individual. The division of responsibilities between the chairman and chief executive should be clearly established, set out in writing and agreed by the board.

A.3 The Chairman

Main Principle

The chairman is responsible for leadership of the board and ensuring its effectiveness on all aspects of its role.

Supporting Principle

The chairman is responsible for setting the board's agenda and ensuring that adequate time is available for discussion of all agenda items, in particular strategic issues. The chairman should also promote a culture of openness and debate by facilitating the effective contribution of non-executive directors in particular and ensuring constructive relations between executive and non-executive directors.

The chairman is responsible for ensuring that the directors receive accurate, timely and clear information. The chairman should ensure effective communication with shareholders.

Code Provisions

A.3.1. The chairman should on appointment meet the independence criteria set out in B.1.1 below. A chief executive should not go on to be chairman of the same company. If exceptionally a board decides that a chief executive should become chairman, the board should consult major shareholders in advance and should set out its reasons to shareholders at the time of the appointment and in the next annual report.[3]

A.4 Non-executive Directors

Main Principle

As part of their role as members of a unitary board, non-executive directors should constructively challenge and help develop proposals on strategy.

Supporting Principles

Non-executive directors should scrutinise the performance of management in meeting agreed goals and objectives and monitor the reporting of performance. They should satisfy themselves on the integrity of financial information and that financial controls and systems of risk management are robust and defensible. They are responsible for determining appropriate levels of remuneration of executive directors and have a prime role in appointing and, where necessary, removing executive directors, and in succession planning.

Code Provisions

A.4.1. The board should appoint one of the independent non-executive directors to be the senior independent director to provide a sounding board for the chairman and to serve as an intermediary for the other directors when necessary. The senior independent director should be available to shareholders if they have concerns which contact through the normal channels of chairman, chief executive or other executive directors has failed to resolve or for which such contact is inappropriate.

A.4.2. The chairman should hold meetings with the non-executive directors without the executives present. Led by the senior independent director, the non-executive directors should meet without the chairman present at least annually to appraise the chairman's performance and on such other occasions as are deemed appropriate.

A.4.3. Where directors have concerns which cannot be resolved about the running of the company or a proposed action, they should ensure that their concerns are recorded in the board minutes. On resignation, a non-executive director should provide a written statement to the chairman, for circulation to the board, if they have any such concerns.

SECTION B: EFFECTIVENESS

B.1 The Composition of the Board

Main Principle

The board and its committees should have the appropriate balance of skills, experience, independence and knowledge of the company to enable them to discharge their respective duties and responsibilities effectively.

Supporting Principles

The board should be of sufficient size that the requirements of the business can be met and that changes to the board's composition and that of its committees can be managed without undue disruption, and should not be so large as to be unwieldy.

The board should include an appropriate combination of executive and non-executive directors (and, in particular, independent non-executive directors) such that no individual or small group of individuals can dominate the board's decision taking.

The value of ensuring that committee membership is refreshed and that undue reliance is not placed on particular individuals should be taken into account in deciding chairmanship and membership of committees.

No one other than the committee chairman and members is entitled to be present at a meeting of the nomination, audit or remuneration committee, but others may attend at the invitation of the committee.

Code Provisions

B.1.1. The board should identify in the annual report each non-executive director it considers to be independent.[4] The board should determine whether the director is independent in character and judgement and whether there are relationships or circumstances which are likely to affect, or could appear to affect, the director's judgement. The board should state its reasons if it determines that a director is independent notwithstanding the existence of relationships or circumstances which may appear relevant to its determination, including if the director:

- has been an employee of the company or group within the last five years;

- has, or has had within the last three years, a material business relationship with the company either directly, or as a partner, shareholder, director or senior employee of a body that has such a relationship with the company;

- has received or receives additional remuneration from the company apart from a director's fee, participates in the company's share option or a performance-related pay scheme, or is a member of the company's pension scheme;

- has close family ties with any of the company's advisers, directors or senior employees;

- holds cross-directorships or has significant links with other directors through involvement in other companies or bodies;

- represents a significant shareholder; or

- has served on the board for more than nine years from the date of their first election.

B.1.2. Except for smaller companies,[5] at least half the board, excluding the chairman, should comprise non-executive directors determined by the board to be independent. A smaller company should have at least two independent non-executive directors.

B.2 Appointments to the Board

Main Principle

There should be a formal, rigorous and transparent procedure for the appointment of new directors to the board.

Supporting Principles

The search for board candidates should be conducted, and appointments made, on merit, against objective criteria and with due regard for the benefits of diversity on the board, including gender.

The board should satisfy itself that plans are in place for orderly succession for appointments to the board and to senior management, so as to maintain an appropriate balance of skills and experience within the company and on the board and to ensure progressive refreshing of the board.

Code Provisions

B.2.1. There should be a nomination committee which should lead the process for board appointments and make recommendations to the board. A majority of members of the nomination committee should be independent non-executive directors. The chairman or an independent non-executive director should chair the committee, but the chairman should not chair the nomination committee when it is dealing with the appointment of a successor to the chairmanship. The nomination committee should make available its terms of reference, explaining its role and the authority delegated to it by the board.[6]

B.2.2. The nomination committee should evaluate the balance of skills, experience, independence and knowledge on the board and, in the light of this evaluation, prepare a description of the role and capabilities required for a particular appointment.

B.2.3. Non-executive directors should be appointed for specified terms subject to re-election and to statutory provisions relating to the removal of a director. Any term beyond six years for a non-executive director should be subject to particularly rigorous review, and should take into account the need for progressive refreshing of the board.

B.2.4. A separate section of the annual report should describe the work of the nomination committee,[7] including the process it has used in relation to board appointments. This section should include a description of the board's policy on diversity, including gender, any measurable objectives that it has set for implementing the policy, and progress on achieving the objectives. An explanation should be given if neither an external search consultancy nor open advertising has been used in the appointment of a chairman or a non-executive director. Where an external search consultancy has been used, it should be identified in the annual report and a statement made as to whether it has any other connection with the company.

B.3 Commitment

Main Principle

All directors should be able to allocate sufficient time to the company to discharge their responsibilities effectively.

Code Provisions

B.3.1. For the appointment of a chairman, the nomination committee should prepare a job specification, including an assessment of the time commitment expected, recognising the need for availability in the event of crises. A chairman's other significant commitments should be disclosed to the board before appointment and included in the annual report. Changes to such commitments should be reported to the board as they arise, and their impact explained in the next annual report.

B.3.2. The terms and conditions of appointment of non-executive directors should be made available for inspection.[8] The letter of appointment should set out the expected time commitment. Non-executive directors should undertake that they will have sufficient time to meet what is expected of them. Their other significant commitments should be disclosed to the board before appointment, with a broad indication of the time involved and the board should be informed of subsequent changes.

B.3.3. The board should not agree to a full time executive director taking on more than one non-executive directorship in a FTSE 100 company nor the chairmanship of such a company.

B.4 Development

Main Principle

All directors should receive induction on joining the board and should regularly update and refresh their skills and knowledge.

Supporting Principles

The chairman should ensure that the directors continually update their skills and the knowledge and familiarity with the company required to fulfil their role both on the board and on board committees.

The company should provide the necessary resources for developing and updating its directors' knowledge and capabilities.

To function effectively all directors need appropriate knowledge of the company and access to its operations and staff.

Code Provisions

B.4.1. The chairman should ensure that new directors receive a full, formal and tailored induction on joining the board. As part of this, directors should avail themselves of opportunities to meet major shareholders.

B.4.2. The chairman should regularly review and agree with each director their training and development needs.

B.5 Information and Support

Main Principle

The board should be supplied in a timely manner with information in a form and of a quality appropriate to enable it to discharge its duties.

Supporting Principles

The chairman is responsible for ensuring that the directors receive accurate, timely and clear information. Management has an obligation to provide such information but directors should seek clarification or amplification where necessary.

Under the direction of the chairman, the company secretary's responsibilities include ensuring good information flows within the board and its committees and between senior management and non-executive directors, as well as facilitating induction and assisting with professional development as required.

The company secretary should be responsible for advising the board through the chairman on all governance matters.

Code Provisions

B.5.1. The board should ensure that directors, especially non-executive directors, have access to independent professional advice at the company's expense where they judge it necessary to discharge their responsibilities as directors. Committees should be provided with sufficient resources to undertake their duties.

B.5.2. All directors should have access to the advice and services of the company secretary, who is responsible to the board for ensuring that board procedures are complied with. Both the appointment and removal of the company secretary should be a matter for the board as a whole.

B.6 Evaluation

Main Principle

The board should undertake a formal and rigorous annual evaluation of its own performance and that of its committees and individual directors.

Supporting Principles

Evaluation of the board should consider the balance of skills, experience, independence and knowledge of the company on the board, its diversity, including gender, how the board works together as a unit, and other factors relevant to its effectiveness.

The chairman should act on the results of the performance evaluation by recognising the strengths and addressing the weaknesses of the board and, where appropriate, proposing new members be appointed to the board or seeking the resignation of directors.

Individual evaluation should aim to show whether each director continues to contribute effectively and to demonstrate commitment to the role (including commitment of time for board and committee meetings and any other duties).

Code Provisions

B.6.1. The board should state in the annual report how performance evaluation of the board, its committees and its individual directors has been conducted.

B.6.2. Evaluation of the board of FTSE 350 companies should be externally facilitated at least every three years. The external facilitator should be identified in the annual report and a statement made as to whether they have any other connection with the company.

B.6.3. The non-executive directors, led by the senior independent director, should be responsible for performance evaluation of the chairman, taking into account the views of executive directors.

B.7 Re-election

Main Principle

All directors should be submitted for re-election at regular intervals, subject to continued satisfactory performance.

Code Provisions

B.7.1. All directors of FTSE 350 companies should be subject to annual election by shareholders. All other directors should be subject to election by shareholders at the first annual general meeting after their appointment, and to re-election thereafter at intervals of no more than three years. Non-executive directors who have served longer than nine years should be subject to annual re-election. The names of directors submitted for election or re-election should be accompanied by sufficient biographical details and any other relevant information to enable shareholders to take an informed decision on their election.

B.7.2. The board should set out to shareholders in the papers accompanying a resolution to elect a non-executive director why they believe an individual should be elected. The chairman should confirm to shareholders when proposing re-election that, following formal performance evaluation, the individual's performance continues to be effective and to demonstrate commitment to the role.

SECTION C: ACCOUNTABILITY

C.1 Financial And Business Reporting

Main Principle

The board should present a fair, balanced and understandable assessment of the company's position and prospects.

Supporting Principle

The board's responsibility to present a fair, balanced and understandable assessment extends to interim and other price-sensitive public reports and reports to regulators as well as to information required to be presented by statutory requirements.

The board should establish arrangements that will enable it to ensure that the information presented is fair, balanced and understandable.

Code Provisions

C.1.1. The directors should explain in the annual report their responsibility for preparing the annual report and accounts, and state that they consider the annual report and accounts, taken as a whole, is fair, balanced and understandable and provides the information necessary for shareholders to assess the company's performance, business model and strategy. There should be a statement by the auditor about their reporting responsibilities.[9]

C.1.2. The directors should include in the annual report an explanation of the basis on which the company generates or preserves value over the longer term (the business model) and the strategy for delivering the objectives of the company.[10]

C.1.3. The directors should report in annual and half-yearly financial statements that the business is a going concern, with supporting assumptions or qualifications as necessary.[11]

C.2 Risk Management and Internal Control[12]

Main Principle

The board is responsible for determining the nature and extent of the significant risks it is willing to take in achieving its strategic objectives. The board should maintain sound risk management and internal control systems.

Code Provision

C.2.1. The board should, at least annually, conduct a review of the effectiveness of the company's risk management and internal control systems and should report to shareholders that they have done so.[13] The review should cover all material controls, including financial, operational and compliance controls.

C.3 Audit Committee and Auditors[14]

Main Principle

The board should establish formal and transparent arrangements for considering how they should apply the corporate reporting and risk management and internal control principles and for maintaining an appropriate relationship with the company's auditors.

Code Provisions

C.3.1. The board should establish an audit committee of at least three, or in the case of smaller companies[15] two, independent non-executive directors. In smaller companies the company chairman may be a member of, but not chair, the committee in addition to the independent non-executive directors, provided he or she was considered independent on appointment as chairman. The board should satisfy itself that at least one member of the audit committee has recent and relevant financial experience.[16]

C.3.2. The main role and responsibilities of the audit committee should be set out in written terms of reference[17] and should include:

- to monitor the integrity of the financial statements of the company and any formal announcements relating to the company's financial performance, reviewing significant financial reporting judgements contained in them;

- to review the company's internal financial controls and, unless expressly addressed by a separate board risk committee composed of independent directors, or by the board itself, to review the company's internal control and risk management systems;

- to monitor and review the effectiveness of the company's internal audit function;

- to make recommendations to the board, for it to put to the shareholders for their approval;

- in general meeting, in relation to the appointment, re-appointment and removal of the external auditor and to approve the remuneration and terms of engagement of the external auditor;

- to review and monitor the external auditor's independence and objectivity and the effectiveness of the audit process, taking into consideration relevant UK professional and regulatory requirements;

- to develop and implement policy on the engagement of the external auditor to supply non-audit services, taking into account relevant ethical guidance regarding the provision of non-audit services by the external audit firm;

- to report to the board, identifying any matters in respect of which it considers that action or improvement is needed and making recommendations as to the steps to be taken; and

- to report to the board on how it has discharged its responsibilities.

C.3.3. The terms of reference of the audit committee, including its role and the authority delegated to it by the board, should be made available.[18]

C.3.4. Where requested by the board, the audit committee should provide advice on whether the annual report and accounts, taken as a whole, is fair, balanced and understandable and provides the information necessary for shareholders to assess the company's performance, business model and strategy.

C.3.5. The audit committee should review arrangements by which staff of the company may, in confidence, raise concerns about possible improprieties in matters of financial reporting or other matters. The audit committee's objective should be to ensure that arrangements are in place for the proportionate and independent investigation of such matters and for appropriate follow-up action.

C.3.6. The audit committee should monitor and review the effectiveness of the internal audit activities. Where there is no internal audit function, the audit committee should consider annually whether there is a need for an internal audit function and make a recommendation to the board, and the reasons for the absence of such a function should be explained in the relevant section of the annual report.

C.3.7. The audit committee should have primary responsibility for making a recommendation on the appointment, reappointment and removal of the external auditors. FTSE 350 companies should put the external audit contract out to tender at least every ten years. If the board does not accept the audit committee's recommendation, it should include in the annual report, and in any papers recommending appointment or re-appointment, a statement from the audit committee explaining the recommendation and should set out reasons why the board has taken a different position.

C.3.8. A separate section of the annual report should describe the work of the committee in discharging its responsibilities.[19] The report should include:

- the significant issues that the committee considered in relation to the financial statements, and how these issues were addressed;

- an explanation of how it has assessed the effectiveness of the external audit process and the approach taken to the appointment or reappointment of the external auditor, and information on the length of tenure of the current audit firm and when a tender was last conducted; and

- if the external auditor provides non-audit services, an explanation of how auditor objectivity and independence is safeguarded.

SECTION D: REMUNERATION

D.1 The Level and Components of Remuneration

Main Principle

Levels of remuneration should be sufficient to attract, retain and motivate directors of the quality required to run the company successfully, but a company should avoid paying more than is necessary for this purpose. A significant proportion of executive directors' remuneration should be structured so as to link rewards to corporate and individual performance.

Supporting Principle

The performance-related elements of executive directors' remuneration should be stretching and designed to promote the long-term success of the company.

The remuneration committee should judge where to position their company relative to other companies. But they should use such comparisons with caution, in view of the risk of an upward ratchet of remuneration levels with no corresponding improvement in performance.

They should also be sensitive to pay and employment conditions elsewhere in the group, especially when determining annual salary increases.

Code Provisions

D.1.1. In designing schemes of performance-related remuneration for executive directors, the remuneration committee should follow the provisions in Schedule A to this Code.

D.1.2. Where a company releases an executive director to serve as a non-executive director elsewhere, the remuneration report[20] should include a statement as to whether or not the director will retain such earnings and, if so, what the remuneration is.

D.1.3. Levels of remuneration for non-executive directors should reflect the time commitment and responsibilities of the role. Remuneration for non-executive directors should not include share options or other performance-related elements. If, exceptionally, options are granted, shareholder approval should be sought in advance and any shares acquired by exercise of the options should be held until at least one year after the non-executive director leaves the board. Holding of share options could be relevant to the determination of a non-executive director's independence (as set out in provision B.1.1).

D.1.4. The remuneration committee should carefully consider what compensation commitments (including pension contributions and all other elements) their directors' terms of appointment would entail in the event of early termination. The aim should be to avoid rewarding poor performance. They should take a robust line on reducing compensation to reflect departing directors' obligations to mitigate loss.

D.1.5. Notice or contract periods should be set at one year or less. If it is necessary to offer longer notice or contract periods to new directors recruited from outside, such periods should reduce to one year or less after the initial period.

D.2 Procedure

Main Principle

There should be a formal and transparent procedure for developing policy on executive remuneration and for fixing the remuneration packages of individual directors. No director should be involved in deciding his or her own remuneration.

Supporting Principles

The remuneration committee should consult the chairman and/or chief executive about their proposals relating to the remuneration of other executive directors. The remuneration committee should also be responsible for appointing any consultants in respect of executive director remuneration. Where executive directors or senior management are involved in advising or supporting the remuneration committee, care should be taken to recognise and avoid conflicts of interest.

The chairman of the board should ensure that the company maintains contact as required with its principal shareholders about remuneration.

Code Provisions

D.2.1. The board should establish a remuneration committee of at least three, or in the case of smaller companies[21] two, independent non-executive directors. In addition the company chairman may also be a member of, but not chair, the committee if he or she was considered independent on appointment as chairman. The remuneration committee should make available its terms of reference, explaining its role and the authority delegated to it by the board.[22] Where remuneration consultants are appointed, they should be identified in the annual report and a statement made as to whether they have any other connection with the company.

D.2.2. The remuneration committee should have delegated responsibility for setting remuneration for all executive directors and the chairman, including pension rights and any compensation payments. The committee should also recommend and monitor the level and structure of remuneration for senior management. The definition of 'senior management' for this purpose should be determined by the board but should normally include the first layer of management below board level.

D.2.3. The board itself or, where required by the Articles of Association, the shareholders should determine the remuneration of the non-executive directors within the limits set in the Articles of Association. Where permitted by the Articles, the board may however delegate this responsibility to a committee, which might include the chief executive.

D.2.4. Shareholders should be invited specifically to approve all new long-term incentive schemes (as defined in the Listing Rules[23]) and significant changes to existing schemes, save in the circumstances permitted by the Listing Rules.

SECTION E: RELATIONS WITH SHAREHOLDERS

E.1 Dialogue with Shareholders

Main Principle

There should be a dialogue with shareholders based on the mutual understanding of objectives. The board as a whole has responsibility for ensuring that a satisfactory dialogue with shareholders takes place.[24]

Supporting Principles

Whilst recognising that most shareholder contact is with the chief executive and finance director, the chairman should ensure that all directors are made aware of their major shareholders' issues and concerns.

The board should keep in touch with shareholder opinion in whatever ways are most practical and efficient.

Code Provisions

E.1.1. The chairman should ensure that the views of shareholders are communicated to the board as a whole. The chairman should discuss governance and strategy with major shareholders. Non-executive directors should be offered the opportunity to attend scheduled meetings with major shareholders and should expect to attend meetings if requested by major shareholders. The senior independent director should attend sufficient meetings with a range of major shareholders to listen to their views in order to help develop a balanced understanding of the issues and concerns of major shareholders.

E.1.2. The board should state in the annual report the steps they have taken to ensure that the members of the board, and in particular the non-executive directors, develop an understanding of the views of major shareholders about the company, for example through direct face-to-face contact, analysts' or brokers' briefings and surveys of shareholder opinion.

E.2 Constructive Use of the AGM

Main Principle

The board should use the AGM to communicate with investors and to encourage their participation.

Code Provisions

E.2.1. At any general meeting, the company should propose a separate resolution on each substantially separate issue, and should in particular propose a resolution at the AGM relating to the report and accounts. For each resolution, proxy appointment forms should provide shareholders with the option to direct their proxy to vote either for or against the resolution or to withhold their vote. The proxy form and any announcement of the results of a vote should make it clear that a 'vote withheld' is not a vote in law and will not be counted in the calculation of the proportion of the votes for and against the resolution.

E.2.2. The company should ensure that all valid proxy appointments received for general meetings are properly recorded and counted. For each resolution, where a vote has been taken on a show of hands, the company should ensure that the following information is given at the meeting and made available as soon as reasonably practicable on a website which is maintained by or on behalf of the company:

- the number of shares in respect of which proxy appointments have been validly made;

- the number of votes for the resolution;

- the number of votes against the resolution; and

- the number of shares in respect of which the vote was directed to be withheld.

E.2.3. The chairman should arrange for the chairmen of the audit, remuneration and nomination committees to be available to answer questions at the AGM and for all directors to attend.

E.2.4. The company should arrange for the Notice of the AGM and related papers to be sent to shareholders at least 20 working days before the meeting.

SCHEDULE A: THE DESIGN OF PERFORMANCE-RELATED REMUNERATION FOR EXECUTIVE DIRECTORS

The remuneration committee should consider whether the directors should be eligible for annual bonuses. If so, performance conditions should be relevant, stretching and designed to promote the long-term success of the company. Upper limits should be set and disclosed. There may be a case for part payment in shares to be held for a significant period.

The remuneration committee should consider whether the directors should be eligible for benefits under long-term incentive schemes. Traditional share option schemes should be weighed against other kinds of long-term incentive scheme. Executive share options should not be offered at a discount save as permitted by the relevant provisions of the Listing Rules.

In normal circumstances, shares granted or other forms of deferred remuneration should not vest, and options should not be exercisable, in less than three years. Directors should be encouraged to hold their shares for a further period after vesting or exercise, subject to the need to finance any costs of acquisition and associated tax liabilities.

Any new long-term incentive schemes which are proposed should be approved by shareholders and should preferably replace any existing schemes or, at least, form part of a well considered overall plan incorporating existing schemes. The total rewards potentially available should not be excessive.

Payouts or grants under all incentive schemes, including new grants under existing share option schemes, should be subject to challenging performance criteria reflecting the company's objectives, including nonfinancial performance metrics where appropriate. Remuneration incentives should be compatible with risk policies and systems.

Grants under executive share option and other long-term incentive schemes should normally be phased rather than awarded in one large block.

Consideration should be given to the use of provisions that permit the company to reclaim variable components in exceptional circumstances of misstatement or misconduct.

In general, only basic salary should be pensionable. The remuneration committee should consider the pension consequences and associated costs to the company of basic salary increases and any other changes in pensionable remuneration, especially for directors close to retirement.

SCHEDULE B: DISCLOSURE OF CORPORATE GOVERNANCE ARRANGEMENTS

Corporate governance disclosure requirements are set out in three places:

- FSA Disclosure and Transparency Rules sub-chapters 7.1 and 7.2 (which set out certain mandatory disclosures);

- FSA Listing Rules 9.8.6 R, 9.8.7 R, and 9.8.7A R (which includes the 'comply or explain' requirement); and

- The UK Corporate Governance Code (in addition to providing an explanation where they choose not to comply with a provision, companies must disclose specified information in order to comply with certain provisions).

These requirements are summarised below. The full text of Disclosure and Transparency Rules 7.1 and 7.2 and Listing Rules 9.8.6 R, 9.8.7 R, 9.8.7A R are contained in the relevant chapters of the FSA Handbook.

The Disclosure and Transparency Rules sub-chapters 7.1 and 7.2 apply to issuers whose securities are admitted to trading on a regulated market (this includes all issuers with a Premium or Standard listing). The Listing Rules 9.8.6 R, 9.8.7 R and 9.8.7A R and UK Corporate Governance Code apply to issuers of Premium listed equity shares only.

There is some overlap between the mandatory disclosures required under the Disclosure and Transparency Rules and those expected under the UK Corporate Governance Code. Areas of overlap are summarised in the Appendix to this Schedule. In respect of disclosures relating to the audit committee and the composition and operation of the board and its committees, compliance with the relevant provisions of the Code will result in compliance with the relevant Rules.

Disclosure and Transparency Rules

Sub-chapter 7.1 of the Disclosure and Transparency Rules concerns audit committees or bodies carrying out equivalent functions.

DTR 7.1.1 R and 7.1.3 R set out requirements relating to the composition and functions of the committee or equivalent body:

- DTR 7.1.1 R states than an issuer must have a body which is responsible for performing the functions set out in DTR 7.1.3 R, and that at least one member of that body must be independent and at least one member must have competence in accounting and/or auditing.

- DTR 7.1.2 G states that the requirements for independence and competence in accounting and/or auditing may be satisfied by the same member or by different members of the relevant body.

- DTR 7.1.3 R states that an issuer must ensure that, as a minimum, the relevant body must:

    1. monitor the financial reporting process;

    2. monitor the effectiveness of the issuer's internal control, internal audit where applicable, and risk management systems;

3. monitor the statutory audit of the annual and consolidated accounts;

4. review and monitor the independence of the statutory auditor, and in particular the provision of additional services to the issuer.

- DTR 7.1.5 R sets out what disclosure is required. Specifically:

  - DTR 7.1.5 R states that the issuer must make a statement available to the public disclosing which body carries out the functions required by DTR 7.1.3 R and how it is composed.

  - DTR 7.1.6 G states that this can be included in the corporate governance statement required under sub-chapter DTR 7.2 (see below).

  - DTR 7.1.7 G states that compliance with the relevant provisions of the UK Corporate Governance Code (as set out in the Appendix to this Schedule) will result in compliance with DTR 7.1.1 R to 7.1.5 R.

Sub-chapter 7.2 concerns corporate governance statements. Issuers are required to produce a corporate governance statement that must be either included in the directors' report (DTR 7.2.1 R); or in a separate report published together with the annual report; or on the issuer's website, in which case there must be a cross-reference in the directors' report (DTR 7.2.9 R).

DTR 7.2.2 R requires that the corporate governance statements must contain a reference to the corporate governance code to which the company is subject (for companies with a Premium listing this is the UK Corporate Governance Code). DTR 7.2.3 R requires that, to the extent that it departs from that code, the company must explain which parts of the code it departs from and the reasons for doing so. DTR 7.2.4 G states that compliance with LR 9.8.6 R (6) (the 'comply or explain' rule in relation to the UK Corporate Governance Code) will also satisfy these requirements.

DTR 7.2.5 R, DTR 7.2.7 R and DTR 7.2.10 R set out certain information that must be disclosed in the corporate governance statement:

- DTR 7.2.5 R states that the corporate governance statement must contain a description of the main features of the company's internal control and risk management systems in relation to the financial reporting process. DTR 7.2.10 R states that an issuer which is required to prepare a group directors' report within the meaning of Section 415(2) of the Companies Act 2006 must include in that report a description of the main features of the group's internal control and risk management systems in relation to the process for preparing consolidated accounts.

- DTR 7.2.6 R states that the corporate governance statement must contain the information required by paragraph 13(2)(c), (d), (f), (h) and (i) of Schedule 7 to the Large and Medium-sized Companies and Groups (Accounts and Reports) Regulations 2008 (SI 2008/410) where the issuer is subject to the requirements of that paragraph.

- DTR 7.2.7 R states that the corporate governance statement must contain a description of the composition and operation of the issuer's administrative, management and supervisory bodies and their committees. DTR 7.2.8 G states that compliance with the relevant provisions of the UK Corporate Governance Code (as set out in the Appendix to this Schedule) will satisfy these requirements.

Listing Rules

Listing Rules 9.8.6 R (for UK incorporated companies) and 9.8.7 R (for overseas incorporated companies) state that in the case of a company that has a Premium listing of equity shares, the following items must be included in its annual report and accounts:

- a statement of how the listed company has applied the Main Principles set out in the UK Corporate Governance Code, in a manner that would enable shareholders to evaluate how the principles have been applied;

- a statement as to whether the listed company has:

  - complied throughout the accounting period with all relevant provisions set out in the UK Corporate Governance Code; or

  - not complied throughout the accounting period with all relevant provisions set out in the UK Corporate Governance Code, and if so, setting out:

    i. those provisions, if any, it has not complied with;

    ii. in the case of provisions whose requirements are of a continuing nature, the period within which, if any, it did not comply with some or all of those provisions; and

    iii. the company's reasons for non-compliance.

The UK Corporate Governance Code

In addition to the "comply or explain" requirement in the Listing Rules, the Code includes specific requirements for disclosure which must be provided in order to comply. These are summarised below.

The annual report should include:

- a statement of how the board operates, including a high level statement of which types of decisions are to be taken by the board and which are to be delegated to management (A.1.1);

- the names of the chairman, the deputy chairman (where there is one), the chief executive, the senior independent director and the chairmen and members of the board committees (A.1.2);

- the number of meetings of the board and those committees and individual attendance by directors (A.1.2);

- where a chief executive is appointed chairman, the reasons for their appointment (this only needs to be done in the annual report following the appointment) (A.3.1);

- the names of the non-executive directors whom the board determines to be independent, with reasons where necessary (B.1.1);

- a separate section describing the work of the nomination committee, including the process it has used in relation to board appointments; a description of the board's policy on diversity, including gender; any measurable objectives that it has set for implementing the policy, and progress on achieving the objectives. An explanation should be given if neither external search consultancy nor open advertising has been used in the appointment of a chairman or a non-executive director. Where an external search consultancy has been used it should be identified and a statement made as to whether it has any other connection with the company (B.2.4);

- any changes to the other significant commitments of the chairman during the year (B.3.1);

- a statement of how performance evaluation of the board, its committees and its directors has been conducted (B.6.1). Where an external facilitator has been used, they should be identified and a statement made as to whether they have any other connection to the company (B.6.2);

- an explanation from the directors of their responsibility for preparing the accounts and a statement that they consider that the annual report and accounts, taken as a whole, is fair, balanced and understandable and provides the information necessary for shareholders to assess and provide the company's performance, business model and strategy. There should also be a statement by the auditor about their reporting responsibilities (C.1.1);

- an explanation from the directors of the basis on which the company generates or preserves value over the longer term (the business model) and the strategy for delivering the objectives of the company (C.1.2);

- a statement from the directors that the business is a going concern, with supporting assumptions or qualifications as necessary (C.1.3);

- a report that the board has conducted a review of the effectiveness of the company's risk management and internal controls systems (C.2.1);

- where there is no internal audit function, the reasons for the absence of such a function (C.3.6);

- where the board does not accept the audit committee's recommendation on the appointment, reappointment or removal of an external auditor, a statement from the audit committee explaining the recommendation and the reasons why the board has taken a different position (C.3.7);

- a separate section describing the work of the audit committee in discharging its responsibilities, including: the significant issues that it considered in relation to the financial statements, and how these issues were addressed; an explanation of how it has assessed the effectiveness of the external audit process and the approach taken to the appointment or reappointment of the external auditor, including the length of tenure of the current audit firm and when a tender was last conducted; and, if the external auditor provides non-audit services, an explanation of how auditor objectivity and independence is safeguarded (C.3.8);

- a description of the work of the remuneration committee as required under the Large and Medium-Sized Companies and Groups (Accounts and Reports) Regulations 2008, including, where an executive director serves as a non-executive director elsewhere, whether or not the director will retain such earnings and, if so, what the remuneration is (D.1.2);

- where remuneration consultants are appointed they should be identified and a statement made as to whether they have any other connection with the company (D.2.1); and

- the steps the board has taken to ensure that members of the board, and in particular the non-executive directors, develop an understanding of the views of major shareholders about their company (E.1.2).

The following information should be made available (which may be met by placing the information on a website that is maintained by or on behalf of the company):

- the terms of reference of the nomination, audit and remuneration committees, explaining their role and the authority delegated to them by the board (B.2.1, C.3.3 and D.2.1); and

- the terms and conditions of appointment of non-executive directors (B.3.2) (see footnote 9).

The board should set out to shareholders in the papers accompanying a resolution to elect or re-elect directors:

- sufficient biographical details to enable shareholders to take an informed decision on their election or re-election (B.7.1);

- why they believe an individual should be elected to a non-executive role (B.7.2); and

- on re-election of a non-executive director, confirmation from the chairman that, following formal performance evaluation, the individual's performance continues to be effective and to demonstrate commitment to the role (B.7.2).

The board should set out to shareholders in the papers recommending appointment or reappointment of an external auditor:

- if the board does not accept the audit committee's recommendation, a statement from the audit committee explaining the recommendation and from the board setting out reasons why they have taken a different position (C.3.6).

Additional guidance

The FRC publishes guidance on going concern, risk management and internal control and audit committees, which contain further suggestions as to information that might usefully be disclosed in the statement that the business is a going concern (C.1.3), the statement on the board's review of the company's risk management and internal control systems (C.2.1) and the report of the audit committee (C.3.8) respectively. This guidance is available on the FRC website.

APPENDIX

OVERLAP BETWEEN THE DISCLOSURE AND TRANSPARENCY RULES AND THE UK CORPORATE GOVERNANCE CODE

Disclosure and transparency rules	UK Corporate Governance Code
D.T.R 7.1.1 R Sets out minimum requirements on composition of the audit committee or equivalent body.	**Provision C.3.1** Sets out recommended composition of the audit committee.
D.T.R 7.1.3 R Sets out minimum functions of the audit committee or equivalent body.	**Provision C.3.2** Sets out the recommended minimum terms of reference for the audit committee.
D.T.R 7.1.5 R The composition and function of the audit committee or equivalent body must be disclosed in the annual report *DTR 7.1.7 R states that compliance with Code provisions A.1.2, C.3.1, C.3.2 and C.3.3 will result in compliance with DTR 7.1.1 R to DTR 7.1.5 R.*	**Provision A.1.2** The annual report should identify members of the board committees. **Provision C.3.8** The annual report should describe the work of the audit committee.
D.T.R 7.2.5 R The corporate governance statement must include a description of the main features of the company's internal control and risk management systems in relation to the financial reporting process. While this requirement differs from the requirement in the UK Corporate Governance Code, it is envisaged that both could be met by a single internal control statement.	**Provision C.2.1** The Board must report that a review of the effectiveness of the risk management and internal control systems has been carried out.

DTR 7.2.7 R	This requirement overlaps with a
The corporate governance statement must include a description of the composition and operation of the administrative, management and supervisory bodies and their committees. *DTR 7.2.8 R states that compliance with Code provisions A.1.1, A.1.2, A.4.6, B.2.1 and C.3.3 will result in compliance with DTR 7.2.7 R.*	number of different provisions of the Code: **A.1.1**: the annual report should include a statement of how the board operates. **A.1.2**: the annual report should identify members of the board and board committees. **B.2.4**: the annual report should describe the work of the nomination committee. **C.3.8**: the annual report should describe the work of the audit committee. **D.2.1**: a description of the work of the remuneration committee should be made available. [*Note: in order to comply with DTR 7.2.7 R this information will need to be included in the corporate governance statement*].

The FRC is responsible for promoting high quality corporate governance and reporting to foster investment. We set the UK Corporate Governance and Stewardship Codes as well as UK standards for accounting, auditing and actuarial work. We represent UK interests in international standard-setting. We also monitor and take action to promote the quality of corporate reporting and auditing. We operate independent disciplinary arrangements for accountants and actuaries; and oversee the regulatory activities of the accountancy and actuarial professional bodies.

Financial Reporting Council

5th Floor, Aldwych House 71–91 Aldwych London WC2B 4HN

+44 (0)20 7492 2300

www.frc.org.uk

UP/FRC-BI12001

© The Financial Reporting Council Limited 2013

The Financial Reporting Council Limited is a company limited by guarantee. Registered in England number 2486368.

Registered Office: 5th Floor, Aldwych House, 71-91 Aldwych, London WC2B 4HN.

Notes

1 For directors of UK incorporated companies, these duties are set out in the Sections 170 to 177 of the Companies Act 2006.
2 Provisions A.1.1 and A.1.2 overlap with FSA Rule DTR 7.2.7 R; Provision A.1.2 also overlaps with DTR 7.1.5 R (see Schedule B).
3 Compliance or otherwise with this provision need only be reported for the year in which the appointment is made.

4 A.3.1 states that the chairman should, on appointment, meet the independence criteria set out in this provision, but thereafter the test of independence is not appropriate in relation to the chairman.

5 A smaller company is one that is below the FTSE 350 throughout the year immediately prior to the reporting year.

6 The requirement to make the information available would be met by including the information on a website that is maintained by or on behalf of the company.

7 This provision overlaps with FSA Rule DTR 7.2.7 R (see Schedule B).

8 The terms and conditions of appointment of non-executive directors should be made available for inspection by any person at the company's registered office during normal business hours and at the AGM (for 15 minutes prior to the meeting and during the meeting).

9 This requirement may be met by the disclosures about the audit scope and responsibilities of the auditor included, or referred to, in the auditor's report pursuant to the requirements of ISA (UK and Ireland) 700, "The Auditor's Report on Financial Statements". Copies are available from the FRC website.

10 It would be desirable if the explanation were located in the same part of the annual report as the Business Review required by Section 417 of the Companies Act 2006. Guidance as to the matters that should be considered in an explanation of a business model is provided in "Reporting Statement: Operating And Financial Review". Copies are available from the FRC website.

11 "Going Concern and Liquidity Risk: Guidance for Directors of UK Companies 2009" suggests means of applying this part of the Code. Copies are available from the FRC website.

12 "Internal Control: Guidance to Directors" suggests means of applying this part of the Code. Copies are available from the FRC website.

13 In addition FSA Rule DTR 7.2.5 R requires companies to describe the main features of the internal control and risk management systems in relation to the financial reporting process.

14 'Guidance on Audit Committees' suggests means of applying this part of the Code. Copies are available from the FRC website.

15 See footnote 6.

16 This provision overlaps with FSA Rule DTR 7.1.1 R (see Schedule B).

17 This provision overlaps with FSA Rules DTR 7.1.3 R (see Schedule B).

18 See footnote 7.

19 This provision overlaps with FSA Rules DTR 7.1.5 R and 7.2.7 R (see Schedule B).

20 As required for UK incorporated companies under the Large and Medium-Sized Companies and Groups (Accounts and Reports) Regulations 2008.

21 See footnote 6.

22 This provision overlaps with FSA Rule DTR 7.2.7 R (see Schedule B).

23 Listing Rules LR 9.4. Copies are available from the FSA website.

24 Nothing in these principles or provisions should be taken to override the general requirements of law to treat shareholders equally in access to information.

Appendix 2

ICSA Guidance Note: Joining the right board: due diligence for prospective directors
May 2011

1 Why undertake due diligence?

1.1 The review carried out by the late Sir Derek Higgs in 2003 on the role and effectiveness of non-executive directors recommended that before accepting an appointment, prospective non-executive directors should undertake their own thorough examination of the company to satisfy themselves that it is an organisation in which they can have confidence and in which they will be well suited to working. This advice clearly remains relevant today: by making the right enquiries, a prospective director can reduce the risk of unwelcome surprises and dramatically increase the likelihood of success.

2 How to undertake due diligence?

2.1 The prospective director should look at the company's annual report and website to see how the company articulates its position on the following matters: the company's business model, its governance, the market environment and dynamics, recent operational performance, strategy, risks and uncertainties, sustainability and financial performance. He/she should also look at the company's website to review regulatory and media announcements issued since the last annual report was published. There is a range of other sources of information listed in 4 below. Published material is unlikely to reveal wrongdoing; however a lack of transparency may be a reason to proceed with caution.

2.2 There follows in section 3 a list of questions of the type which the prospective director may want to consider. The list is not intended to be exhaustive, but is intended to be a helpful basis for the pre-appointment due diligence process that all directors should undertake. The answers to some of the questions can be found by reviewing the documents listed in 4 below. Where answers cannot be found, or should supplementary questions develop, the company should be approached for the answers, possibly at the one-to one meetings suggested in 2.3.

2.3 Before accepting a role, a prospective director should have pre-appointment meetings with the chairman, CEO, CFO, company secretary and all members of the nomination committee, if not the entire board. It may be beneficial to meet some directors in pairs, or in small groups (rather than solely relying on one-to one meetings) as this can give an indication of the dynamics between board members.

If the individual is joining with the intention of taking on the role of chairman of the company or chair of the audit or remuneration committee, meetings should also be set up with the auditors, the head of internal audit or the remuneration advisers as appropriate. All prospective directors should consider whether there are any other external advisers to the company, for example the corporate broker, with whom a meeting could provide relevant insights. Further information may be obtained from discussions with senior management, employees, suppliers and customers although care should be taken to preserve confidentiality as the fact that an approach to the individual, as a prospective director, has been made will usually be deemed to be price sensitive information.

2.4   The prospective director should check scheduled board dates for the year ahead at an early stage in the due diligence process to ensure he/she will be able to attend most, if not all, of the planned meetings in the first year.

2.5   The prospective director should be aware that the company will be unable to disclose certain confidential or price sensitive information prior to the formal appointment and should make him/herself aware of, and observe, the insider trading and market abuse laws and regulations in respect of inside information.

3   Due diligence questions

3.1   The business

- What are the exact nature and extent of the company's business activities?

- What is the company's current financial position and what has its financial track record been over the last three years?

- What is the company's strategy?

- What are the company's culture and values as set by the board?

- Who are the company's stakeholders?

- What are the key dependencies (eg regulatory approvals, key licences)?

- What is the company's competitive position and market share in its main business areas?

- If the company operates in a regulated sector, what is the relationship with the regulator?

- What are the key issues being faced by the board at the moment?

3.2   Governance

- How well does the company articulate its position on governance in the annual report?

- What record does the company have on corporate governance issues?

- Does the company secretary have a reporting line into the chairman on board governance matters?

- Does the chairman report personally on governance, and about the role and effectiveness of the board?

- Is the company embracing or developing best practice?

- Does the governance report go further than the provisions of the UK Corporate Governance Code, for example giving a detailed explanation of the output from the board evaluation process?

- Is each board committee report headed by an introductory letter by the committee chairman setting out the key issues?

- Is succession at both management and board levels covered, and in what kind of detail?

- Are you satisfied that the internal regulation of the company is sound and that you can operate effectively within its stated corporate governance framework?

3.3 The board

3.3.1 Board composition

- Who are the current executive and non-executive directors, what is their background and record and how long have they served on the board?

- Is the board composition suitably diverse to stimulate independent challenge and thought?

- Are there groups with a common agenda on the board, and what is their impact?

- Are you being brought on to the board to bolster an existing group, or to bring something new? If the latter, what is being expected of you and can you deliver it?

- Is there a range of skills on the board and are those skills and experiences aligned with the company's strategic direction, or does the strategy/journey represent new territory for all the board members?

- Is the board composition keeping pace with the speed of change at the company? Does it meet the needs of the business?

- Is there the right balance of executives to non-executives to ensure that there is enough expert knowledge on the board of the company's operations?

- How is board composition and succession planning reviewed by the board?

3.3.2 Boardroom behaviours

- What are the dynamics of the relationships between chairman/CEO, chairman/ senior independent director, chairman/company secretary, executive/ non-executive directors and the company secretary/other directors etc?

- How is the leadership of the chairman perceived?

- Does the chairman set clear expectations concerning the company's culture, values and behaviours, and the style and tone of board discussions?

- Is constructive challenge from the non-executive directors welcomed?

- Does the chairman allow adequate time for debate?

- Does the board have a high level of visibility and lead by example?

- What is the level of communication among board members between meetings?

3.3.3 Operational matters

- Has adequate thought been given to the board's decision-making processes?

- Do board papers provide high quality information, at a time far enough in advance of the meetings, to enable informed debate and high-quality decision making?

- Does the board agenda focus on the right things? Have you seen the schedule of matters reserved for the board's decision?

- Are board committee meetings structured so that there is sufficient time to allow a report to the board meeting and is adequate time allowed in board meetings to discuss committee matters?

- What is the attitude to site visits? How often does the board collectively or individually visit key locations?

- How is the strategy away-day handled? What matters have been covered on previous away-days?

- What is the practice in a typical board meeting week? Are there dinners before or after the meetings enabling the directors to get to know each other better, meet management below board level and discuss wider issues in a less formal and time-constrained environment?

3.3.4 Board evaluation

- Are there rigorous evaluations of the effectiveness of the board, its committees and the individual directors?

- Have external evaluations been undertaken?

- What are the key issues that came out of the last board evaluation?

- Does the chairman act on the results of board, committee and individual director evaluations?

- Are there areas for development on the board and what plans are there to tackle them?

3.4 The role of the non-executive director

- Is the company clear and specific about the qualities, knowledge, skills and experience that it needs to complement the existing board? Will you be able to make a positive contribution?

- Can the chairman explain why you are suited to the role?

- What is the time commitment required and can you make this commitment? Could you find the time to deal with emergency situations outside of the routine board and committee meetings?

- If the company is not performing particularly well is there potential to turn it round and do you have the time, desire and capability to make a positive impact?

- Does the company offer a suitable director induction programme and adequate ongoing training/professional development? Is it clear from the company how you will acquire an understanding of the main areas of business activity, especially areas involving significant risk?

- Is there adequate internal support for the non-executives (typically from the company secretariat)?

- What are the internal protocols: does a new non-executive director channel everything through the chairman, CEO or company secretary, or is it accepted practice to contact the CFO, risk officer, head of internal audit etc directly if felt appropriate?

- Would accepting the non-executive directorship put you in a position of having a conflict of interest?

- Is it a good career move? Will you grow in terms of experience and/or ability as a result of joining the board?

3.5 Remuneration

- How well does the company articulate its position on remuneration in the annual report?

- What record does the company have on director remuneration issues?

- Are remuneration targets aligned with the long-term interests of shareholders?

- To what extent did shareholders support the remuneration report in the advisory vote at the last AGM?

3.6 Investor relations

- Who owns the company, ie who are the company's main shareholders and how has the profile changed over recent years?

- What is the company's attitude towards, and relationship with, its shareholders?

- What questions were raised at the previous AGM?

- How often does the chairman meet shareholders; what kind of questions do they ask?

- When do the non-executive directors typically have the opportunity to meet with shareholders?

3.7 Risk management

- What are the main risks the company faces, and how are these risks managed?

- What is the risk appetite or tolerance of the company in the achievement of its strategic objectives?

- Are the risk assessments underpinned by proper analysis?

- Does the company have sound and effective systems of internal controls?

- What is the company's attitude towards, and relationship with, its stakeholders?

- Does the chairman ensure effective communication with the company's stakeholders?

- Is there anything about the nature and extent of the company's business activities that would cause you concern both in terms of risk and any personal ethical considerations?

- Is any material litigation presently being undertaken or threatened, either by the company or against it?

- What insurance cover is available to directors and what is the company's policy on indemnifying directors?

4 Further sources of information

- Company report and accounts, and/or any listing prospectus

- Company website

- Any corporate social responsibility or environmental report issued by the company

- Voting services reports

- Press reports

- Analysts' reports

- Rating agency reports.

Appendix 3
ICSA Guidance Note: Induction of directors
June 2012

Since the publication of the ICSA Best Practice Guide *The Appointment and Induction of Directors*, it has become apparent that some newly appointed directors have been completely overwhelmed with the sheer volume of documents and other papers provided by the well-meaning company secretary to such an extent that some have been completely put off by it.

The objective of induction is to inform the director such that he or she can become as effective as possible in their new role as soon as possible. The provision of reams of paper in one go is, obviously, not conducive to this process. It is therefore recommended that, on appointment, a new director be provided with certain key, essential information together with a comprehensive list of other information that will be made available subsequently.

More recently we have seen the publication of the Higgs Report on the role and effectiveness of non-executive directors. That report includes various recommendations including, as Annex I, an induction checklist. ICSA worked closely with the Higgs review team on the creation of that checklist and, in order to enable it to be kept brief and to the point, undertook to produce this Guidance Note providing more comprehensive details of the material that should be considered for inclusion in an induction pack provided to new directors on, or during the weeks immediately following their appointment.

The following list is divided into three parts. The first includes the essential material that should be provided immediately and the second, material that should be provided over the first few weeks following the appointment, as and when deemed most appropriate. The director should, however, be provided immediately with a comprehensive list of the material being made available in total, together with an undertaking to provide it earlier if required. The third list covers items which the company secretary might consider making the director aware of. Note that some information may have already been provided during the director's due diligence process prior to appointment, or along with the appointment letter. Whilst duplication should be avoided, care should be taken to provide any updates that may be necessary.

The topics contained within this note should be supplied to all newly appointed directors, both executive and non-executive, however the secretary will need to gauge the level of previous knowledge and adjust them accordingly, particularly in regard to the appointment of executive directors.

Essential information to be provided immediately

The following information is felt to be essential and needs to be given to the director prior to the first board meeting. Methods of delivery vary, some of the information needs to be sent to the director with his appointment letter; but some could be deferred until a meeting after the board papers have been issued, so that the company secretary can review the board pack with the director before the first meeting highlighting any relevant issues.

Directors duties

- Brief outline of the role of a director and a summary of his/her responsibilities and ongoing obligations under legislation, regulation and best practice.

- Copy of UKLA Model Code, and details of the company's procedure regarding directors' share dealings and the disclosure of price sensitive information.

- The company's guidelines on:

    - Matters reserved for the board.

    - Delegated authorities.

    - The policy for obtaining independent professional advice for directors.

    - Other standing orders, policies and procedures of which the director should be aware.

    - 'Fire drill' procedures. (the procedures in place to deal with situations such as hostile takeover bids).

    - The company's business.

    - Current strategic/business plan, market analysis and budgets for the year with revised forecast, and three-/five-year plan.

    - Latest annual report and accounts, and interims as appropriate.

    - Explanation of key performance indicators.

    - List of major domestic and overseas subsidiaries, associated companies and joint ventures, including any parent company(ies).

    - Summary details of major group insurance policies including D & O liability insurance.

    - Details of any major litigation, either current or potential, being undertaken by the company or against the company.

    - Treasury issues.

    - Funding position and arrangements.

    - Dividend policy.

    - The corporate brochure, mission statement and any other reports issued by the company such as an environmental report, with a summary of the main events (such as mergers, divestments, introductions of new products, diversification into new areas, restructuring etc.) over the last three years.

Board issues

- Up-to-date copy of the company's Memorandum and Articles of Association/ Constitution, with a summary of the most important provisions.

- Minutes of the last three to six board meetings.

- Schedule of dates of future board meetings and board subcommittees if appropriate.

- Description of board procedures covering details such as when papers are sent out, the normal location of meetings, how long they last and an indication of the routine business transacted.

- Brief biographical and contact details of all directors of the company, the company secretary and other key executives. This should include any executive responsibilities of directors, their dates of appointment and any board committees upon which individual directors sit.

- Details of board subcommittees together with terms of reference and, where the director will be joining a committee, copies of the minutes of meetings of that committee during the previous 12 months.

Additional material to be provided during the first few months

The following information is crucial to assist the director to develop his knowledge of the company, its operations and staff, but is not necessary for him to commence his involvement. It is suggested, however, that a detailed schedule of the information available is provided to him, and the information is supplied either on request or within three months of appointment. It would also be appropriate to involve senior members of staff in the induction programme, for example the investor relations manager could give a presentation on the IR programme, so that the non-executive director begins to get a view of the depth of management available and the executive director is exposed to areas of the business he has less previous knowledge of.

- Copies of the company's main product/service brochures.

- Copies of recent press cuttings, reports and articles concerning the company.

- Details of the company's advisers (lawyers, bankers, auditors, registrars etc.), both internal and external, with the name of the partner dealing with the company's affairs.

- The company's risk management procedures and relevant disaster recovery plans.

- An outline of the provisions of the Combined Code as appended to the UK Listing Rules together with details of the company's corporate governance guidelines and any Investor's corporate governance guidelines which the company seeks to follow.

- Brief history of the company including when it was incorporated and any significant events during its history.

- Notices of any general meetings held in the last three years, and accompanying circulars as appropriate.

- Company organisation chart and management succession plans.
- Copy of all management accounts prepared since the company's last audited accounts.
- The company's investor relations policy and details of the major shareholders.
- Details of the five largest customers with the level of business done over the last five years.
- Details of the five largest suppliers to the company.
- Policies as regards:
  - Health and safety;
  - The environment;
  - Ethics and whistleblowing;
  - Charitable & political donations; and
  - Internal company telephone directory (including any overseas contact numbers and names).

Additional information which the company secretary might consider making the director aware of

The final section includes information which will differ for all companies depending on the sector and the company secretary will need to use his experience and knowledge to pass on information to allow the director to feel accustomed to the business as soon as possible.

- Protocol, procedures and dress code for:
  - Board meetings;
  - General meetings;
  - Formal dinners, staff social events, site visits etc. including the involvement of partners where appropriate.
- Procedures for:
  - Accounts sign off;
  - Results announcements;
  - Items requiring approval outside of board meetings;
  - Expenses policy and method of re-imbursement.

Appendix 4

ICSA Guidance Note: Directors' Service Contracts
October 2008

Extract on key provisions

Set out below is a checklist of key points to be covered in the contract. Although a director's service contract may or may not create an employer/employee relationship with the company,[1] the list includes all the clauses which would be required if the contract was to be a valid statement of main terms of employment for the purposes of s. 1 of the Employment Rights Act of 1996:

- name of the company and the director;

- appointment commencement date, date of commencement of continuous employment, and reference to the retirement position. (Legal advice should be obtained on an appropriate form of words taking account of age discrimination legislation[2]);

- duties required of the director including provision for service on other boards within the Group, service on other boards or for the benefit of other companies within the group;

- amount of time to be spent on those duties, including normal hours of work, and provision to comply with working time regulations;

- any limitations on the director engaging in business or professional activities outside the relationship with the company, requirements for the disclosure of those activities to the company, and the method of obtaining the company's prior approval for such activities if appropriate;

- remuneration details – salary, eligibility for annual bonus and long-term incentive schemes, medical insurance, company car, pension (including whether there is a contracting out certificate in force) and other benefits, including any flexibility for the company to review, amend or withdraw such benefits (particularly any benefits provided through insurance), and payment intervals;

- the level of expenses claimable and method of authorisation;

- details of the director's principal place of work, any requirement for business travel or future change of location, and any terms relating to work outside the country of employment or residence for periods of more than one month;

- holiday entitlement and holiday pay due to the director or to be repaid to the company on termination of the contract;

- entitlement to pay during periods of absence for sickness and absence;

- right for the company to require the director to undergo a reasonable medical examination and for the report to be disclosed to the company;

- requirement for the protection of confidential company information and the employer's intellectual property, including any works created by the director in the course of his contract;

- reference to the existence of any grievance or disciplinary appeal procedures and where they can be found, details of who will take any decision in the first instance, and who will hear any appeal, and details of any right to suspend;

- details of the notice period to be given by the company to the director and vice versa (see separate section below) or the date of expiry of any fixed term;

- other provisions relating to the termination of contract including the right for the company to give pay in lieu of notice or place the director on gardening leave;

- specific circumstances in which the contract may be terminated without notice, e.g. act of gross misconduct, negligence, bankruptcy, criminal conviction, retirement through ill health or because of accident/disability, and, for FSA-related companies, the loss of approved person status;

- any provision for the removal of a director from office as a director of any Group company, including any power of attorney to enable the company to effect the removal, and any indemnity available to protect the director in the event of litigation;

- any constraints on a director on leaving the company e.g. working for a competing organisation, poaching staff, soliciting or dealing with clients. (However, such provisions need to be carefully drafted to ensure they would be considered by the court to be no wider than is reasonably necessary to protect the company's legitimate business interests); and

- specification of the law which governs the agreement and the jurisdiction in which any dispute will be heard.

Notes

1 If the service is provided via a service company then the employment contract will be between the service company and the director. The service to the end company will be a matter of contract between that company and the service company.

2 Until the conclusive outcome of the *Heyday* case in the European Court of Justice is known, the legal position on retirement will not be clear, and there is a risk that any compulsory retirement at 65 could give rise to an age discrimination claim.

Appendix 5

ICSA Guidance Note: Sample non-executive director's appointment letter
December 2011

i Introduction

This sample letter is not intended to be a prescriptive template. It reflects the various practices of some of the larger companies and aims to provide an initial checklist of the elements a company may wish to cover in its appointment letters. The text and content should be adapted to suit the company's own circumstances.

As well as incorporating standard contract terms, the sample letter covers the reference in the Financial Reporting Council (FRC)'s 'Guidance on Board Effectiveness' to time commitment:

'Non-executive directors need to make sufficient time available to discharge their responsibilities effectively. The letter of appointment should state the minimum time that the non-executive director will be required to spend on the company's business, and seek the individual's confirmation that he or she can devote that amount of time to the role, consistent with other commitments. The letter should also indicate the possibility of additional time commitment when the company is undergoing a period of particularly increased activity, such as an acquisition or takeover, or as a result of some major difficulty with one or more of its operations.'

ii Sample letter

I am pleased to confirm that upon the recommendation of the nomination committee, the Board has approved your appointment as [an independent/a non-independent] non-executive director of [name of company] ('the Company'). This letter sets out the main terms of your appointment.

It is agreed that, on acceptance of this offer, this letter will constitute a contract for services and not a contract of employment.

1 Appointment

1.1 Subject to the remaining provisions of this letter, [your appointment is for an initial term of three years commencing on [date]] [your appointment is for an initial term, from [date] until the conclusion of the Company's Annual General Meeting (AGM) occurring approximately three years from that date], unless terminated earlier by either party giving to the other party [one/three] month[s] written notice.

1.2 Your appointment is subject to the articles of association. Nothing in this letter shall be taken to exclude or vary the terms of the articles of association as they apply to you as a director of the Company. Your continued appointment as non-executive director is subject to election by the Company's shareholders at the AGM scheduled to be held on [date] and to re-election at any subsequent AGM at which either the articles of association of the Company require, or the Board resolves, that you stand for re-election.

[The Board has resolved to apply Provision B.7.1 of the FRC's UK Corporate Governance Code 2010, whereby all directors will be subject to annual election at the [year] AGM, and expects to do so in subsequent years.]

If the shareholders do not re-elect you as a director, or you are retired from office under the articles of association, your appointment shall terminate automatically, with immediate effect and without compensation.

1.3 Continuation of your contract of appointment is also contingent on satisfactory performance and any relevant statutory provisions relating to the removal of a director.

1.4 Non-executive directors are typically expected to serve two three-year terms but may be invited by the Board to serve for an additional period. Any term renewal is subject to Board review and AGM re-election. Notwithstanding any mutual expectation, there is no right to re-nomination by the Board, either annually or after any three-year period.

1.5 You [will/may] be required to serve on one or more committees of the Board. You will be provided with the relevant terms of reference on your appointment to such a committee. [You also [will/may] be asked to serve as a non-executive director on the board of any of the Company's subsidiaries or joint ventures, or as Senior Independent Director.] Any such appointment will be covered in a separate communication.

1.6 Notwithstanding paragraphs 1.1–1.5, we may terminate your appointment with immediate effect if you:

(a) commit a material breach of your obligations under this letter; or

(b) commit any serious or repeated breach or non-observance of your obligations to the Company (which include an obligation not to breach your duties to the Company, whether statutory, fiduciary or common-law); or

(c) are guilty of any fraud or dishonesty or acted in a manner which, in the opinion of the Company acting reasonably, brings or is likely to bring you or the Company into disrepute or is materially adverse to the interests of the Company; or

(d) are convicted of any arrestable criminal offence [other than an offence under road traffic legislation in the UK or elsewhere for which a fine or non-custodial penalty is imposed]; or

(e) are declared bankrupt or have made an arrangement with or for the benefit of your creditors; or

(f) are disqualified from acting as a director.

1.7 On termination of your appointment, you shall at the request of the Company resign from your office as a director of the Company [and all offices held by you in any Group company].

1.8 If there are matters which arise which cause you concern about your role you should discuss them with me [or the Senior Independent Director]. If you have any concerns which cannot be resolved, and you choose to resign for that, or any other, reason, you should provide an appropriate written statement to me [or the Senior Independent Director] for circulation to the Board.

2 Time commitment

2.1 You will be expected to devote such time as is necessary for the proper performance of your duties and you should be prepared to spend at least [number of days] days per [month/year] on company business after the induction phase. This is based on preparation for and attendance at:

- scheduled Board meetings
- [Board dinners]
- [the annual Board strategy away-day(s)]
- the AGM
- [site visits]
- meetings of the non-executive directors
- meetings with shareholders
- updating meetings/training
- meetings as part of the Board evaluation process.

[Meetings may involve you in some overseas travel.] Unless urgent and unavoidable circumstances prevent you from doing so, it is expected that you will attend the meetings outlined above.

2.2 The nature of the role makes it impossible to be specific about the maximum time commitment, and there is always the possibility of additional time commitment in respect of preparation time and ad hoc matters which may arise from time to time, and particularly when the Company is undergoing a period of increased activity. At certain times it may be necessary to convene additional Board, committee or shareholder meetings.

2.3 The average time commitment stated in 2.1 will increase should you become a committee member or chair, or if you are given additional responsibilities, such as being appointed the Senior Independent Director, or non-executive director on the boards of any of the Company's subsidiaries. Details of the expected increase in time commitment will be covered in any relevant communication confirming the additional responsibility.

2.4 By accepting this appointment you undertake that, taking into account all other commitments you may have, you are able to, and will, devote sufficient time to your duties as a non-executive director.

3 Duties

3.1 You will be expected to perform your duties, whether statutory, fiduciary or common law, faithfully, efficiently and diligently to a standard commensurate with both the functions of your role and your knowledge, skills and experience.

3.2 You will exercise your powers in your role as a non-executive director having regard to relevant obligations under prevailing law and regulation, including the Companies Act 2006, the UK Corporate Governance Code and associated guidance1[1] and the UK Listing Authority's Listing, Prospectus, and Disclosure and Transparency Rules. [You are also required to comply with the requirements of the [New York Stock Exchange]. You will be advised by the Company Secretary where these differ from requirements in the UK.]

3.3 You will have particular regard to the general duties of directors as set out in Part 10, Chapter 2 of the Companies Act 2006, including the duty to promote the success of the company:

'A director of a company must act in the way he considers, in good faith, would be most likely to promote the success of the company for the benefit of its members as a whole, and in doing so have regard (amongst other matters) to –

(a) the likely consequences of any decision in the long term,

(b) the interests of the company's employees,

(c) the need to foster the company's business relationships with suppliers, customers and others,

(d) the impact of the company's operations on the community and the environment,

(e) the desirability of the company maintaining a reputation for high standards of business conduct, and

(f) the need to act fairly as between members of the company.'

3.4 You will have particular regard to the FRC's UK Corporate Governance Code (the 'Code') and associated Guidance on Board Effectiveness in respect of the role of the board[2] and the role of the non-executive director.

In your role as non-executive director you will be required to:

- constructively challenge and help develop proposals on strategy;

- scrutinise the performance of management in meeting agreed goals and objectives and monitor the reporting of performance;

- satisfy yourself on the integrity of financial information and that financial controls and systems of risk management are robust and defensible;

- determine appropriate levels of remuneration of executive directors and have a prime role in appointing and, where necessary, removing executive directors, and in succession planning;

- devote time to developing and refreshing your knowledge and skills;

- uphold high standards of integrity and probity and support me and the other directors in instilling the appropriate culture, values and behaviours in the boardroom and beyond;

- insist on receiving high-quality information sufficiently in advance of board meetings; and

- take into account the views of shareholders and other stakeholders where appropriate.

3.5 You will be required to exercise relevant powers under, and abide by, the Company's articles of association.

3.6 You will be required to exercise your powers as a director in accordance with the Company's policies and procedures [and internal control framework].

3.7 You will disclose any direct or indirect interest which you may have in any matter being considered at a board meeting or committee meeting and, save as permitted under the articles of association, you will not vote on any resolution of the Board, or of one of its committees, on any matter where you have any direct or indirect interest.

3.8 You will immediately report to me your own wrongdoing or the wrongdoing or proposed wrongdoing of any employee or director of which you become aware.

3.9 Unless specifically authorised to do so by the Board, you will not enter into any legal or other commitment or contract on behalf of the Company.

4 Remuneration and expenses

4.1 The annual fee rate as at the date of this letter is £[amount] gross per annum, paid [monthly/quarterly] in arrears. This fee covers all duties, including service on any board committee or company subsidiary, with the exception of committee chairmanships and certain additional responsibilities, such as taking on the role of Senior Independent Director. [In your case, a further fee of £[amount] is payable as at the date of this letter for taking on [chairmanship of the [name of committee] Committee] [./and] [the role of Senior Independent Director].]

4.2 All fees will be paid through PAYE and are subject to income tax and other statutory deductions.

4.3 Fees will be subject to an [annual/periodic] review by the Board.

[4.4 [You will comply with the Company's requirements regarding the minimum share-holding level (agreed from time to time by the Board).]]

4.5 The Company will reimburse you for all reasonable and properly-documented expenses you incur in performing the duties of your office. The procedure and other guidance in respect of expense claims is set out in [name of document].

4.6 On termination of the appointment you shall only be entitled to such fees as may have accrued to the date of termination, together with reimbursement in the normal way of any expenses properly incurred prior to that date.

5 Independence and outside interests

5.1 [The Board of the Company has determined you to be independent, taking account of the guidance contained in B.1.1 of the UK Corporate Governance Code.]

5.2 You have already disclosed to the Board the significant commitments you have outside this role. You must inform me in advance of any changes to these commitments. In certain circumstances the agreement of the Board may have to be sought before accepting further commitments which either might give rise to a conflict of interest or a conflict of any of your duties to the Company, or which might impact on the time that you are able to devote to your role at the Company.

5.3 It is accepted and acknowledged that you have business interests other than those of the Company and have declared any conflicts that are apparent at present. In the event that you become aware of any further potential or actual conflicts of interest, these should be disclosed to me and the Company Secretary as soon as they become apparent and, again, the agreement of the Board may have to be sought.

6 Confidentiality

6.1 You acknowledge that all information acquired during your appointment is confidential to the Company and should not be released, communicated, nor disclosed either during your appointment or following termination (by whatever means), to third parties without my prior clearance.

6.2 This restriction shall cease to apply to any confidential information which may (other than by reason of your breach) become available to the public generally.

6.3 You acknowledge the need to hold and retain company information (in whatever format you may receive it) under appropriately secure conditions.

6.4 You hereby waive all rights arising by virtue of Chapter IV of Part I of the Copyright Designs and Patents Act 1988 in respect of all copyright works created by you in the course of performing your duties hereunder.

7 Price-sensitive information and dealing in the Company's shares

7.1 Your attention is drawn to the requirements under both law and regulation regarding the disclosure of price-sensitive information, and in particular to the Disclosure and Transparency Rules of the UK Listing Authority and s 52 of the Criminal Justice Act 1993 on insider dealing. You should avoid making any statements that might risk a breach of these requirements. If in doubt please contact me or the Company Secretary.

7.2 During your period of appointment you are required to comply with the provisions of the Model Code, as annexed to the Listing Rules of the UK Listing Authority, in relation to dealing in the Company's listed securities, and any such other code as the Company may adopt from time to time which sets out the terms for dealings by directors in the Company's listed securities. A copy of the current share dealing code adopted by the Company will be provided to you separately.

8 Induction

8.1 Immediately after appointment, the Company will provide a comprehensive, formal and tailored induction [which will involve travel overseas]. You will be expected to make yourself available during your first year of appointment for not less than an additional [10] days for the purposes of the induction. The Company Secretary will be in touch with further details.

9 Review process

9.1 The performance of individual directors and the whole Board and its committees is evaluated annually.

10 Training

10.1 On an ongoing basis, and further to the annual evaluation process, we will make arrangements for you to develop and refresh your skills and knowledge in areas which we mutually identify as being likely to be required, or of benefit to you, in carrying out your duties effectively. You should endeavour to make yourself available for any relevant training sessions which may be organised for the Board.

11 Insurance and indemnity

11.1 The Company has directors' and officers' liability insurance in place and it is intended to maintain such cover for the full term of your appointment. You have been informed of the current indemnity limit, on which the Board is updated from time to time. Other details of the cover are available from the Company Secretary.

11.2 You will also be granted a deed of indemnity by the Company.

12 Independent professional advice

12.1 Circumstances may occur when it will be appropriate for you to seek advice from independent advisers at the Company's expense. A copy of the Board's agreed procedure under which directors may obtain independent advice will be provided by the Company Secretary. The Company will reimburse the reasonable cost of expenditure incurred by you in accordance with its policy.

13 Changes to personal details

13.1 You shall advise the Company Secretary promptly of any change in address or other personal contact details.

14 Return of property

14.1 Upon termination of your appointment with the Company (for whatever cause), you shall deliver to the Company all documents, records, papers or other company property which may be in your possession or under your control, and which relate in any way to the business affairs of the Company, and you shall not retain any copies thereof.

[15 Non-compete clause

15.1 By countersignature of this letter and in consideration for the fees payable to you under the terms of this letter, you now agree that you will not (without the previous consent in writing of the Company), for the period of six months immediately after the termination of your office, whether as principal or agent and whether alone or jointly with, or as a director, manager, partner, shareholder, employee or consultant of, any other person, carry on or be engaged, concerned or interested in any business which is similar to or competes with any business being carried on by the Company [or any company in the Group.]]

16 Data protection

16.1 By signing this letter you consent to the Company holding and processing information about you for legal, personnel, administrative and management purposes and in particular to the processing of any sensitive personal data (as defined in the Data Protection Act 1998) including, as and when appropriate:

(a) information about your physical or mental health or condition in order to monitor sick leave and take decisions as to your fitness to perform your duties;

(b) information about you that may be relevant to ensuring equality of opportunity and treatment in line with the Company's equal opportunities policy and in compliance with equal opportunities legislation; and

(c) information relating to any criminal proceedings in which you have been involved, for insurance purposes and in order to comply with legal requirements and obligations to third parties.

You consent to the transfer of such personal information to other offices the Company may have [or to a company in the Group] or to other third parties, whether or not outside the European Economic Area, for administration purposes and other purposes in connection with your appointment, where it is necessary or desirable for the Company to do so.

16.2 You will comply at all times with the Company's data protection policy, a copy of which will be provided to you.

17 Rights of third parties

17.1 The Contracts (Rights of Third Parties) Act 1999 shall not apply to this letter. No person other than you and the Company shall have any rights under this letter and the terms of this letter shall not be enforceable by any person other than you and the Company.

18 Law

18.1 Your engagement with the Company is governed by and shall be construed in accordance with the laws of [country] and your engagement shall be subject to the jurisdiction of the courts of [country].

18.2 This letter constitutes the entire terms and conditions of your appointment and no waiver or modification thereof shall be valid unless in writing and signed by the parties hereto.

If you are willing to accept these terms of appointment, please confirm your acceptance by signing and returning to me the enclosed copy of this letter.

Yours sincerely

[Name]

Chairman

I confirm and agree to the terms of my appointment as a non-executive director of [name of company] as set out in this letter.

_____

[Name]

_____

[Date]

Appendix A

The UK Corporate Governance Code on the role of the board:

' A.1 The Role of the Board

Main Principle

Every company should be headed by an effective board which is collectively responsible for the long-term success of the company.

Supporting Principles

The board's role is to provide entrepreneurial leadership of the company within a framework of prudent and effective controls which enables risk to be assessed and managed. The board should set the company's strategic aims, ensure that the necessary financial and human resources are in place for the company to meet its objectives and review management performance. The board should set the company's values and standards and ensure that its obligations to its shareholders and others are understood and met.

All directors must act in what they consider to be the best interests of the company, consistent with their statutory duties.'

The FRC Guidance on Board Effectiveness states that an effective board:

- provides direction for management;

- demonstrates ethical leadership, displaying – and promoting throughout the company – behaviours consistent with the culture and values it has defined for the organisation;

- creates a performance culture that drives value creation without exposing the company to excessive risk of value destruction;

- makes well-informed and high-quality decisions based on a clear line of sight into the business;

- creates the right framework for helping directors meet their statutory duties under the Companies Act 2006, and/or other relevant statutory and regulatory regimes;

- is accountable, particularly to those that provide the company's capital; and

- thinks carefully about its governance arrangements and embraces evaluation of their effectiveness.

Complete versions of the UK Corporate Governance Code and the FRC Guidance on Board Effectiveness can be found at: http://www.frc.org.uk/corporate/ukcgcode.cfm.

Notes

1 The FRC's associated guidance comprises: i. Guidance on Board Effectiveness, ii. Going Concern and Liquidity Risk: Guidance for Directors of UK Companies, iii. Internal Control: Revised Guidance for Directors and iv. Guidance on Audit Committees.

2 Excerpts from the Code and Guidance on Board Effectiveness on the role of the board have been appended to this contract in Appendix A.

Appendix 6

Final Recommendations of the Walker Review

Board size, composition and qualification

Recommendation 1

To ensure that NEDs have the knowledge and understanding of the business to enable them to contribute effectively, a BOFI board should provide thematic business awareness sessions on a regular basis and each NED should be provided with a substantive personalised approach to induction, training and development to be reviewed annually with the chairman. Appropriate provision should be made similarly for executive board members in business areas other than those for which they have direct responsibility.

Recommendation 2

A BOFI board should provide for dedicated support for NEDs on any matter relevant to the business on which they require advice separately from or additional to that available in the normal board process.

Recommendation 3

The overall time commitment of NEDs as a group on a FTSE 100-listed bank or life assurance company board should be greater than has been normal in the past. How this is achieved in particular board situations will depend on the composition of the NED group on the board. For several NEDs, a minimum expected time commitment of 30 to 36 days in a major bank board should be clearly indicated in letters of appointment and will in some cases limit the capacity of an individual NED to retain or assume board responsibilities elsewhere. For any prospective director where so substantial a time commitment is not envisaged or practicable, the letter of appointment should specify the time commitment agreed between the individual and the board. The terms of letters of appointment should be available to shareholders on request.

Recommendation 4

The FSA's ongoing supervisory process should give closer attention to the overall balance of the board in relation to the risk strategy of the business, taking into account the experience, behavioural and other qualities of individual directors and their access to fully adequate induction and development programmes. Such programmes should be designed to assure a sufficient continuing level of financial industry awareness so that NEDs are equipped to engage proactively in BOFI board deliberation, above all on risk strategy.

Recommendation 5

The FSA's interview process for NEDs proposed for FTSE 100-listed bank and life assurance company boards should involve questioning and assessment by one or more (retired or otherwise non-conflicted) senior advisers with relevant industry experience at or close to board level of a similarly large and complex entity who might be engaged by the FSA for the purpose, possibly on a part-time panel basis.

Functioning of the board and evaluation of performance

Recommendation 6

As part of their role as members of the unitary board of a BOFI, NEDs should be ready, able and encouraged to challenge and test proposals on strategy put forward by the executive. They should satisfy themselves that board discussion and decision-taking on risk matters is based on accurate and appropriately comprehensive information and draws, as far as they believe it to be relevant or necessary, on external analysis and input.

Recommendation 7

The chairman of a major bank should be expected to commit a substantial proportion of his or her time, probably around two-thirds, to the business of the entity, with clear understanding from the outset that, in the event of need, the bank chairmanship role would have priority over any other business time commitment. Depending on the balance and nature of their business, the required time commitment should be proportionately less for the chairman of a less complex or smaller bank, insurance or fund management entity.

Recommendation 8

The chairman of a BOFI board should bring a combination of relevant financial industry experience and a track record of successful leadership capability in a significant board position. Where this desirable combination is only incompletely achievable at the selection phase, and provided that there is an adequate balance of relevant financial industry experience among other board members, the board should give particular weight to convincing leadership experience since financial industry experience without established leadership skills in a chairman is unlikely to suffice. An appropriately intensive induction and continuing business awareness programme should be provided for the chairman to ensure that he or she is kept well informed and abreast of significant new developments in the business.

Recommendation 9

The chairman is responsible for leadership of the board, ensuring its effectiveness in all aspects of its role and setting its agenda so that fully adequate time is available for substantive discussion on strategic issues. The chairman should facilitate, encourage and expect the informed and critical contribution of the directors in particular in discussion and decision-taking on matters of risk and strategy and should promote effective communication between executive and non-executive directors. The chairman is responsible for ensuring that the directors receive all information that is relevant to discharge of their obligations in accurate, timely and clear form.

Recommendation 10

The chairman of a BOFI board should be proposed for election on an annual basis. The board should keep under review the possibility of transitioning to annual election of all board members.

Recommendation 11

The role of the senior independent director (SID) should be to provide a sounding board for the chairman, for the evaluation of the chairman and to serve as a trusted intermediary for the NEDs, when necessary. The SID should be accessible to shareholders in the event that communication with the chairman becomes difficult or inappropriate.

Recommendation 12

The board should undertake a formal and rigorous evaluation of its performance, and that of committees of the board, with external facilitation of the process every second or third year. The evaluation statement should either be included as a dedicated section of the chairman's statement or as a separate section of the annual report, signed by the chairman. Where an external facilitator is used, this should be indicated in the statement, together with their name and a clear indication of any other business relationships with the company and that the board is satisfied that any potential conflict given such other business relationship has been appropriately managed.

Recommendation 13

The evaluation statement on board performance and governance should confirm that a rigorous evaluation process has been undertaken and describe the process for identifying the skills and experience required to address and challenge adequately key risks and decisions that confront, or may confront, the board. The statement should provide such meaningful, high-level information as the board considers necessary to assist shareholders' understanding of the main features of the process, including an indication of the extent to which issues raised in the course of the evaluation have been addressed. It should also provide an indication of the nature and extent of communication with major shareholders and confirmation that the board were fully apprised of views indicated by shareholders in the course of such dialogue.

The role of institutional shareholders: communication and engagement

Recommendation 14

Boards should ensure that they are made aware of any material cumulative changes in the share register as soon as possible, understand as far as possible the reasons for such changes and satisfy themselves that they have taken steps, if any are required, to respond. Where material cumulative changes take place over a short period, the FSA should be promptly informed.

Recommendation 15

Deleted.

Recommendation 16

The remit of the FRC should be explicitly extended to cover the development and encouragement of adherence to principles of best practice in stewardship by institutional investors and fund managers. This new role should be clarified by separating the content of the present Combined Code, which might be described as the Corporate Governance Code, from what might most appropriately be described as the Stewardship Code.

Recommendation 17

The Code on the Responsibilities of Institutional Investors, prepared by the Institutional Shareholders' Committee, should be ratified by the FRC and become the Stewardship Code. By virtue of the independence and authority of the FRC, this transition to sponsorship by the FRC should give materially greater weight to the Stewardship Code. Its status should be akin to that of the Combined Code as a statement of best practice, with observance on a similar 'comply or explain' basis.

Recommendation 18

The FRC should oversee a review of the Stewardship Code on a regular basis, in close consultation with institutional shareholders, fund managers and other interested parties, to ensure its continuing fitness for purpose in the light of experience and make proposals for any appropriate adaptation.

Recommendation 18B

All fund managers that indicate commitment to engagement should participate in a survey to monitor adherence to the Stewardship Code. Arrangements should be put in place under the guidance of the FRC for appropriately independent oversight of this monitoring process which should publish an engagement survey on an annual basis.

Recommendation 19

Fund managers and other institutions authorised by the FSA to undertake investment business should signify on their websites or in another accessible form whether they commit to the Stewardship Code. Disclosure of such commitment should be accompanied by an indication whether their mandates from life assurance, pension fund and other major clients normally include provisions in support of engagement activity and of their engagement policies on discharge of the responsibilities set out in the Stewardship Code. Where a fund manager or institutional investor is not ready to commit and to report in this sense, it should provide, similarly on the website, a clear explanation of its alternative business model and the reasons for the position it is taking.

Recommendation 20

The FSA should require institutions that are authorised to manage assets for others to disclose clearly on their websites, or in other accessible form, the nature of their commitment to the Stewardship Code or their alternative business model.

Recommendation 20B

In view of the importance of facilitating enhanced engagement between shareholders and investee companies, the FSA, in consultation with the FRC and Takeover Panel, should keep under review the adequacy of the what is in effect 'safe harbour' interpretation and guidance that has been provided as a means of minimising regulatory impediments to such engagement.

Recommendation 21

Institutional investors and fund managers should actively seek opportunities for collective engagement where this has the potential to enhance their ownership influence in promoting sustainable improvement in the performance of their investee companies. Initiative should be taken by the FRC and major UK fund managers and institutional investors to invite potentially interested major foreign institutional investors, such as sovereign wealth funds, public sector pension funds and endowments, to commit to the Stewardship Code and its provisions on collective engagement.

Recommendation 22

Voting powers should be exercised, fund managers and other institutional investors should disclose their voting record, and their policies in respect of voting should be described in statements on their websites or in another publicly accessible form.

Governance of risk

Recommendation 23

The board of a FTSE 100-listed bank or life insurance company should establish a board risk committee separately from the audit committee. The board risk committee should have responsibility for oversight and advice to the board on the current risk exposures of the entity and future risk strategy, including strategy for capital and liquidity management, and the embedding and maintenance throughout the entity of a supportive culture in relation to the management of risk alongside established prescriptive rules and procedures. In preparing advice to the board on its overall risk appetite, tolerance and strategy, the board risk committee should ensure that account has been taken of the current and prospective macroeconomic and financial environment drawing on financial stability assessments such as those published by the Bank of England, the FSA and other authoritative sources that may be relevant for the risk policies of the firm.

Recommendation 24

In support of board-level risk governance, a BOFI board should be served by a CRO who should participate in the risk management and oversight process at the highest level on an enterprise-wide basis and have a status of total independence from individual business units. Alongside an internal reporting line to the CEO or CFO, the CRO should report to the board risk committee, with direct access to the chairman of the committee in the event of need. The tenure and independence of the CRO should be underpinned by a provision that removal from office would require the prior agreement of the board. The remuneration of the CRO should be subject to approval by the chairman or chairman of the board remuneration committee.

Recommendation 25

The board risk committee should be attentive to the potential added value from seeking external input to its work as a means of taking full account of relevant experience elsewhere and in challenging its analysis and assessment.

Recommendation 26

In respect of a proposed strategic transaction involving acquisition or disposal, it should as a matter of good practice be for the board risk committee in advising the board to ensure that a due diligence appraisal of the proposition is undertaken, focusing in particular on risk aspects and implications for the risk appetite and tolerance of the entity, drawing on independent external advice where appropriate and available, before the board takes a decision whether to proceed.

Recommendation 27

The board risk committee (or board) risk report should be included as a separate report within the annual report and accounts. The report should describe thematically the strategy of the entity in a risk management context, including information on the key risk exposures inherent in the strategy, the associated risk appetite and tolerance and how the actual risk appetite is assessed over time covering both banking and trading book exposures and the effectiveness of the risk management process over such exposures. The report should also provide at least high-level information on the scope and outcome of the stress-testing programme. An indication should be given of the membership of the committee, of the frequency of its meetings, whether external advice was taken and, if so, its source.

Remuneration

Recommendation 28

The remuneration committee should have a sufficient understanding of the company's approach to pay and employment conditions to ensure that it is adopting a coherent approach to remuneration in respect of all employees. The terms of reference of the remuneration committee should accordingly include responsibility for setting the over-arching principles and parameters of remuneration policy on a firm-wide basis.

Recommendation 29

The terms of reference of the remuneration committee should be extended to oversight of remuneration policy and outcomes in respect of all 'high end' employees.

Recommendation 30

In relation to 'high end' employees, the remuneration committee report should confirm that the committee is satisfied with the way in which performance objectives and risk adjustments are reflected in the compensation structures for this group and explain the principles underlying the performance objectives, risk adjustments and the related compensation structure if these differ from those for executive board members.

Recommendation 31

For FTSE 100-listed banks and comparable unlisted entities such as the largest building societies, the remuneration committee report for the 2010 year of account and thereafter should disclose in bands the number of 'high end' employees, including executive board members, whose total expected remuneration in respect of the reported year is in a range of £1 million to £2.5 million, in a range of £2.5 million to £5 million and in £5 million bands thereafter and, within each band, the main elements of salary, cash bonus, deferred shares, performance-related long-term awards and pension contribution. Such disclosures should be accompanied by an indication to the extent possible of the areas of business activity to which these higher bands of remuneration relate.

Recommendation 32

FSA-authorised banks that are UK-domiciled subsidiaries of non-resident entities should disclose for the 2010 year of account and thereafter details of total remuneration bands (including remuneration received outside the UK) and the principal elements within such remuneration for their 'high end' employees on a comparable basis and timescale to that required for UK-listed banks.

Recommendation 33

Deferral of incentive payments should provide the primary risk adjustment mechanism to align rewards with sustainable performance for executive board members and 'high end' employees in a BOFI included within the scope of the FSA Remuneration Code. Incentives should be balanced so that at least one-half of variable remuneration offered in respect of a financial year is in the form of a long-term incentive scheme with vesting subject to a performance condition with half of the award vesting after not less than three years and of the remainder after five years. Short-term bonus awards should be paid over a three-year period with not more than one-third in the first year. Clawback should be used as the means to reclaim amounts in circumstances of misstatement and misconduct. This recommended structure should be incorporated in the FSA Remuneration Code review process next year and the remuneration committee report for 2010 and thereafter should indicate on a 'comply or explain' basis the conformity of an entity's 'high end' remuneration arrangements with this recommended structure.

Recommendation 34

Executive board members and 'high end' employees should be expected to maintain a shareholding or retain a portion of vested awards in an amount in line with their total compensation on a historic or expected basis, to be built up over a period at the discretion of the remuneration committee. Vesting of stock for this group should not normally be accelerated on cessation of employment other than on compassionate grounds.

Recommendation 35

The remuneration committee should seek advice from the board risk committee on specific risk adjustments to be applied to performance objectives set in the context of incentive packages; in the event of any difference of view, appropriate risk adjustments should be decided by the chairman and NEDs on the board.

Recommendation 36

If the non-binding resolution on a remuneration committee report attracts less than 75 per cent of the total votes cast, the chairman of the committee should stand for re-election in the following year irrespective of his or her normal appointment term.

Recommendation 37

The remuneration committee report should state whether any executive board member or 'high end' employee has the right or opportunity to receive enhanced benefits, whether while in continued employment or on termination, resignation, retirement or in the wake of any other event such as a change of control, beyond those already disclosed in the directors' remuneration report and whether the committee has exercised its discretion during the year to enhance such benefits either generally or for any member of this group.

Recommendation 38/39

Remuneration consultants should put in place a formal constitution for the professional group that has now been formed, with provision: for independent oversight and review of the remuneration consultants code; that this code and an indication of those committed to it should be lodged on the FRC website; and that all remuneration committees should use the code as the basis for determining the contractual terms of engagement of their advisers; and that the remuneration committee report should indicate the source of consultancy advice and whether the consultant has any other advisory engagement with the company.

Appendix 7
Turnbull Report: Internal Control – Guidance for Directors on the Combined Code
Introduction

Internal control requirements of the Combined Code

1. When the Combined Code of the Committee on Corporate Governance (the Code) was published, the Institute of Chartered Accountants in England & Wales agreed with the London Stock Exchange that it would provide guidance to assist listed companies to implement the requirements in the Code relating to internal control.

2. Principle d.2 of the Code states that 'The board should maintain a sound system of internal control to safeguard shareholders' investment and the company's assets'.

3. Provision d.2.1 states that 'The directors should, at least annually, conduct a review of the effectiveness of the group's system of internal control and should report to shareholders that they have done so. The review should cover all controls, including financial, operational and compliance controls and risk management'.

4. Provision d.2.2 states that 'Companies which do not have an internal audit function should from time to time review the need for one'.

5. Paragraph 12.43a of the London Stock Exchange Listing Rules states that 'in the case of a company incorporated in the United Kingdom, the following additional items must be included in its annual report and accounts:

    (a) a narrative statement of how it has applied the principles set out in Section 1 of the Combined Code, providing explanation which enables its shareholders to evaluate how the principles have been applied;

    (b) a statement as to whether or not it has complied throughout the accounting period with the Code provisions set out in Section 1 of the Combined Code. A company that has not complied with the Code provisions, or complied with only some of the Code provisions or (in the case of provisions whose require-ments are of a continuing nature) complied for only part of an accounting period, must specify the Code provisions with which it has not complied, and (where relevant) for what part of the period such non compliance continued, and give reasons for any non-compliance'.

6. The Preamble to the Code, which is appended to the Listing Rules, makes it clear that there is no prescribed form or content for the statement setting out how the various principles in the Code have been applied. The intention is that companies should have a free hand to explain their governance policies in the light of the principles, including any special circumstances which have led to them adopting a particular approach.

7. The guidance in this document should be followed by boards of listed companies in:

    - assessing how the company has applied Code principle d.2;

    - implementing the requirements of Code provisions d.2.1 and d.2.2; and

    - reporting on these matters to shareholders in the annual report and accounts.

Objectives of the guidance

8. This guidance is intended to:

    - reflect sound business practice whereby internal control is embedded in the business processes by which a company pursues its objectives;

    - remain relevant over time in the continually evolving business environment; and

    - enable each company to apply it in a manner which takes account of its particular circumstances.

    The guidance requires directors to exercise judgement in reviewing how the company has implemented the requirements of the Code relating to internal control and reporting to shareholders thereon.

9. The guidance is based on the adoption by a company's board of a risk-based approach to establishing a sound system of internal control and reviewing its effectiveness. This should be incorporated by the company within its normal management and governance processes. It should not be treated as a separate exercise undertaken to meet regulatory requirements.

The importance of internal control and risk management

10. A company's system of internal control has a key role in the management of risks that are significant to the fulfilment of its business objectives. A sound system of internal control contributes to safeguarding the shareholders' investment and the company's assets.

11. Internal control (as referred to in paragraph 20) facilitates the effectiveness and efficiency of operations, helps ensure the reliability of internal and external reporting and assists compliance with laws and regulations.

12. Effective financial controls, including the maintenance of proper accounting records, are an important element of internal control. They help ensure that the company is not unnecessarily exposed to avoidable financial risks and that financial information used within the business and for publication is reliable. They also contribute to the safeguarding of assets, including the prevention and detection of fraud.

13. A company's objectives, its internal organisation and the environment in which it operates are continually evolving and, as a result, the risks it faces are continually

changing. A sound system of internal control therefore depends on a thorough and regular evaluation of the nature and extent of the risks to which the company is exposed. Since profits are, in part, the reward for successful risk taking in business, the purpose of internal control is to help manage and control risk appropriately rather than to eliminate it.

Groups of companies

14. Throughout this guidance, where reference is made to 'company' it should be taken, where applicable, as referring to the group of which the reporting company is the parent company. For groups of companies, the review of effectiveness of internal control and the report to the shareholders should be from the perspective of the group as a whole.

The Appendix

15. The Appendix to this document contains questions which boards may wish to consider in applying this guidance.

Maintaining a sound system of internal control

Responsibilities

16. The board of directors is responsible for the company's system of internal control. It should set appropriate policies on internal control and seek regular assurance that will enable it to satisfy itself that the system is functioning effectively. The board must further ensure that the system of internal control is effective in managing risks in the manner which it has approved.

17. In determining its policies with regard to internal control, and thereby assessing what constitutes a sound system of internal control in the particular circumstances of the company, the board's deliberations should include consideration of the following factors:

- the nature and extent of the risks facing the company;

- the extent and categories of risk which it regards as acceptable for the company to bear;

- the likelihood of the risks concerned materialising; and

- the company's ability to reduce the incidence and impact on the business of risks that do materialise; and the costs of operating particular controls relative to the benefit thereby obtained in managing the related risks.

18. It is the role of management to implement board policies on risk and control. In fulfilling its responsibilities, management should identify and evaluate the risks faced by the company for consideration by the board and design, operate

and monitor a suitable system of internal control which implements the policies adopted by the board.

19. All employees have some responsibility for internal control as part of their accountability for achieving objectives. They, collectively, should have the necessary knowledge, skills, information and authority to establish, operate and monitor the system of internal control. This will require an understanding of the company, its objectives, the industries and markets in which it operates, and the risks it faces.

20. An internal control system encompasses the policies, processes, tasks, behaviours and other aspects of a company that, taken together:

    • facilitate its effective and efficient operation by enabling it to respond appropriately to significant business, operational, financial, compliance and other risks to achieving the company's objectives. This includes the safeguarding of assets from inappropriate use or from loss and fraud, and ensuring that liabilities are identified and managed;

    • help ensure the quality of internal and external reporting. This requires the maintenance of proper records and processes that generate a flow of timely, relevant and reliable information from within and outside the organisation; and

    • help ensure compliance with applicable laws and regulations, and also with internal policies with respect to the conduct of business.

21. A company's system of internal control will reflect its control environment which encompasses its organisational structure. The system will include:

    • control activities;

    • information and communications processes; and

    • processes for monitoring the continuing effectiveness of the system of internal control.

22. The system of internal control should:

    • be embedded in the operations of the company and form part of its culture; l be capable of responding quickly to evolving risks to the business arising from factors within the company and to changes in the business environment; and

    • include procedures for reporting immediately to appropriate levels of management any significant control failings or weaknesses that are identified together with details of corrective action being undertaken.

23. A sound system of internal control reduces, but cannot eliminate, the possibility of poor judgement in decision-making; human error; control processes being deliberately circumvented by employees and others; management overriding controls; and the occurrence of unforeseeable circumstances.

24. A sound system of internal control therefore provides reasonable, but not absolute, assurance that a company will not be hindered in achieving its business objectives, or in the orderly and legitimate conduct of its business, by circumstances which

may reasonably be foreseen. A system of internal control cannot, however, provide protection with certainty against a company failing to meet its business objectives or all material errors, losses, fraud, or breaches of laws or regulations.

Reviewing the effectiveness of internal control

Responsibilities

25. Reviewing the effectiveness of internal control is an essential part of the board's responsibilities. The board will need to form its own view on effectiveness after due and careful enquiry based on the information and assurances provided to it. Management is accountable to the board for monitoring the system of internal control and for providing assurance to the board that it has done so.

26. The role of board committees in the review process, including that of the audit committee, is for the board to decide and will depend upon factors such as the size and composition of the board; the scale, diversity and complexity of the company's operations; and the nature of the significant risks that the company faces. To the extent that designated board committees carry out, on behalf of the board, tasks that are attributed in this guidance document to the board, the results of the relevant committees' work should be reported to, and considered by, the board. The board takes responsibility for the disclosures on internal control in the annual report and accounts.

The process for reviewing effectiveness

27. Effective monitoring on a continuous basis is an essential component of a sound system of internal control. The board cannot, however, rely solely on the embedded monitoring processes within the company to discharge its responsibilities. It should regularly receive and review reports on internal control. In addition, the board should undertake an annual assessment for the purposes of making its public statement on internal control to ensure that it has considered all significant aspects of internal control for the company for the year under review and up to the date of approval of the annual report and accounts.

28. The reference to 'all controls' in Code Provision d.2.1 should not be taken to mean that the effectiveness of every internal control (including controls designed to manage immaterial risks) should be subject to review by the board. Rather it means that, for the purposes of this guidance, internal controls considered by the board should include all types of controls including those of an operational and compliance nature, as well as internal financial controls.

29. The board should define the process to be adopted for its review of the effectiveness of internal control. This should encompass both the scope and frequency of the reports it receives and reviews during the year, and also the process for its annual assessment, such that it will be provided with sound, appropriately documented, support for its statement on internal control in the company's annual report and accounts.

30. The reports from management to the board should, in relation to the areas covered by them, provide a balanced assessment of the significant risks and the effectiveness

of the system of internal control in managing those risks. Any significant control failings or weaknesses identified should be discussed in the reports, including the impact that they have had, could have had, or may have, on the company and the actions being taken to rectify them. It is essential that there be openness of communication by management with the board on matters relating to risk and control.

31. When reviewing reports during the year, the board should:

- consider what are the significant risks and assess how they have been identified, evaluated and managed;

- assess the effectiveness of the related system of internal control in managing the significant risks, having regard, in particular, to any significant failings or weaknesses in internal control that have been reported;

- consider whether necessary actions are being taken promptly to remedy any significant failings or weaknesses; and

- consider whether the findings indicate a need for more extensive monitoring of the system of internal control.

32. Additionally, the board should undertake an annual assessment for the purpose of making its public statement on internal control. The assessment should consider issues dealt with in reports reviewed by it during the year together with any additional information necessary to ensure that the board has taken account of all significant aspects of internal control for the company for the year under review and up to the date of approval of the annual report and accounts.

33. The board's annual assessment should, in particular, consider:

- the changes since the last annual assessment in the nature and extent of significant risks, and the company's ability to respond to changes in its business and the external environment;

- the scope and quality of management's ongoing monitoring of risks and of the system of internal control, and, where applicable, the work of its internal audit function and other providers of assurance;

- the extent and frequency of the communication of the results of the monitoring to the board (or board committee(s)) which enables it to build up a cumulative assessment of the state of control in the company and the effectiveness with which risk is being managed;

- the incidence of significant control failings or weaknesses that have been identified at any time during the period and the extent to which they have resulted in unforeseen outcomes or contingencies that have had, could have had, or may in the future have, a material impact on the company's financial performance or condition; and

- the effectiveness of the company's public reporting processes.

34. Should the board become aware at any time of a significant failing or weakness in internal control, it should determine how the failing or weakness arose and re-assess the effectiveness of management's ongoing processes for designing, operating and monitoring the system of internal control.

The board's statement on internal control

35. In its narrative statement of how the company has applied Code principle d.2, the board should, as a minimum, disclose that there is an ongoing process for identifying, evaluating and managing the significant risks faced by the company, that it has been in place for the year under review and up to the date of approval of the annual report and accounts, that it is regularly reviewed by the board and accords with the guidance in this document.

36. The board may wish to provide additional information in the annual report and accounts to assist understanding of the company's risk management processes and system of internal control.

37. The disclosures relating to the application of principle d.2 should include an acknowledgement by the board that it is responsible for the company's system of internal control and for reviewing its effectiveness. It should also explain that such a system is designed to manage rather than eliminate the risk of failure to achieve business objectives, and can only provide reasonable and not absolute assurance against material misstatement or loss.

38. In relation to Code provision d.2.1, the board should summarise the process it (where applicable, through its committees) has applied in reviewing the effectiveness of the system of internal control. It should also disclose the process it has applied to deal with material internal control aspects of any signi. cant problems disclosed in the annual report and accounts.

39. Where a board cannot make one or more of the disclosures in paragraphs 35 and 38, it should state this fact and provide an explanation. The Listing Rules require the board to disclose if it has failed to conduct a review of the effectiveness of the company's system of internal control.

40. The board should ensure that its disclosures provide meaningful, high-level information and do not give a misleading impression.

41. Where material joint ventures and associates have not been dealt with as part of the group for the purposes of applying this guidance, this should be disclosed.

Internal audit

42. Provision d.2.2 of the Code states that companies which do not have an internal audit function should from time to time review the need for one.

43. The need for an internal audit function will vary depending on company-specific factors including the scale, diversity and complexity of the company's activities and the number of employees, as well as cost–benefit considerations. Senior management and the board may desire objective assurance and advice on risk and control. An adequately resourced internal audit function (or its equivalent where, for example, a third party is contracted to perform some or all of the work concerned) may provide such assurance and advice. There may be other functions within the company that also provide assurance and advice covering specialist areas such as health and safety, regulatory and legal compliance and environmental issues.

44. In the absence of an internal audit function, management needs to apply other monitoring processes in order to assure itself and the board that the system of internal control is functioning as intended. In these circumstances, the board will need to assess whether such processes provide sufficient and objective assurance.

45. When undertaking its assessment of the need for an internal audit function, the board should also consider whether there are any trends or current factors relevant to the company's activities, markets or other aspects of its external environment, that have increased, or are expected to increase, the risks faced by the company. Such an increase in risk may also arise from internal factors such as organisational restructuring or from changes in reporting processes or underlying information systems. Other matters to be taken into account may include adverse trends evident from the monitoring of internal control systems or an increased incidence of unexpected occurrences.

46. The board of a company that does not have an internal audit function should assess the need for such a function annually having regard to the factors referred to in paragraphs 43 and 45 above. Where there is an internal audit function, the board should annually review its scope of work, authority and resources, again having regard to those factors.

47. If the company does not have an internal audit function and the board has not reviewed the need for one, the Listing Rules require the board to disclose these facts.

Appendix

Assessing the effectiveness of the company's risk and control processes

Some questions which the board may wish to consider and discuss with management when regularly reviewing reports on internal control and carrying out its annual assessment are set out below. The questions are not intended to be exhaustive and will need to be tailored to the particular circumstances of the company.

This Appendix should be read in conjunction with the guidance set out in this document.

1. Risk assessment

   • Does the company have clear objectives and have they been communicated so as to provide effective direction to employees on risk assessment and control issues? For example, do objectives and related plans include measurable performance targets and indicators?

   • Are the significant internal and external operational, financial, compliance and other risks identified and assessed on an ongoing basis? (Significant risks may, for example, include those related to market, credit, liquidity, techno-logical, legal, health, safety and environmental, reputation, and business probity issues.)

   • Is there a clear understanding by management and others within the company of what risks are acceptable to the board?

2.   Control environment and control activities

- Does the board have clear strategies for dealing with the significant risks that have been identified? Is there a policy on how to manage these risks?

- Do the company's culture, code of conduct, human resource policies and performance reward systems support the business objectives and risk management and internal control system?

- Does senior management demonstrate, through its actions as well as its policies, the necessary commitment to competence, integrity and fostering a climate of trust within the company?

- Are authority, responsibility and accountability defined clearly such that decisions are made and actions taken by the appropriate people? Are the decisions and actions of different parts of the company appropriately coordinated?

- Does the company communicate to its employees what is expected of them and the scope of their freedom to act? This may apply to areas such as customer relations; service levels for both internal and outsourced activities; health, safety and environmental protection; security of tangible and intangible assets; business continuity issues; expenditure matters; accounting; and financial and other reporting.

- Do people in the company (and in its providers of outsourced services) have the knowledge, skills and tools to support the achievement of the company's objectives and to manage effectively risks to their achievement?

- How are processes/controls adjusted to reflect new or changing risks, or operational deficiencies?

3.   Information and communication

- Do management and the board receive timely, relevant and reliable reports on progress against business objectives and the related risks that provide them with the information, from inside and outside the company, needed for decision-making and management review purposes? This could include performance reports and indicators of change, together with qualitative information such as on customer satisfaction, employee attitudes etc.

- Are information needs and related information systems reassessed as objectives and related risks change or as reporting deficiencies are identified?

- Are periodic reporting procedures, including half-yearly and annual reporting, effective in communicating a balanced and understandable account of the company's position and prospects?

- Are there established channels of communication for individuals to report suspected breaches of laws or regulations or other improprieties?

4.   Monitoring

- Are there ongoing processes embedded within the company's overall business operations, and addressed by senior management, which monitor the effective application of the policies, processes and activities related to internal control and risk management? (Such processes may include control self-assessment, confirmation by personnel of compliance with policies and codes of conduct, internal audit reviews or other management reviews.)

- Do these processes monitor the company's ability to re-evaluate risks and adjust controls effectively in response to changes in its objectives, its business, and its external environment?

- Are there effective follow-up procedures to ensure that appropriate change or action occurs in response to changes in risk and control assessments?

- Is there appropriate communication to the board (or board committees) on the effectiveness of the ongoing monitoring processes on risk and control matters? This should include reporting any significant failings or weaknesses on a timely basis.

- Are there special arrangements for management monitoring and reporting to the board on risk and control matters of particular importance? These could include, for example, actual or suspected fraud and other illegal or irregular acts, or matters that could adversely affect the company's reputation or financial position?

The FRC is responsible for promoting high quality corporate governance and reporting to foster investment. We set the UK Corporate Governance and Stewardship Codes as well as UK standards for accounting, auditing and actuarial work. We represent UK interests in international standard-setting. We also monitor and take action to promote the quality of corporate reporting and auditing. We operate independent disciplinary arrangements for accountants and actuaries; and oversee the regulatory activities of the accountancy and actuarial professional bodies.

Financial Reporting Council

5th Floor, Aldwych House 71–91 Aldwych London WC2B 4HN

+44 (0)20 7492 2300

www.frc.org.uk

UP/FRC-BI12001

© The Financial Reporting Council Limited 2013

The Financial Reporting Council Limited is a company limited by guarantee. Registered in England number 2486368.

Registered Office: 5th Floor, Aldwych House, 71-91 Aldwych, London WC2B 4HN.

Appendix 8

The UK Stewardship Code

September 2012

Principle 1

Institutional investors should publicly disclose their policy on how they will discharge their stewardship responsibilities

Guidance

Stewardship activities include monitoring and engaging with companies on matters such as strategy, performance, risk, capital structure, and corporate governance, including culture and remuneration. Engagement is purposeful dialogue with companies on those matters as well as on issues that are the immediate subject of votes at general meetings.

The policy should disclose how the institutional investor applies stewardship with the aim of enhancing and protecting the value for the ultimate beneficiary or client.

The statement should reflect the institutional investor's activities within the investment chain, as well as the responsibilities that arise from those activities. In particular, the stewardship responsibilities of those whose primary activities are related to asset ownership may be different from those whose primary activities are related to asset management or other investment-related services.

Where activities are outsourced, the statement should explain how this is compatible with the proper exercise of the institutional investor's stewardship responsibilities and what steps the investor has taken to ensure that they are carried out in a manner consistent with the approach to stewardship set out in the statement.

The disclosure should describe arrangements for integrating stewardship within the wider investment process.

Principle 2

Institutional investors should have a robust policy on managing conflicts of interest in relation to stewardship which should be publicly disclosed

Guidance

An institutional investor's duty is to act in the interests of its clients and/or beneficiaries.

Conflicts of interest will inevitably arise from time to time, which may include when voting on matters affecting a parent company or client.

Institutional investors should put in place, maintain and publicly disclose a policy for identifying and managing conflicts of interest with the aim of taking all reasonable steps to put the interests of their client or beneficiary first. The policy should also address how matters are handled when the interests of clients or beneficiaries diverge from each other.

Principle 3

Institutional investors should monitor their investee companies

Guidance

Effective monitoring is an essential component of stewardship. It should take place regularly and be checked periodically for effectiveness.

When monitoring companies, institutional investors should seek to:

- keep abreast of the company's performance;

- keep abreast of developments, both internal and external to the company, that drive the company's value and risks;

- satisfy themselves that the company's leadership is effective;

- satisfy themselves that the company's board and committees adhere to the spirit of the UK Corporate Governance Code, including through meetings with the chairman and other board members;

- consider the quality of the company's reporting; and

- attend the General Meetings of companies in which they have a major holding, where appropriate and practicable.

Institutional investors should consider carefully explanations given for departure from the UK Corporate Governance Code and make reasoned judgements in each case. They should give a timely explanation to the company, in writing where appropriate, and be prepared to enter a dialogue if they do not accept the company's position.

Institutional investors should endeavour to identify at an early stage issues that may result in a significant loss in investment value. If they have concerns, they should seek to ensure that the appropriate members of the investee company's board or management are made aware.

Institutional investors may or may not wish to be made insiders. An institutional investor who may be willing to become an insider should indicate in its stewardship statement the willingness to do so, and the mechanism by which this could be done.

Institutional investors will expect investee companies and their advisers to ensure that information that could affect their ability to deal in the shares of the company concerned is not conveyed to them without their prior agreement.

Principle 4

Institutional investors should establish clear guidelines on when and how they will escalate their stewardship activities

Guidance

Institutional investors should set out the circumstances in which they will actively intervene and regularly assess the outcomes of doing so. Intervention should be considered regardless of whether an active or passive investment policy is followed. In addition, being underweight is not, of itself, a reason for not intervening. Instances when institutional investors may want to intervene include, but are not limited to, when they have concerns about the company's strategy, performance, governance, remuneration or approach to risks, including those that may arise from social and environmental matters.

Initial discussions should take place on a confidential basis. However, if companies do not respond constructively when institutional investors intervene, then institutional investors should consider whether to escalate their action, for example, by:

- holding additional meetings with management specifically to discuss concerns;
- expressing concerns through the company's advisers;
- meeting with the chairman or other board members;
- intervening jointly with other institutions on particular issues;
- making a public statement in advance of General Meetings;
- submitting resolutions and speaking at General Meetings; and
- requisitioning a General Meeting, in some cases proposing to change board membership.

Principle 5

Institutional investors should be willing to act collectively with other investors where appropriate

Guidance

At times collaboration with other investors may be the most effective manner in which to engage.

Collective engagement may be most appropriate at times of significant corporate or wider economic stress, or when the risks posed threaten to destroy significant value.

Institutional investors should disclose their policy on collective engagement, which should indicate their readiness to work with other investors through formal and informal groups when this is necessary to achieve their objectives and ensure companies are aware of concerns. The disclosure should also indicate the kinds of circumstances in which the institutional investor would consider participating in collective engagement.

Principle 6

Institutional investors should have a clear policy on voting and disclosure of voting activity

Guidance

Institutional investors should seek to vote all shares held. They should not automatically support the board.

If they have been unable to reach a satisfactory outcome through active dialogue then they should register an abstention or vote against the resolution. In both instances, it is good practice to inform the company in advance of their intention and the reasons why.

Institutional investors should disclose publicly voting records.

Institutional investors should disclose the use made, if any, of proxy voting or other voting advisory services. They should describe the scope of such services, identify the providers and disclose the extent to which they follow, rely upon or use recommendations made by such services.

Institutional investors should disclose their approach to stock lending and recalling lent stock.

Principle 7

Institutional investors should report periodically on their stewardship and voting activities

Guidance

Institutional investors should maintain a clear record of their stewardship activities.

Asset managers should regularly account to their clients or beneficiaries as to how they have discharged their responsibilities. Such reports will be likely to comprise qualitative as well as quantitative information. The particular information reported and the format used, should be a matter for agreement between agents and their principals.

Asset owners should report at least annually to those to whom they are accountable on their stewardship policy and its execution.

Transparency is an important feature of effective stewardship. Institutional investors should not, however, be expected to make disclosures that might be counterproductive. Confidentiality in specific situations may well be crucial to achieving a positive outcome.

Asset managers that sign up to this Code should obtain an independent opinion on their engagement and voting processes having regard to an international standard or a UK framework such as AAF 01/06.[1] The existence of such assurance reporting should be publicly disclosed. If requested, clients should be provided access to such assurance reports.

Note

1 Assurance reports on internal controls of service organisations made available to third parties: http://www.icaew. com/en/technical/audit-and-assurance/assurance/technical-release-aaf-01-06.

Appendix 9
LR 9 Annex 1 THE MODEL CODE (R)

This annex is referred to in LR 9.2 (Requirements with continuing application) and LR 15 (Investment entities).

Introduction

This code imposes restrictions on dealing in the *securities* of a *listed company* beyond those imposed by law. Its purpose is to ensure that *persons discharging managerial responsibilities* do not abuse, and do not place themselves under suspicion of abusing, *inside information* that they may be thought to have, especially in periods leading up to an announcement of the *company's* results.

Nothing in this code sanctions a breach of section 118 of the *Act* (Market abuse), the insider dealing provisions of the Criminal Justice Act or any other relevant legal or regulatory requirements.

Definitions

1   In this code the following definitions, in addition to those contained in the *listing rules*, apply unless the context requires otherwise:

    (a)   *close period* means:

        (i)   the period of 60 days immediately preceding a preliminary announcement of the *listed company's* annual results or, if shorter, the period from the end of the relevant financial year up to and including the time of announcement; or

        (ii) the period of 60 days immediately preceding the publication of its annual financial report or if shorter the period from the end of the relevant financial year up to and including the time of such publication; and

        (iii) if the *listed company* reports on a half-yearly basis the period from the end of the relevant financial period up to and including the time of such publication; and

        (iv) if the *listed company* reports on a quarterly basis the period of 30 days immediately preceding the announcement of the quarterly results or, if shorter, the period from the end of the relevant financial period up to and including the time of the announcement;

    (b)   *connected person* has the meaning given in section 96B (2) of the *Act* (Persons discharging managerial responsibilities and connected persons);

(c) dealing includes:

   (i) any acquisition or disposal of, or agreement to acquire or dispose of any of the *securities* of the *company*;

   (ii) entering into a contract (including a contract for difference) the purpose of which is to secure a profit or avoid a loss by reference to fluctuations in the price of any of the *securities* of the *company*;

   (iii) the grant, acceptance, acquisition, disposal, exercise or discharge of any option (whether for the call, or put or both) to acquire or dispose of any of the *securities* of the *company*;

   (iv) entering into, or terminating, assigning or novating any stock lending agreement in respect of the *securities* of the *company*;

   (v) using as security, or otherwise granting a charge, lien or other encumbrance over the *securities* of the *company*;

   (vi) any transaction, including a transfer for nil consideration, or the exercise of any power or discretion effecting a change of ownership of a beneficial interest in the *securities* of the *company*; or

   (vii) any other right or obligation, present or future, conditional or unconditional, to acquire or dispose of any *securities* of the *company*;

(d) [deleted]

(e) *prohibited period* means:

   (i) any *close period*; or

   (ii) any period when there exists any matter which constitutes *inside information* in relation to the *company*;

(f) *restricted person* means a *person discharging managerial responsibilities*; and

(g) *securities* of the *company* means any publicly traded or quoted *securities* of the *company* or any member of its *group* or any securities that are convertible into such *securities*.

Dealings not subject to the provisions of this code

2 The following dealings are not subject to the provisions of this code:

(a) undertakings or elections to take up entitlements under a rights issue or other offer (including an offer of *securities* of the *company* in lieu of a cash dividend);

(b) the take up of entitlements under a rights issue or other offer (including an offer of *securities* of the *company* in lieu of a cash dividend);

(c) allowing entitlements to lapse under a rights issue or other offer (including an offer of *securities* of the *company* in lieu of a cash dividend);

(d) the sale of sufficient entitlements nil-paid to take up the balance of the entitlements under a rights issue;

(e) undertakings to accept, or the acceptance of, a takeover offer;

(f) dealing where the beneficial interest in the relevant *security* of the *company* does not change;

(g) transactions conducted between a *person discharging managerial responsibilities* and their spouse, civil partner, child or step-child (within the meaning of section 96B(2) of the *Act*);

(h) transfers of *shares* arising out of the operation of an *employees' share scheme* into a savings scheme investing in *securities* of the *company* following:

    (i) exercise of an option under an approved SAYE option scheme; or

    (ii) release of *shares* from a HM Revenue and Customs approved share incentive plan ;

(i) with the exception of a disposal of *securities* of the *company* received by a *restricted person* as a participant, dealings in connection with the following *employees' share schemes*;

    (i) an HM Revenue and Customs approved SAYE option scheme or share incentive plan, under which participation is extended on similar terms to all or most employees of the participating *companies* in that scheme; or

    (ii) a scheme on similar terms to a HM Revenue and Customs approved SAYE option scheme or share incentive plan, under which participation is extended on similar terms to all or most employees of the participating *companies* in that scheme; or

(j) the cancellation or surrender of an option under an *employees' share scheme*;

(k) transfers of the *securities* of the *company* by an independent trustee of an *employees' share scheme* to a beneficiary who is not a restricted person;

(l) transfers of *securities* of the *company* already held by means of a matched sale and purchase into a saving scheme or into a pension scheme in which the *restricted person* is a participant or beneficiary;

(m) an investment by a *restricted person* in a scheme or arrangement where the assets of the scheme (other than a scheme investing only in the *securities* of the *company*) or arrangement are invested at the discretion of a third party;

(n) a dealing by a *restricted person* in the units of an authorised unit trust or in *shares* in an *open-ended investment company*; and

(o) bona fide gifts to a restricted person by a third party.

Dealing by restricted persons

3 A *restricted person* must not deal in any *securities* of the *company* without obtaining clearance to deal in advance in accordance with paragraph 4 of this code.

Clearance to deal

4   (a)   A *director* (other than the chairman or chief executive) or *company* secretary must not deal in any *securities* of the *company* without first notifying the chairman (or a *director* designated by the board for this purpose) and receiving clearance to deal from him.

    (b)   The chairman must not deal in any *securities* of the *company* without first notifying the chief executive and receiving clearance to deal from him or, if the chief executive is not present, without first notifying the senior independent *director*, or a committee of the board or other officer of the *company* nominated for that purpose by the chief executive, and receiving clearance to deal from that *director*, committee or officer.

    (c)   The chief executive must not deal in any *securities* of the *company* without first notifying the chairman and receiving clearance to deal from him or, if the chairman is not present, without first notifying the senior independent director, or a committee of the board or other officer of the *company* nominated for that purpose by the chairman, and receiving clearance to deal from that director, committee or officer.

    (d)   If the role of chairman and chief executive are combined, that person must not deal in any *securities* of the *company* without first notifying the board and receiving clearance to deal from the board.

    (e)   *Persons discharging managerial responsibilities* (who are not *directors*) must not deal in any *securities* of the *company* without first notifying the company secretary or a designated *director* and receiving clearance to deal from him.

5   A response to a request for clearance to deal must be given to the relevant *restricted person* within five *business days* of the request being made.

6   The *company* must maintain a record of the response to any dealing request made by a *restricted person* and of any clearance given. A copy of the response and clearance (if any) must be given to the restricted person concerned.

7   A *restricted person* who is given clearance to deal in accordance with paragraph 4 must deal as soon as possible and in any event within two *business days* of clearance being received.

Circumstances for refusal

8   A *restricted person* must not be given clearance to deal in any *securities* of the *company*:

    (a)   during a prohibited period; or

    (b)   on considerations of a short term nature. An investment with a maturity of one year or less will always be considered to be of a short term nature.

Dealings permitted during a *prohibited period*

Dealing in exceptional circumstances

9   A restricted person, who is not in possession of *inside information* in relation to the *company*, may be given clearance to deal if he is in severe financial difficulty or there are other exceptional circumstances. Clearance may be given for such a *person* to sell (but not purchase) *securities* of the *company* when he would otherwise be prohibited by this code from doing so. The determination of whether the *person* in question is in severe financial difficulty or whether there are other exceptional circumstances can only be made by the *director* designated for this purpose.

10   A *person* may be in severe financial difficulty if he has a pressing financial commitment that cannot be satisfied otherwise than by selling the relevant *securities* of the *company*. A liability of such a *person* to pay tax would not normally constitute severe financial difficulty unless the *person* has no other means of satisfying the liability. A circumstance will be considered exceptional if the *person* in question is required by a court order to transfer or sell the *securities* of the *company* or there is some other overriding legal requirement for him to do so.

11   The *FSA* should be consulted at an early stage regarding any application by a restricted person to deal in exceptional circumstances.

Awards of securities and options

12   The grant of options by the board of *directors* under an *employees' share scheme* to individuals who are not *restricted persons* may be permitted during a prohibited period if such grant could not reasonably be made at another time and failure to make the grant would be likely to indicate that the *company* was in a prohibited period.

13   The award by the *company* of *securities*, the grant of options and the grant of rights (or other interests) to acquire *securities* of the *company* to restricted persons is permitted in a prohibited period if:

    (a)   the award or grant is made under the terms of an *employees' share scheme* and the scheme was not introduced or amended during the relevant prohibited period; and

    (b)   either:

        (i)   the terms of such *employees' share scheme* set out the timing of the award or grant and such terms have either previously been approved by shareholders or summarised or described in a document sent to shareholders, or

        (ii)   the timing of the award or grant is in accordance with the timing of previous awards or grants under the scheme; and

    (c)   the terms of the *employees' share scheme* set out the amount or value of the award or grant or the basis on which the amount or value of the award or grant is calculated and do not allow the exercise of discretion; and

(d)   the failure to make the award or grant would be likely to indicate that the *company* is in a prohibited period.

Exercise of options

14   Where a *company* has been in an exceptionally long prohibited period or the *company* has had a number of consecutive prohibited periods, clearance may be given to allow the exercise of an option or right under an *employees' share scheme*, or the conversion of a convertible security, where the final date for the exercise of such option or right, or conversion of such security, falls during a prohibited period and the restricted person could not reasonably have been expected to exercise it at a time when he was free to deal.

15   Where the exercise or conversion is permitted pursuant to paragraph 14, clearance may not be given for the sale of the *securities* of the *company* acquired pursuant to such exercise or conversion including the sale of sufficient *securities* of the *company* to fund the costs of the exercise or conversion and/or any tax liability arising from the exercise or conversion unless a binding undertaking to do so was entered into when the *company* was not in a prohibited period.

Qualification shares

16   Clearance may be given to allow a *director* to acquire qualification *shares* where, under the *company's constitution*, the final date for acquiring such *shares* falls during a prohibited period and the *director* could not reasonably have been expected to acquire those shares at another time.

Saving schemes

17   A restricted person may enter into a scheme under which only the *securities* of the *company* are purchased pursuant to a regular standing order or direct debit or by regular deduction from the *person's* salary, or where such *securities* are acquired by way of a standing election to re-invest dividends or other distributions received, or are acquired as part payment of the *person's* remuneration without regard to the provisions of this code, if the following provisions are complied with:

(a)   the restricted person does not enter into the scheme during a prohibited period, unless the scheme involves the part payment of remuneration in the form of *securities* of the *company* and is entered into upon the commencement of the *person's* employment or in the case of a non-executive *director* his appointment to the board;

(b)   the *restricted person* does not carry out the purchase of the *securities* of the *company* under the scheme during a prohibited period, unless the restricted person entered into the scheme at a time when the *company* was not in a prohibited period and that person is irrevocably bound under the terms of the scheme to carry out a purchase of *securities* of the *company* (which may include the first purchase under the scheme) at a fixed point in time which falls *in a prohibited period*;

(c)   the restricted person does not cancel or vary the terms of his participation, or carry out sales of *securities* of the *company* within the scheme during a prohibited period; and

(d)   before entering into the scheme, cancelling the scheme or varying the terms of his participation or carrying out sales of the *securities* of the *company* within the scheme, the *restricted person* obtains clearance in accordance with paragraph 4.

Acting as a trustee

18   Where a restricted person is acting as a trustee, dealing in the *securities* of the *company* by that trust is permitted during a prohibited period where:

(a)   the restricted person is not a beneficiary of the trust; and

(b)   the decision to deal is taken by the other trustees or by investment managers on behalf of the trustees independently of the restricted person.

19   The other trustees or investment managers acting on behalf of the trustees can be assumed to have acted independently where the decision to deal:

(a)   was taken without consultation with, or other involvement of, the restricted person; or

(b)   as delegated to a committee of which the restricted person is not a member.

Dealing by connected persons and investment managers

20   A *person discharging managerial responsibilities* must take reasonable steps to prevent any dealings by or on behalf of any *connected person* of his in any *securities* of the *company* on considerations of a short term nature.

21   A *person discharging managerial responsibilities* must seek to prohibit any dealings in the *securities* of the *company* during a *close period*:

(a)   by or on behalf of any *connected person* of his; or

(b)   by an investment manager on his behalf or on behalf of any *person* connected with him where either he or any *person* connected has funds under management with that investment fund manager, whether or not discretionary (save as provided by paragraphs 17 and 18).

22   A *person discharging managerial responsibilities* must advise all of his *connected person*s and investment managers acting on his behalf:

(a)   of the name of the *listed company* within which he is a *person discharging managerial responsibilities*;

(b) of the *close period*s during which they cannot deal in the *securities* of the *company*; and

(c) that they must advise the *listed company* immediately after they have dealt in *securities* of the *company*.

Dealing under a trading plan

23 A restricted person may deal in *securities* of a *company* pursuant to a *trading plan* if clearance has first been given in accordance with paragraph 4 of this Code to the person entering into the plan and to any amendment to the plan. A restricted person must not cancel a *trading plan* unless clearance has first been given in accordance with paragraph 4 of this Code for its cancellation.

24 A restricted person must not enter into a *trading plan* or amend a *trading plan* during a *prohibited period* and clearance under paragraph 4 of this Code must not be given during a *prohibited period* to the entering into, or amendment of, a *trading plan*. Clearance under paragraph 4 of this Code may be given during a *prohibited period* to the cancellation of a *trading plan* but only in the exceptional circumstances referred to in paragraphs 9 and 10 of this Code.

25 A restricted person may deal in *securities* of a *company* during a *prohibited period* pursuant to a *trading plan* if:

(a) the *trading plan* was entered into before the *prohibited period*;

(b) clearance under paragraph 4 of this Code has been given to the person entering into the *trading plan* and to any amendment to the *trading plan* before the *prohibited period*; and

(c) the *trading plan* does not permit the restricted person to exercise any influence or discretion over how, when, or whether to effect dealings.

26 Where a transaction occurs in accordance with a *trading plan*, the *restricted person* must notify the *issuer* at the same time as he makes the notification required by DTR 3.1.2 R of:

(a) the fact that the transaction occurred in accordance with a *trading plan*; and

(b) the date on which the relevant *trading plan* was entered into.

© Financial Services Authority 2013.

Appendix 10

Data protection principles

1   Personal data must be fairly and lawfully processed.

2   Personal data shall be obtained only for specified and limited purposes, and shall not be further processed in any manner incompatible with those purposes.

3   The amount of personal data held shall be adequate, relevant and not excessive in relation to the purposes for which it is held.

4   Personal data must be accurate.

5   Personal data shall not be kept longer than necessary.

6   Personal data shall be processed in accordance with individuals' rights.

7   Personal data shall be secured against unauthorised or unlawful processing, accidental loss, destruction or damage.

8   Personal data must not be transferred to a country outside the European Economic Area without adequate protection.

Appendix 11

Schedule of recommended retention periods

Note: recommendations are based upon statutory requirements and principles of 'best' practice for commercial and damage limitation reasons.

Type of document	Statutory minimum retention period	Recommended period of retention
Incorporation documents		
Certificate of Incorporation and certificates on change of name	N/A	Permanently
Certificate to commence business (public company)	N/A	Permanently
Memorandum and Articles of Association (originals and updated copies)	Permanently	Permanently
Printed copy of resolutions submitted to Companies House	Permanently	Permanently
Statutory returns, records and registers		
Annual return (copy)	N/A	At least 3 years (original at Companies House)
Return of allotments (copy)	N/A	At least 3 years (original at Companies House)
Directors' service contracts	1 year after cessation (and be available for inspection during that time (CA 2006, 228(3))	6 years after cessation
Register of directors and secretaries (original)	Permanently	Permanently
Register of interests in voting shares	Permanently	Permanently
Register of charges	Permanently	Permanently

Type of document	Statutory minimum retention period	Recommended period of retention
Register of documents sealed (if applicable)	N/A	Permanently
Minutes of meetings		
Directors' meetings	10 years after the date of the meeting (CA 2006, s 248)	Life of company
General meetings	10 years after the date of the meeting (CA 2006, s 355(1)(b))	Life of company
Resolutions of members (passed otherwise than at a general meeting)	10 years after the date of the resolution (CA 2006, s 355(1)(a))	Life of company
Share registration documents		
Register of members	Permanently	Permanently
Register of debenture and loan stock holders	N/A	Permanently/7 years after redemption of stock
Letters and forms applying for shares, debentures, etc	N/A	12 years from. issue, with a permanent microfilmed record
Renounceable letters of allotment and acceptances	N/A	12 years from renunciation, with a permanent microfilmed record
Renounced share certificates	N/A	As above
Contracts for purchase of own shares by company	10 years from date of purchase	10 years from date of purchase
Share and stock transfer forms and letters of request	N/A	20 years after date of transfer, with permanent microfilmed record
Requests for designating or redesignating accounts	N/A	20 years after request, with permanent microfilmed record

Type of document	Statutory minimum retention period	Recommended period of retention
Cancelled share/stock certificate	N/A	1 year from date of cancellation
Stop notices and other court orders	N/A	20 years from cessation of order
Letters of indemnity for lost certificates	N/A	Permanently
Powers of attorney	N/A	12 years after ceasing to be valid
Dividend and interest payment lists	3 years private company, 6 years public company after audit	3–6 years after audit of the dividend payment
Paid dividend and interest warrants	3 years private company, 6 years public company after audit	6 years after date of payment
Unpaid dividend records	N/A	12 years after dividend declared
Dividend and interest mandate forms	N/A	6 years from when the instruction ceased to be valid
Notification of address change by member	N/A	2 years after notification
Trust deed securing issue of debentures or loan stock	N/A stock	12 years after stock redeemed
Accounting and tax records		
Accounting records (as required by CA 2006, s388(4))		
• public company	6 years	10 years
• limited company	3 years	10 years
Annual report and accounts (signed) Annual report and accounts (unsigned)	N/A	Permanently (keep sufficient copies to meet requests)
Interim report and accounts	N/A	Permanently (as above)

Type of document	Statutory minimum retention period	Recommended period of retention
Budgets, forecasts and periodic internal financial reports	N/A	6 years
Taxation records and tax returns	Inspection possible up to 6 years after tax/accounting period	Permanently
VAT records and Customs & Excise returns	Inspection may be conducted up to 6 years after period	Permanently
PAYE records	3 years after end of tax year (6 years after period of expiry of contract for payroll records)	Permanently
Expense accounts	N/A	6 years
Bank records		
Cheques, bills of exchange and other negotiable instruments	6 years public company, 3 years private company	3/6 years
Paying-in counterfoils	6 years public company, 3 years private company	3/6 years
Statements from and instructions to bank	6 years public company, 3 years private company	3/6 years
Charity donation documents		
Deeds of Covenant	6 years after last payment	12 years after last payment
Documents supporting entries in accounts for donations	3 or 6 years	6 years
Contracts		
Contracts executed under seal	N/A	12 years after expiry

Type of document	Statutory minimum retention period	Recommended period of retention
Contracts with customers, suppliers, agents or others	N/A	6 years after expiry or contract completion
Rental and hire purchase agreements	N/A	6 years after expiry
Licensing agreements	N/A	6 years after expiry
Contracts relating to building work and maintenance	N/A	15 years after completion/performance
Employee records		
Job applications and interview records (for unsuccessful candidates)	N/A	6 months to 1 year from notification
Contracts of employment or changes to terms	N/A	6 years after employment ceases for a public company and 3 years for private company
Personnel records	N/A	6 years after employment ceases, with permanent microfilm record
Senior executive records	N/A	Permanently
Training records	N/A	6 years after employment ceases
Employment agreements	N/A	Permanently
Payroll and wage records (including details on overtime, bonuses and expenses)	6 years	12 years
Salary records	6 years	6 years
Time cards and piecework records	N/A	2 years after audit
Details of benefits in kind	6 years	12 years

Type of document	Statutory minimum retention period	Recommended period of retention
Income tax records (p 4 5, p 60, p 58, p 48, etc)	3 years after end of tax year	12 years
Annual return of taxable pay and tax paid	3 years after end of tax year	12 years
Labour agreements	N/A	10 years after ceasing to be effective
Works council minutes	N/A	Permanently
Consents to the processing of personal and sensitive data	6 years after processing ceases	6 years after processing ceases
CRB checks and disclosures of criminal records	Delete on completion of recruitment process unless relevant to ongoing employment. Delete when conviction spent unless in an excluded profession	Delete on completion of recruitment process unless relevant to ongoing employment. Delete when conviction spent unless in an excluded profession
Immigration checks	2 years after employment ceases	2 years after employment ceases
Employee records from closed units	6 years	12 years
Health and safety		
Record of consultations with safety representative and	50 years	Permanently
Health and safety policy documents (old and revised copies)	Implied permanently by Health & Safety at Work etc. Act 1974 s 2(3)	Permanently
Assessment of risks under health and safety regulations (including routine assessment, monitoring and maintenance records for aspects in workplace such as air quality, levels of pollution, noise level, use of hazardous substances, etc.)	Until revised (Management of Health & Safety at Work Regulations 1999	Permanently (old and current copies)

Type of document	Statutory minimum retention period	Recommended period of retention
Accident report book and relevant records/ correspondence	3 years from date of last entry (RIDDOR 1995)	Permanently
Medical records (generally):	N/A	12 years
• Radiation accident assessment	50 years	Permanently
• Radiation dosage summary	2 years from the end of the calendar year	Permanently
• Under Control of Lead at Work Regulations 1998 (replaced 1980 regulations)	40 years from date of last entry	Permanently
• Under Control of Asbestos at Work Regulations 1987	40 years	Permanently
• Under Control of Substances Hazardous to Health Regulations 1994 ('COSHH' Regulations)	40 years	Permanently
Insurance		
Public liability policies	N/A	Permanently
Product liability policies	N/A	Permanently
Employers' liability policies	40 years	Permanently
Sundry insurance policies and insurance schedules	N/A	Until claims under policy are barred or 3 years after policy lapses, whichever is longer
Group health policies	N/A	12 years after final cessation of benefit
Group personal accident policies	N/A	12 years after final cessation of benefit
Claims correspondence	N/A	3 years after settlement

Type of document	Statutory minimum retention period	Recommended period of retention
Intellectual property records		
Certificates of registration of trade/service marks (current and lapsed)	N/A	Permanently or 6 years after cessation of registration
Documents evidencing assignment of trade/service marks	N/A	6 years after cessation of registration
Intellectual property agreements and licences	N/A	6 years after expiry
Material with copyright protection:		
• Literary, dramatic and musical works	N/A	Life plus 50 years
• Artistic works, recordings, films and photos	N/A	50 years broadcasts
Pension scheme documents (unapproved schemes)		
Trust deeds and scheme rules	N/A	Permanently for life of scheme
Trustees' minute books	N/A	Permanently for life of scheme
Record of pensioners	N/A	12 years after cessation of benefit
Money purchase details	N/A	6 years after transfer or value taken
Pension scheme investment policies	N/A	12 years after cessation of benefit payable
Pension scheme documents (HMRC approved and statutory pension schemes)		
Pension fund accounts and supporting documents	6 years from date accounts signed	Permanently
Actuarial valuation reports	6 years from date report signed	Permanently
HMRC approvals	N/A	Permanently

Type of document	Statutory minimum retention period	Recommended period of retention
Property documents		
Title deeds for property	N/A	Permanently or until sold or transferred
Leases	N/A	15 years after lease and liabilities under the lease have terminated
Licences (signed)	N/A	15 years after surrender, expiry or termination
Sub-letting agreements (signed	N/A	12 years after surrender, expiry or termination

Appendix 12
FRC GUIDANCE ON AUDIT COMMITTEES
September 2012

1.   Introduction

1.1   This guidance is designed to assist company boards in making suitable arrangements for their audit committees, and to assist directors serving on audit
committees in carrying out their role. While boards are not required to follow
this guidance, it is intended to assist them when implementing the relevant
provisions of the UK Corporate Governance Code. Companies with a Premium
listing of equity shares in the UK are required under the Listing Rules either to
comply with the provisions of the Code or to explain to shareholders why they
have not done so.

1.2   Best practice requires that every board should consider in detail what arrangements for its audit committee are best suited for its particular circumstances.
Audit committee arrangements need to be proportionate to the task, and will
vary according to the size, complexity and risk profile of the company.

1.3   While all directors have a duty to act in the interests of the company the audit
committee has a particular role, acting independently from the executive, to
ensure that the interests of shareholders are properly protected in relation to
financial reporting and internal control.

1.4   Nothing in the guidance should be interpreted as a departure from the principle
of the unitary board. All directors remain equally responsible for the company's
affairs as a matter of law. The audit committee, like other committees to which
particular responsibilities are delegated (such as the remuneration committee),
remains a committee of the board. Any disagreement within the board,
including disagreement between the audit committee's members and the rest of
the board, should be resolved at board level.

1.5   The Code provides that a separate section of the annual report should describe
the work of the committee. This deliberately puts the spotlight on the audit
committee and gives it an authority that it might otherwise lack. This is not
incompatible with the principle of the unitary board.

1.6   The guidance contains recommendations about the conduct of the audit
committee's relationship with the board, with the executive management and
with internal and external auditors. However, the most important features of
this relationship cannot be drafted as guidance or put into a code of practice:
a frank, open working relationship and a high level of mutual respect are
essential, particularly between the audit committee chairman and the board
chairman, the chief executive and the finance director. The audit committee
must be prepared to take a robust stand, and all parties must be prepared to

make information freely available to the audit committee, to listen to their views and to talk through the issues openly.

1.7 In particular, the management is under an obligation to ensure the audit committee is kept properly informed, and should take the initiative in supplying information rather than waiting to be asked. The board should make it clear to all directors and staff that they must cooperate with the audit committee and provide it with any information it requires. In addition, executive board members will have regard to their duty to provide all directors, including those on the audit committee, with all the information they need to discharge their responsibilities as directors of the company.

1.8 Many of the core functions of audit committees set out in this guidance are expressed in terms of 'oversight', 'assessment' and 'review' of a particular function. It is not the duty of audit committees to carry out functions that properly belong to others, such as the company's management in the preparation of the financial statements or the auditors in the planning or conducting of audits. To do so could undermine the responsibility of management and auditors. Audit committees should, for example, satisfy themselves that there is a proper system and allocation of responsibilities for the day-to-day monitoring of financial controls but they should not seek to do the monitoring themselves.

1.9 However, the high-level oversight function may lead to detailed work. The audit committee must intervene if there are signs that something may be seriously amiss. For example, if the audit committee is uneasy about the explanations of management and auditors about a particular financial reporting policy decision, there may be no alternative but to grapple with the detail and perhaps to seek independent advice.

1.10 Under this guidance, audit committees have wide-ranging, time-consuming and sometimes intensive work to do. Companies need to make the necessary resources available. This includes suitable payment for the members of audit committees themselves. They – and particularly the audit committee chairman – bear a significant responsibility and they need to commit a significant extra amount of time to the job. Companies also need to make provision for induction and training for new audit committee members and continuing training as may be required.

1.11 For groups, it will usually be necessary for the audit committee of the parent company to review issues that relate to particular subsidiaries or activities carried on by the group. Consequently, the board of a UK-listed parent company with a Premium listing of equity shares in the UK should ensure that there is adequate cooperation within the group (and with internal and external auditors of individual companies within the group) to enable the parent company audit committee to discharge its responsibilities effectively.

2 Establishment and effectiveness of the audit committee

Establishment and terms of reference

2.1 The board should establish an audit committee of at least three, or in the case of smaller companies[1] two, members.

2.2 The main role and responsibilities of the audit committee should be set out in written terms of reference and should include:

- to monitor the integrity of the financial statements of the company and any formal announcements relating to the company's financial performance, reviewing significant financial reporting judgements contained in them;

- to review the company's internal financial controls and, unless expressly addressed by a separate board risk committee composed of independent directors or by the board itself;

- the company's internal control and risk management systems;

- to monitor and review the effectiveness of the company's internal audit function;

- to make recommendations to the board, for it to put to the shareholders for their approval in general meeting, in relation to the appointment of the external auditor and to approve the remuneration and terms of engagement of the external auditor;

- to review and monitor the external auditor's independence and objectivity and the effectiveness of the audit process, taking into consideration relevant UK professional and regulatory requirements;

- to develop and implement policy on the engagement of the external auditor to supply non-audit services, taking into account relevant ethical guidance regarding the provision of non-audit services by the external audit firm; and to report to the board, identifying any matters in respect of which it considers that action or improvement is needed, and making recommendations as to the steps to be taken; and

- to report to the board on how it has discharged its responsibilities.

Membership and appointment

2.3 The board should establish an audit committee of at least three, or in the case of smaller companies two, independent non-executive directors. In smaller companies the company chairman may be a member of, but not chair, the committee in addition to the independent non-executive directors, provided he or she was considered independent on appointment as chairman. The board should satisfy itself that at least one member of the audit committee has recent and relevant financial experience.

2.4 Appointments to the audit committee should be made by the board on the recommendation of the nomination committee, in consultation with the audit committee chairman.

2.5 Appointments should be for a period of up to three years, extendable by no more than two additional three-year periods, so long as members continue to be independent.

Meetings of the audit committee

2.6 It is for the audit committee chairman, in consultation with the company secretary, to decide the frequency and timing of its meetings. There should be as many meetings as the audit committee's role and responsibilities require. It is recommended there should be not fewer than three meetings during the year, held to coincide with key dates within the financial reporting and audit cycle.[2] However, most audit committee chairmen will wish to call more frequent meetings.

2.7 No one other than the audit committee's chairman and members is entitled to be present at a meeting of the audit committee. It is for the audit committee to decide if non-members should attend for a particular meeting or a particular agenda item. It is to be expected that the external audit lead partner will be invited regularly to attend meetings as well as the finance director. Others may be invited to attend.

2.8 Sufficient time should be allowed to enable the audit committee to undertake as full a discussion as may be required. A sufficient interval should be allowed between audit committee meetings and main board meetings to allow any work arising from the audit committee meeting to be carried out and reported to the board as appropriate.

2.9 The audit committee should, at least annually, meet the external and internal auditors, without management, to discuss matters relating to its remit and any issues arising from the audit.

2.10 Formal meetings of the audit committee are the heart of its work. However, they will rarely be sufficient. It is expected that the audit committee chairman, and to a lesser extent the other members, will wish to keep in touch on a continuing basis with the key people involved in the company's governance, including the board chairman, the chief executive, the finance director, the external audit lead partner and the head of internal audit.

Resources

2.11 The audit committee should be provided with sufficient resources to undertake its duties.

2.12 The audit committee should have access to the services of the company secretariat on all audit committee matters including: assisting the chairman in planning the audit committee's work, drawing up meeting agendas, maintenance of minutes, drafting of material about its activities for the annual report, collection and distribution of information and provision of any necessary practical support.

2.13 The company secretary should ensure that the audit committee receives information and papers in a timely manner to enable full and proper consideration to be given to the issues.

2.14   The board should make funds available to the audit committee to enable it to take independent legal, accounting or other advice when the audit committee reasonably believes it necessary to do so.

Remuneration

2.15   In addition to the remuneration paid to all non-executive directors, each company should consider the further remuneration that should be paid to members of the audit committee to recompense them for the additional responsibilities of membership. Consideration should be given to the time members are required to give to audit committee business, the skills they bring to bear and the onerous duties they take on, as well as the value of their work to the company. The level of remuneration paid to the members of the audit committee should take into account the level of fees paid to other members of the board. The chairman's responsibilities and time demands will generally be heavier than the other members of the audit committee and this should be reflected in his or her remuneration.

Skills, experience and training

2.16   It is desirable that the committee member whom the board considers to have recent and relevant financial experience should have a professional qualification from one of the professional accountancy bodies. The need for a degree of financial literacy among the other members will vary according to the nature of the company, but experience of corporate financial matters will normally be required. The availability of appropriate financial expertise will be particularly important where the company's activities involve specialised financial activities.

2.17   The company should provide an induction programme for new audit committee members. This should cover the role of the audit committee, including its terms of reference and expected time commitment by members; and an overview of the company's business model and strategy, identifying the main business and financial dynamics and risks. It could also include meeting some of the company staff.

2.18   Training should also be provided to members of the audit committee on an ongoing and timely basis and should include an understanding of the principles of and developments in financial reporting and related company law. In appropriate cases, it may also include, for example, understanding financial statements, applicable accounting standards and recommended practice; the regulatory framework for the company's business; the role of internal and external auditing and risk management.

2.19   The induction programme and ongoing training may take various forms, including attendance at formal courses and conferences, internal company talks and seminars, and briefings by external advisers.

3   Relationship with the Board

3.1   The role of the audit committee is for the board to decide and to the extent that the audit committee undertakes tasks on behalf of the board, the results should be reported to, and considered by, the board. In doing so it should identify any matters in respect of which it considers that action or improvement is needed, and make recommendations as to the steps to be taken.

3.2   The terms of reference should be tailored to the particular circumstances of the company.

3.3   The audit committee should review annually its terms of reference and its own effectiveness and recommend any necessary changes to the board. The board should also review the audit committee's effectiveness annually.

3.4   The audit committee should report to the board on how it has discharged its responsibilities, including:

- The significant issues that it considered in relation to the financial statements and how these issues were addressed;

- Its assessment of the effectiveness of the external audit process and its recommendation on the appointment or reappointment of the external auditor; and

- Any other issues on which the board has requested the committee's opinion.

3.5   Where there is disagreement between the audit committee and the board, adequate time should be made available for discussion of the issue with a view to resolving the disagreement. Where any such disagreements cannot be resolved, the audit committee should have the right to report the issue to the shareholders as part of the report on its activities in the annual report.

4   Role and responsibilities

Financial reporting

4.1   The audit committee should review, and report to the board on, the significant financial reporting issues and judgements made in connection with the preparation of the company's financial statements (having regard to matters communicated to it by the auditor[3]), interim reports, preliminary announcements and related formal statements.

4.2   It is management's, not the audit committee's, responsibility to prepare complete and accurate financial statements and disclosures in accordance with financial reporting standards and applicable rules and regulations. However the audit committee should consider significant accounting policies, any changes to them and any significant estimates and judgements. The management should inform the audit committee of the methods used to account for significant or unusual transactions where the accounting treatment is open to different approaches. Taking into account the external auditor's view, the audit committee should consider whether the company has adopted appropriate accounting policies and, where necessary, made appropriate estimates and judgements. The audit committee should review the clarity and completeness of disclosures in the financial statements and consider whether the disclosures made are set properly in context.

4.3 Where, following its review, the audit committee is not satisfied with any aspect of the proposed financial reporting by the company, it shall report its views to the board.

4.4 The audit committee should review related information presented with the financial statements, including the business review, and corporate governance statements relating to the audit and to risk management. Similarly, where board approval is required for other statements containing financial information (for example, summary financial statements, significant financial returns to regulators and release of price sensitive information), whenever practicable the audit committee should review such statements first (without being inconsistent with any requirement for prompt reporting under the Listing Rules).

Narrative Reporting

4.5 Where requested by the board, the audit committee should review the content of the annual report and accounts and advise the board on whether, taken as a whole, it is fair, balanced and understandable and provides the information necessary for shareholders to assess the company's performance, business model and strategy.

4.6 This report will inform the board's statement on these matters required under Section C.1.1 of the UK Corporate Governance Code.[4] In order for the board to make that statement, any review undertaken by the committee would need to assess whether the narrative in the front of the report was consistent with the accounting information in the back, so as to ensure that there were no surprises hidden in the accounts.

Whistleblowing

4.7 The audit committee should review arrangements by which staff of the company may, in confidence, raise concerns about possible improprieties in matters of financial reporting or other matters. The audit committee's objective should be to ensure that arrangements are in place for the proportionate and independent investigation of such matters and for appropriate follow-up action.

Internal controls and risk management systems

4.8 The audit committee should review the company's internal financial controls (that is, the systems established to identify, assess, manage and monitor financial risks); and, unless expressly addressed by a separate board risk committee comprised of independent directors or by the board itself, the company's internal control and risk management systems.[5]

4.9 The company's management is responsible for the identification, assessment, management and monitoring of risk, for developing, operating and monitoring the system of internal control and for providing assurance to the board that it has done so. Except where the board or a risk committee is expressly responsible for reviewing the effectiveness of the internal control and risk management systems, the audit committee should receive reports from management on the effectiveness of the systems they have established and the conclusions of any testing carried out by internal and external auditors.

4.10 Except to the extent that this is expressly dealt with by the board or risk committee, the audit committee should review and approve the statements included in the annual report in relation to internal control and the management of risk.

The internal audit process

4.11 The audit committee should monitor and review the effectiveness of the company's internal audit function. Where there is no internal audit function, the audit committee should consider annually whether there is a need for an internal audit function and make a recommendation to the board, and the reasons for the absence of such a function should be explained in the relevant section of the annual report.

4.12 The need for an internal audit function will vary depending on company specific factors including the scale, diversity and complexity of the company's activities and the number of employees, as well as cost/benefit considerations. Senior management and the board may desire objective assurance and advice on risk and control. An adequately resourced internal audit function (or its equivalent where, for example, a third party is contracted to perform some or all of the work concerned) may provide such assurance and advice. There may be other functions within the company that also provide assurance and advice covering specialist areas such as health and safety, regulatory and legal compliance and environmental issues.

4.13 When undertaking its assessment of the need for an internal audit function, the audit committee should also consider whether there are any trends or current factors relevant to the company's activities, markets or other aspects of its external environment, that have increased, or are expected to increase, the risks faced by the company. Such an increase in risk may also arise from internal factors such as organisational restructuring or from changes in reporting processes or underlying information systems. Other matters to be taken into account may include adverse trends evident from the monitoring of internal control systems or an increased incidence of unexpected occurrences.

4.14 In the absence of an internal audit function, management needs to apply other monitoring processes in order to assure itself, the audit committee and the board that the system of internal control is functioning as intended. In these circumstances, the audit committee will need to assess whether such processes provide sufficient and objective assurance.

4.15 If the external auditor is being considered to undertake aspects of the internal audit function, the audit committee should consider the effect this may have on the effectiveness of the company's overall arrangements for internal control and investor perceptions in this regard. Investor perceptions are likely to be influenced by:

- the rationale set out in the annual report for the work being performed by the external auditor;

- the nature and extent of the work performed by the external auditor;

- how the independence and objectivity of the external auditor and internal audit function have been safeguarded; and

- whether, in the absence of internal audit work, the audit committee is wholly reliant on the views of the external auditor about the effectiveness of its system of controls relating to core activities and significant locations.

4.16   The audit committee should review and approve the internal audit function's remit, having regard to the complementary roles of the internal and external audit functions. The audit committee should ensure that the function has the necessary resources and access to information to enable it to fulfil its mandate, and is equipped to perform in accordance with appropriate professional standards for internal auditors.[6]

4.17   The audit committee should approve the appointment or termination of appointment of the head of internal audit.

4.18   In its review of the work of the internal audit function, the audit committee should:

- ensure that the internal auditor has direct access to the board chairman and to the audit committee, and is accountable to the audit committee;

- review and assess the annual internal audit work plan;

- receive a report on the results of the internal auditors' work on a periodic basis;

- review and monitor management's responsiveness to the internal auditor's findings and recommendations;

- meet with the head of internal audit at least once a year without the presence of management; and

- monitor and assess the role and effectiveness of the internal audit function in the overall context of the company's risk management system.

The external audit process

4.19   The audit committee is the body responsible for overseeing the company's relations with the external auditor.

Appointment and tendering

4.20   The audit committee should have primary responsibility for making a recommendation on the appointment, reappointment and removal of the external auditors. If the board does not accept the audit committee's recommendation, it should include in the annual report, and in any papers recommending appointment or reappointment, a statement from the audit committee explaining its recommendation and should set out reasons why the board has taken a different position.

4.21   The audit committee's recommendation to the board should be based on the assessments referred to below. If the audit committee recommends considering the selection of possible new appointees as external auditors, it should oversee the selection process, and ensure that all tendering firms have such access as is necessary to information and individuals during the duration of the tendering process.

4.22   The audit committee should annually assess, and report to the board on, the qualification, expertise and resources, and independence of the external auditors and the effectiveness of the audit process, with a recommendation on whether to propose to the shareholders that the external auditor be reappointed. The assessment should cover all aspects of the audit service provided by the audit firm, and include obtaining a report on the audit firm's own internal quality control procedures and consideration of audit firms' annual transparency reports, where available. It might also be appropriate for the audit committee to consider whether there might be any benefit in using firms from more than one audit network.[7]

4.23   FTSE 350 companies should put the audit services contract out to tender at least once every ten years, to enable the audit committee to compare the quality and effectiveness of the services provided by the incumbent auditor with those of other audit firms. So that there is time to undertake an effective tendering process, and to allow shareholders to provide input to the process should they wish, the company should announce its intention in advance of the commencement of the tendering process.

4.24   If the external auditor resigns, the audit committee should investigate the issues giving rise to such resignation and consider whether any action is required.

4.25   The audit committee should evaluate the risks to the quality and effectiveness of the financial reporting process, and should consider the need to include the risk of the withdrawal of their auditor from the market in that evaluation.

4.26   The audit committee section of the annual report should include an explanation of how the committee has assessed the effectiveness of the external audit process and of the approach taken to the appointment or reappointment of the external auditor, in order that shareholders can understand why it recommended either to reappoint or change the auditors. It should also include information on the length of tenure of the current audit firm, when a tender was last conducted, and any contractual obligations that acted to restrict the audit committee's choice of external auditors.

Terms and remuneration

4.27   The audit committee should approve the terms of engagement and the remuneration to be paid to the external auditor in respect of audit services provided.

4.28   The audit committee should review and agree the engagement letter issued by the external auditor at the start of each audit, ensuring that it has been updated to reflect changes in circumstances arising since the previous year. The scope of the external audit should be reviewed by the audit committee with the auditor. If the audit committee is not satisfied as to its adequacy it should arrange for additional work to be undertaken.

4.29   The audit committee should satisfy itself that the level of fee payable in respect of the audit services provided is appropriate and that an effective, high quality, audit can be conducted for such a fee.

Annual audit cycle

4.30   At the start of each annual audit cycle, the audit committee should ensure that appropriate plans are in place for the audit.

4.31   The audit committee should consider whether the auditor's overall work plan, including planned levels of materiality, and proposed resources to execute the audit plan appears consistent with the scope of the audit engagement, having regard also to the seniority, expertise and experience of the audit team.

4.32   The audit committee should review, with the external auditors, the findings of their work. In the course of its review, the audit committee should:

- discuss with the external auditor major issues that arose during the course of the audit and have subsequently been resolved and those issues that have been left unresolved;

- review key accounting and audit judgements; and

- review levels of errors identified during the audit, obtaining explanations from management and, where necessary, the external auditors as to why certain errors might remain unadjusted.

4.33   The audit committee should also review the audit representation letters before signature and give particular consideration to matters where representation has been requested that relate to nonstandard issues.[8] The audit committee should consider whether the information provided is complete and appropriate based on its own knowledge.

4.34   As part of the ongoing monitoring process, the audit committee should review the management letter (or equivalent). The audit committee should review and monitor management's responsiveness to the external auditor's findings and recommendations.

4.35   At the end of the annual audit cycle, the audit committee should assess the effectiveness of the audit process. In the course of doing so, the audit committee should:

- review whether the auditor has met the agreed audit plan and understand the reasons for any changes, including changes in perceived audit risks and the work undertaken by the external auditors to address those risks;

- consider the robustness and perceptiveness of the auditors in their handling of the key accounting and audit judgements identified and in responding to questions from the audit committee, and in their commentary where appropriate on the systems of internal control;

- obtain feedback about the conduct of the audit from key people involved, for example the finance director and the head of internal audit;

- review and monitor the content of the external auditor's management letter, in order to assess whether it is based on a good understanding of the company's business and establish whether recommendations have been acted upon and, if not, the reasons why they have not been acted upon; and

- report to the board on the effectiveness of the external audit process.

Independence, including the provision of non-audit services

4.36 The audit committee should assess the independence and objectivity of the external auditor annually, taking into consideration relevant UK law, regulation and professional requirements. This assessment should involve a consideration of all relationships between the company and the audit firm (including the provision of non-audit services) and any safeguards established by the external auditor. The audit committee should consider whether, taken as a whole and having regard to the views, as appropriate, of the external auditor, management and internal audit, those relationships appear to impair the auditor's independence and objectivity.

4.37 The audit committee should seek reassurance that the auditors and their staff have no financial, business, employment or family and other personal relationship with the company which could adversely affect the auditor's independence and objectivity, taking account of relevant Ethical Standards for Auditors. The audit committee should seek from the audit firm, on an annual basis, information about policies and processes for maintaining independence and monitoring compliance with relevant requirements, including current requirements regarding the rotation of audit partners and staff.

4.38 The audit committee should develop and recommend to the board the company's policy in relation to the provision of non-audit services by the auditor, and keep the policy under review. The audit committee's objective should be to ensure that the provision of such services does not impair the external auditor's independence or objectivity. In this context, the audit committee should consider:

- whether the skills and experience of the audit firm make it the most suitable supplier of the non-audit service;

- whether there are safeguards in place to eliminate or reduce to an acceptable level any threat to objectivity and independence in the conduct of the audit resulting from the provision of such services by the external auditor;

- the nature of the non-audit services;

- the fees incurred, or to be incurred, for non-audit services both for individual services and in aggregate, relative to the audit fee; and

- the criteria which govern the compensation of the individuals performing the audit.

4.39 The audit committee should set and apply a formal policy specifying the types of non-audit service (if any):

- for which the use of the external auditor is pre-approved (i.e. approval has been given in advance as a matter of policy, rather than the specific approval of an engagement being sought before it is contracted);

- for which specific approval from the audit committee is required before they are contracted; and

- from which the external auditor is excluded.

4.40 Pre-approval of the use of the external auditor may be appropriate where the threats to auditor independence are considered low, for example if the engagement is:

- routine in nature and the fee is not significant in the context of the audit fee; or

- for an audit-related service.[9]

4.41 The non-audit services that fall within the second category in paragraph 4.39 are likely to be those which, because of their size or nature or because of special terms and conditions (for example, contingent fee arrangements), are thought to give rise to threats to the auditor's independence. As a consequence, careful consideration will be needed when determining whether it is in the interests of the company that they should be purchased from the audit firm (rather than another supplier) and, if so, whether any safeguards to be put in place by the audit firm are likely to be effective.

4.42 In determining the policy, the audit committee should take into account the possible threats to auditor objectivity and independence[10] and the Ethical Standards for Auditors regarding the provision of non-audit services by the external audit firm.

4.43 The audit committee should agree with the board the company's policy for the employment of former employees of the external auditor, taking into account the Ethical Standards for Auditors and paying particular attention to the policy regarding former employees of the audit firm who were part of the audit team and moved directly to the company. The audit committee should monitor application of the policy, including the number of former employees of the external auditor currently employed in senior positions in the company, and consider whether in the light of this there has been any impairment, or appearance of impairment, of the auditor's independence and objectivity in respect of the audit.

4.44 The audit committee should monitor the external audit firm's compliance with the Ethical Standards for Auditors relating to the rotation of audit partners, the level of fees that the company pays in proportion to the overall fee income of the firm, or relevant part of it,[11] and other related regulatory requirements.

4.45 A degree of flexibility over the timing of rotation of the audit engagement partner is possible where the audit committee decides that it is necessary to safeguard the quality of the audit. In such circumstances, the audit engagement partner may continue in this position for an additional period of up to two years, so that no longer than seven years in total is spent in this position. The audit committee should disclose this fact and the reasons for it to the shareholders as early as practicable.

4.46 The annual report should explain to shareholders how, if the auditor provides non-audit services, auditor objectivity and independence is safeguarded. The explanation should:

- describe the work of the committee in discharging its responsibilities;

- set out the audit committee's policy on the engagement of the external auditor to supply non-audit services in sufficient detail to describe each of the elements in paragraph 4.39, or cross-refer to where this information can be found on the company's website;[12] and

- set out, or cross-refer to, the fees paid to the auditor for audit services, audit related services and other non-audit services; and if the auditor provides non-audit services, other than audit related services, explain for each significant engagement, or category of engagements, what the services are, why the audit committee concluded that it was in the interests of the company to purchase them from the external auditor (rather than another supplier) and how auditor objectivity and independence has been safeguarded.

5 Communications with shareholders

5.1 The terms of reference of the audit committee, including its role and the authority delegated to it by the board, should be made available. A separate section in the annual report should describe the work of the committee in discharging those responsibilities.

5.2 The audit committee section should include, *inter alia*:

- a summary of the role of the audit committee;

- the names and qualifications of all members of the audit committee during the period;

- the number of audit committee meetings;

- the significant issues that the committee considered in relation to the financial statements and how these issues were addressed, having regard to matters communicated to it by the auditors;[13]

- an explanation of how it has assessed the effectiveness of the external audit process and the approach taken to the appointment or reappointment of the external auditor, and information on the length of tenure of the current audit firm, when a tender was last conducted, and any contractual obligations that acted to restrict the audit committee's choice of external auditors (see paragraph 4.26); and

- if the external auditor provides non-audit services, how auditor objectivity and independence is safeguarded (see paragraph 4.46).

5.3 The committee will need to exercise judgement in deciding which of the issues it considered in relation to the financial statements are significant, but should include at least those matters that have informed the board's assessment of whether the company is a going concern. The committee should aim to describe the significant issues in a concise and understandable form. The statement need not repeat information disclosed elsewhere in the annual report and accounts, but could provide cross-references to that information.

5.4　When reporting on the significant issues, the audit committee would not be expected to disclose information which, in its opinion, would be prejudicial to the interests of the company (for example, because it related to impending developments or matters in the course of negotiation).

5.5　The chairman of the audit committee should be present at the AGM to answer questions, through the chairman of the board, on the report on the audit committee's activities and matters within the scope of the audit committee's responsibilities.

Notes

1 Defined in the UK Corporate Governance Code as companies below the FTSE 350 index.

2 For example, when the audit plans (internal and external) are available for review and when interim statements, preliminary announcements and the full annual report are near completion.

3 The auditor is required by auditing standards to communicate to the audit committee the information that the auditor believes will be relevant to the board and the audit committee (in the context of fulfilling their responsibilities respectively under Code provisions C.1.1, C.2.1, C.3.2 and, where applicable, C.3.4) in order to understand the rationale and the evidence relied upon when making significant professional judgments in the course of the audit and reaching an opinion on the financial statements.

4 In addition, the auditor is required by auditing standards to report, in their report on the financial statements, if the board's statement in the annual report is inconsistent with the knowledge acquired by the auditor in the course of performing the audit.

5 'Internal Control: Guidance to Directors' provides further guidance on this subject. Copies are available from the FRC website.

6 Further guidance can be found in the Chartered Institute of Internal Auditors' Code of Ethics and the International Standards for the Professional Practice of Internal Auditing.

7 Guidance on the considerations relevant to the use of firms from more than one audit network can be found on the FRC website.

8 Further guidance can be found in the International Standard on Auditing (UK and Ireland) 580: 'Management Representations'.

9 Audit-related services are those non-audit services specified as such in the Ethical Standards for Auditors as including:

- reporting required by law or regulation to be provided by the auditor;
- reviews of interim financial information;
- reporting on regulatory returns;
- reporting to a regulator on client assets;
- reporting on government grants;
- reporting on internal financial controls when required by law or regulation; and
- extended work that is authorised by those charged with governance on financial information and/or financial controls performed where this work is integrated with the audit work and is performed on the same principal terms and conditions.

10 The Ethical Standards for Auditors explain that threats to auditor objectivity and independence may arise from:

- self-interest threats which arise when the auditor has financial or other interests which might cause it to be reluctant to take actions that would be adverse to the interests of the audit firm or any individual in a position to influence the conduct and outcome of the audit;
- self-review threats which arise when the results of a non-audit service performed by the auditor or others within the firm are reflected in the amounts included or disclosed in the financial statements of the audited entity;
- management threats which arise where partners and employees of the audit firm make judgments or take decisions on behalf of the management of the audited entity;
- advocacy threats which arise when the audit firm undertakes work that involves acting as an advocate for an audited entity and supporting a position taken by management in an adversarial context;
- familiarity threats which arise when the auditor is predisposed to accept or is insufficiently questioning of the audited entity's point of view; and
- intimidation threats which arise when the auditor's conduct is influenced by fear or threats.

11 Where the audit firm's profits are not shared on a firm-wide basis, the relevant part of the firm is that by reference to which the audit engagement partner's profit share is calculated.

12 The statutory requirement for disclosure in the financial statements is contained in the Companies (Disclosure of Auditor Remuneration and Liability Limitation Agreements) Regulations 2008. A template for the provision of this information by the auditors to the audit committee is set out in Appendix A to Ethical Standard 1.

13 The auditor is required by auditing standards to report, in their report on the financial statements, if the section of the annual report describing the work of the audit committee does not appropriately address the matters communicated by the auditor to the audit committee.

Appendix 13

Basic contents of the written statement of employment

1 Names of employer and employee.*

2 Date employment commenced (and the period of continuous employment).*

3 Remuneration and intervals at which it is paid.*

4 Hours of work.*

5 Holiday entitlement.*

6 Sickness entitlement.

7 Pension and pension schemes.

8 Entitlement to notice (this may be by reference to current legal entitlement or terms of a collective agreement).

9 Job title or a brief job description.*

10 Where employment is not permanent, the period for which it is expected to continue or, where it is for a fixed term, the date when employment is to end.

11 Place of work or, if the employee is required or allowed to work in more than one location, an indication of this and of the employer's address.*

12 The existence of any relevant collective agreements that directly affect the terms and conditions of the employee's employment and details of the persons who entered into such agreements.

Notes

- Employment particulars may be given in instalments, the last of which must be provided within two months of the start of the employment. The items identified with an * above must be given in the first instalment.

- Where the employee is normally employed in the UK but will be required to work abroad for the same employer for a period of more than one month, the statement must also include details of:

  - how long they will be working abroad;

  - currency in which they will be paid;

  - any additional pay or benefits;

  - terms on return to the UK.

- Where there are no particulars to be given for any of the items covered in the statement, this will have to be indicated.

- The statement must include a note about the employer's disciplinary and grievance procedures (except where fewer than 20 people are employed) and state whether a pensions 'contracting-out certificate' is in force for the employment in question.

- The statement may refer employees to other accessible documents, which the employee must consult for details of pension schemes, sickness entitlement, disciplinary rules and grievance procedures.

Appendix 14
Duties once placed in liquidation

Duties to the liquidator	Penalty imposed on directors
Where winding up is imminent, directors must not:	Fine, imprisonment or both (IA 1986, s 206).
• conceal any company property or debt;	
• fraudulently remove company property;	
• conceal, destroy, mutilate, falsify or alter company's books or papers;	
• make false entries in books or papers relating the company's property or affairs;	
• fraudulently part with, alter or omit information from documents relating to property or affairs;	
• pawn, pledge or dispose of company property on credit.	
When a company is placed in liquidation, the directors must return to the liquidator all property, books, papers and other documents and items in their possession (IA 1986, s 234).	Fine, which will increase over time (IA 1986, s 235(5)).
When the winding-up order has been issued, directors must ensure that they do not:	Fine, imprisonment or both (IA 1986, s 207).
• make a gift, transfer or create a charge on company property;	
• conceal or remove property of the company.	
During the winding-up the directors have a duty to:	Fine, imprisonment or both (IA 1986, s 208).
• discover and disclose to the liquidator all the company's property, any disposals and the value received;	
• deliver all property, books and papers in their custody to the liquidator;	

- inform the liquidator of a false debt proved in winding up;

- produce all necessary books and papers affecting or relating to the company's property.

Directors must ensure that all books, papers and documents relating to the company's property or securities remain in their original form and are not destroyed, altered or tampered with in any way.

Falsifying books with intent to defraud or deceive creditors is an offence, resulting in a fine, imprisonment or both (IA 1986, s 209).

Any statement of affairs given to the liquidator by the directors must contain all relevant information.

Fine, imprisonment or both (IA 1986, s 210).

All representations made by directors to creditors for their agreement or consent to matters relating to winding up must be correct.

Fine, imprisonment or both (IA 1986, s 211).

Appendix 15
Matters for determining fitness of directors (CDDA 1986, s 9(1A))

Matters applicable in all cases

- Misfeasance or breach of any fiduciary or other duty (including a breach of the statutory statement of directors' duties under CA 2006).

- Misapplication or retention of, or any conduct by the director giving rise to an obligation to account for, any money or other property of the company.

- Responsibility for the company entering into any transactions liable to be set aside under Part XVI of the Insolvency Act 1986 (provisions against debt avoidance).

- Responsibility for any failure by the company to comply with provisions of the Companies Act 2006 in relation to keeping and retaining accounting records and registers of directors, secretaries and shareholders, making annual returns preparing and arranging signature of accounts, and registering charges created by the company.

Matters applicable where the company has become insolvent

- Responsibility for the causes of the company's insolvency.

- The extent to which responsible for failing to supply goods or services that have been paid for.

- Responsibility for the company entering into any transactions or giving any preference.

- Responsibility for any failure by the directors of the company to call a creditors' meeting in a creditors' voluntary winding up.

- Failure by the director to: comply with obligations imposed by or under provisions of the Insolvency Act in respect of statements of affairs where the company is in administration, receivership or is being voluntarily or compulsorily wound up; attend meetings of creditors; deliver company property or co-operate with the liquidator.

Glossary

The following explanations are not intended to be strict legal definitions.

Administrator A person appointed by the court to manage a company in financial difficulties in order to protect creditors and, if possible, avoid liquidation. The administrator has the power to remove and appoint directors.

Agent Someone who is authorised to carry out business transactions on behalf of another (the principal) who is thereby bound by such actions.

AIM Alternative Investment Market.

Annual general meeting (AGM) A general meeting of the company's members which must be held in each period of six months beginning with the day following its accounting reference date.

Articles Articles of Association, a constitutional document setting out the internal regulations of the company. Unless modified or excluded, the specimen articles in Table A have effect. See also *Table A.*

Board (of directors) See *Director.*

Business Enterprise and Regulatory Reform The government department responsible for the administration of company law. The Companies Act confers certain powers on the Secretary of State for Business, Enterprise and Regulatory Reform (formerly the Secretary of State for Trade and Industry).

Case law The principles and rules of law established by judicial decisions. Under this system the decision reached in a particular case creates a precedent: that is, it is regarded as exemplifying rules of broader application which must be followed except by higher courts. See also *Common law.*

Class rights The rights attached to different classes of shares.

Combined Code The Combined Code issued by the Financial Reporting Council and applying to reporting years beginning on or after 1 November 2006.

Common law A body of law based on custom and usage and decisions reached in previous cases. The principles and rules of common law derive from judgments and judicial opinions delivered in response to specific circumstances, not from written legislation. See also *Case law, Statute law.*

Company secretary An officer of the company with a number of statutory duties, such as to sign the annual return and accompanying documents, and usually charged with a range of duties relating to the company's statutory books and records, filing requirements, etc. Until April 2008, every company must have a secretary who, in the case of a public company, must meet the qualification requirements laid down in the Companies Act.

Connected person Includes members of a director's family (including a spouse or civil partner; any other person whom the director lives with as partner in an enduring family relationship and that person's children or stepchildren under the age of 18 years; the director's own children and stepchildren; and the director's parents); a body corporate with which the director is connected (holds an interest in at least 20 per cent of the share capital or may exercise voting rights of more than 20 per cent of voting power); a person acting as trustee of a trust of which the director is a beneficiary or may benefit; a partner of a director or person connected with the director; or any firm of which the director is a partner (CA 2006, ss 252–256).

Director An officer of the company responsible for determining policy, supervising the management of the company's business and exercising the powers of the company. Directors must generally carry out these functions collectively as a board.

Dividends The distribution of a portion of the company's profits to members according to the class and amount of their shareholdings.

DTR Disclosure and Transparency Rules.

General meeting A meeting of the company which all members (subject to restrictions in the Memorandum and Articles) are entitled to attend. See also *Annual general meeting.*

IFRS International Financial Reporting Standards.

Insider dealing Buying or selling shares on the basis of an unfair advantage derived from access to price-sensitive information not generally available.

Liquidation The process under which a company ceases to trade and realises its assets for distribution to creditors and then shareholders. The term 'winding up' is synonymous.

Listed company A company whose shares are dealt on the Official List of the London Stock Exchange.

Listing Rules Published by the UK Listing Authority, these detail the requirements that must be met by companies before their shares can be dealt with on the Official List of the Stock Exchange. For the full requirements, readers should refer to and rely only on the latest edition, available from the UK Listing Authority.

Material interest Any interest other than one where a person is managing investments for another or is operating an authorised unit trust, recognised trust or collective investment scheme; belongs to an open-ended investment company; or where the person is trustee or nominee for another (see ca 1985, s199(2a) for the full definition).

Memorandum Memorandum of Association, a constitutional document governing the company's relationship with the world at large, stating its name, domicile, objects, limitations of liability (if applicable) and authorised share capital.

Misfeasance Improper performance of a lawful action.

Non-cash asset Any property or interest in property other than cash and includes discharge of a person's liability and creation of an interest in property such as a lease (CA 1985, s 739).

Officer Includes a director, manager or secretary of a company. An officer must have a level of supervisory control that reflects the general policy of the company, so not everyone with the title of manager is sufficiently senior to be regarded as an officer.

Ordinary resolution A resolution approved by a simple majority of votes cast in general meeting.

Ordinary shares The most common form of share in a company, giving holders the right to share in the company's profits in proportion to their holdings and the right to vote at general meetings (although nonvoting ordinary shares are occasionally encountered).

Preference shares Shares carrying the right to payment of a fixed dividend out of profits before the payment of an ordinary dividend or the preferential return of capital or both.

Prohibited name In relation to appointment of a director, this means a name for a company which is the same as or similar to the name of a company that went into insolvent liquidation at any time within 12 months of the person being a director (refer to IA 1986, s 216(1) and (2) for the full definition).

Prospectus Any prospectus, notice, circular, advertisement or other invitation to the public to subscribe for or purchase a company's shares or debentures.

Proxy A person authorised by a member to vote on his or her behalf at a general meeting.

Quasi-loan Where one party makes payment to another or incurs expenditure on their behalf without an agreement but on the understanding that the money will be repaid (see CA 1985, s 331(3) for the full definition).

Registered office The address at which legal documents may be served on the company and where the statutory books are normally kept. The registered office need not be the company's place of business and may be changed freely so long as it remains in the country of origin.

Registrar of companies The official responsible for maintaining the company records filed under the requirements of the Companies Act.

Relevant company A public or a private company in a group structure in which another company is a public company (CA 1985, s 331(6)).

Return date Either the anniversary of incorporation or the anniversary of the date shown on the previous year's annual return.

Secretary of State Within this book, refers to the Secretary of State for Business, Enterprise and Regulatory Reform (formerly the Secretary of State for Trade and Industry).

Special resolution A resolution approved by 75 per cent of votes cast.

Statute law The body of law represented by legislation, and thus occurring in authoritative written form. Statute law contrasts with common law, over which it takes precedence.

Statutory books The general term applied to the registers and minute books that the Companies Act requires a company to maintain.

Subscriber A person who subscribes to the Memorandum and agrees to take up shares in the company on incorporation.

Table A The specimen articles of association for a company limited by shares set out in the Companies (Tables A to F) (Amendment) Regulations 2007. Unless specifically modified or excluded, the version of Table A in force at the time of a company's incorporation automatically applies to the company.

Turnbull Report The report *Internal Control: Guidance for Directors on the Combined Code* issued in September 1999 by the Turnbull Working Party.

TVRs Total voting rights.

Tyson Report The Tyson Report on the Recruitment and Development of Non-Executive Directors (June 2003) commissioned by the Department of Trade and Industry.

Written resolution Allows private companies to move any resolution without holding a general meeting. Only those members comprising the requisite majority for the resolution need to sign it to make it effective.

Directory of web resources

ACAS
www.acas.org.uk

Association of British Insurers
www.abi.org.uk

British Chambers of Commerce
www.britishchambers.org.uk

The Competition Commission
www.competition-commision.org.uk

The Confederation of British Industry
www.cbi.org.uk

The Department for Business, Innovation and Skills
www.bis.gov.uk

The Environment Agency
www.environment-agency.gov.uk

Federation of Small Businesses
www.fsb.org.uk

Financial Reporting Council
www.frc.org.uk

Financial Times Non-Executive Directors' Club
www.non-execs.com

GOV.UK
www.gov.uk

Health & Safety Executive
www.hse.gov.uk

HM Revenue & Customs
www.hmrc.gov.uk

The Institute of Chartered Secretaries and Administrators
www.icsaglobal.com

The Information Commissioner
www.ico.gov.uk

The Insolvency Service
www.insolvency.gov.uk

The Institute of Directors
www.iod.com

Institute of Risk Management
www.irm.org

National Association of Pension Funds
www.napf.co.uk

Non-Executive Directors
Association
www.nedaglobal.com

Office of Fair Trading
www.oft.gov.uk

PLUS Markets Group
www.plusmarketsgroup.com

The Quoted Companies Alliance
www.qca.com

The Registrar of Companies for
England and Wales
www.companies-house.gov.uk

Research Recommendations and
Electronic Voting (RREV)
www.rrev.co.uk

The Takeover Panel
www.thetakeoverpanel.org.uk

UK Listing Authority
www.fsa.gov.uk

Index